PAUL OAKENFOLD

READY STEADY GO

PAUL OAKENFOLD

READY STEADY GO

MY UNSTOPPABLE JOURNEY IN DANCE

WELBECK

Published by Welbeck
An imprint of Welbeck Non-Fiction Limited
Part of Welbeck Publishing Group
Based in London and Sydney
www.welbeckpublishing.com

First published by Welbeck in 2022

A CIP catalogue record for this book is available from the British Library

Pages 146–147 reference to Shaun Ryder first appeared in
Paul Oakenfold: The Authorised Biography (Bantam Press, 2007).

ISBN
Hardback – 978-1-80279-074-0
Trade Paperback – 978-1-80279-080-1

Typeset by seagulls.net
Printed in the UK by CPI Group

10 9 8 7 6 5 4 3 2 1

Disclaimer
This is a work of nonfiction. While all the stories in this book are true,
certain names, identifying details, dates, places and events have been changed,
invented and altered to protect the privacy of the people involved.

For Dad, David and Linda.

191

193

CONTENTS

1	Don't Dis the Dyslexia	1
2	Yes, Chef	15
3	Enter Danny	23
4	New York Baby!	37
5	Irons in Plenty of Fires	59
6	The Project Club	73
7	Behind the Decks	85
8	We're Going to Ibiza	91
9	The Reunions	111
10	Here's to the Future	119
11	Mr Remixer	135
12	Call the Cops!	143
13	Even Better Than the Real Thing	153
14	Moving Up a Gear	161
15	Mix Me Some Goa	173
16	Double Cream	181
17	Cracking America	193
18	It's Just Not Cricket	207
19	He Shoots, He Scores	213
20	Madonna	233

21	Viva Las Vegas	237
22	Sound Trek	247
23	Do Stonehenge	259
24	Somebody Special	265
25	Bond vs. Oakenfold	275
26	What Lies Ahead	281
Acknowledgements		287
Picture Credits		288
Index		289

CHAPTER 1

Don't Dis the Dyslexia

It was only when I started writing this book that I began to appreciate what an incredible life I've led – so far. I took on New York City aged eighteen and lived to tell the tale, exported hip hop to the UK and had a hand in making it massive, helped to reinvent modern club culture, as you do, toured the world with the biggest band and the biggest female artist on the planet, broke America, became the world's first ever superstar DJ, had some number ones, wrote the score for a $100-million movie, became the first major DJ to have a residency in Las Vegas, thus opening the door for every other DJ and making it a dance music Mecca, and played football on the pitch at Wembley. Shit, man, I even got myself a *Blue Peter* badge! It's not a bad little list.

The main ingredients for making this happen have been perseverance, hard work, luck, front, a good work ethic and, dare I say it, a little bit of talent. Each element has been as important as the next, although if I had to choose the most prevalent I'd probably go for luck. Not that I consider myself to be an especially lucky person. I don't. What I realised though, a long time ago, is that the harder I try to get where I want to be in life, the luckier I become. It's developed into a kind of self-fulfilling prophecy, in that regardless of how wild or outlandish an ambition might be, I always expect it to happen. And look where's it's got me. Seriously, as both a mindset and a way of going about things, I can heartily recommend it.

You might be asking yourself, how the hell did Paul Oakenfold end up in a position where he was able to do things such as reinvent a culture or have a number one? Come to think of it, how did he end up becoming a DJ? That, my friends, is a very good question.

I used to get a bit envious of people who could pinpoint the exact moment when they were inspired to make music their career. I'm often asked the question myself. The people who ask are hoping I'll blurt out something hackneyed like, 'It was Croydon Town Hall, 1973. I was off my tits on Tizer, had just watched a middle-aged man play 'Tiger Feet' for the tenth time while talking absolute crap and thought, yes please, I'll have a bit of that!'

Until recently, I always thought that my route into the music business, which was actually quite gradual and organic, had never had a magic eureka moment at the start of it. Or should I say, not one that I was aware of. I've now realised that there actually was such a moment, but it's lacking in charm. There's no Tizer and no 'Tiger Feet'. It did take place in Croydon, however, and the other person involved was a middle-aged prat. Two out of four. Not bad.

The realisation that a bizarre event that happened well over forty years ago turned out to be the catalyst for me opening nightclubs, remixing tracks by the Rolling Stones, scoring films and touring the world as a DJ, which I believe to be something quite positive – you may not, that's your prerogative – is almost as implausible as the fact that it all came about because I'm dyslexic. It's true. Watching me try and read a book is like watching a drunk try and stand up after downing a bottle of tequila. In fact, I must be one of the only people on the planet who can probably write a book quicker than he can read one. I'll read through a paragraph, which ultimately won't make any damn sense whatsoever, so I'll start again. And so it goes on. Up, down, up, down. I always get there in the end but by the time I do I've usually lost interest.

I must have talked about dyslexia no more than a few dozen times before now, and never at length. I was always a bit embarrassed by it, to be honest. Not only that, but it was also considered by most people to be something negative and that ain't me at all. I was the model for Mr Smiley Face.

Even so, that perception is ultimately what stopped me from realising that having dyslexia ain't something to feel ashamed or embarrassed about. Anything but. It's just another one of life's obstacles. Something you can either learn to live with and perhaps even turn into an opportunity, as I ended up doing, or let it get the better of you. You do have a choice, regardless of what people might say.

Anyway, shall we spin back a bit?

I, Paul Mark Oakenfold, was born on Friday, 30 August 1963 to Sheila and John Oakenfold. Despite my family living in Highbury at the time, so dangerously close to Arsenal Football Club, I was actually born in Mile End Hospital in the East End. Because Mile End Hospital sits within the sound of Bow Bells, that makes me a true cockney, which is something I'm very proud of. I certainly sound like a cockney so although I never lived there I'm fairly authentic.

My earliest memory is sitting on an outside toilet at my grandmother's house when I was three years old. The reason I remember it is because it was bloody cold and I didn't like it! A year later, when I was four, my dad decided that me and my younger brother, David, would have a much better start in life if we all moved to the countryside. He and Mum eventually decided upon a place called Greenhithe which is near Dartford in Kent. The house we moved into was on a brand new estate, and when

I wasn't either at school or at home asleep, I'd be out playing at a placed called the pit, which was near the local cement works. Very glamorous.

According to my mum I showed leadership qualities from a very early age. To anybody who wasn't my mum that would probably translate into something like, he was a bossy little git who had a right mouth on him. All the local children used to congregate at the pit and Mum reckons I was numero uno. King of the pit. I remember being confident and definitely not shy but I don't remember being bossy. Perhaps I've just got a selective memory? I always had a lot of friends though and we had a lot of freedom and a lot of fun together. That I do remember. I was a lucky boy.

When I was twelve my parents decided that they'd had enough of living in the sticks and we ended up moving to a place called Thornton Heath which is near Croydon in south London. By this time our family had expanded from four members to five with the arrival of my little sister, Linda.

I was about halfway through my first year at secondary school when we moved. Arriving late into a year was always going to be difficult but when the pupils at Croydon's Lanfranc High School, which these days is known as the Archbishop Lanfranc Academy, found out that I supported Chelsea and not Crystal Palace, whose ground is just a couple of miles from the school, they began to express their displeasure, and in a number of different ways.

The reason for me supporting Chelsea and not Arsenal, by the way, which was always David and my dad's team, is about as glamorous and interesting as watching Crystal Palace on a Monday evening in February. When I was about three or four years old, so long before I'd even been to a game of football, somebody bought me a Chelsea shirt. I must have liked the colour or something because until I grew out of it I wore it almost constantly. My poor dad was beside himself but in my young eyes, blue was the colour, football was the game, and Chelsea was the team.

I'm surprised I actually stuck with football to be honest as the first match I went to was Charlton Athletic versus Preston North End. Not exactly a glamour tie. The thing is, I didn't even watch it from the stadium. A friend of my family's called Sid Steele was working on a block of flats overlooking Charlton's ground, The Valley, and after meeting me outside the Galleon pub before the match he took me up to the seventh floor and we watched it from there. The following week my brother David wanted to go, by which point Sid was working on a higher floor which meant we got an even better view.

Fortunately, my dad's love for his children was even stronger than his love for Arsenal FC so instead of making me wait until I could go and see my already beloved Chelsea on my own, he sacrificed himself – literally – by taking me to the Shed End at Stamford Bridge one Saturday afternoon. As sacrifices go, that one was a biggy.

But it wasn't just the colour of the shirt or even the game itself that interested me. It was the whole thing; from putting your scarf on at home and getting on the bus, to arriving at the ground, buying a programme and soaking up the atmosphere. In musical terms it's like a really good album in that it's always greater than the sum of its parts. The aforementioned anticipation, the hope, the passion, the camaraderie, the rivalry and, hopefully, a good game of football. That's what the public want.

The other contributing factor to me eventually going for a job in the music industry, other than the story I'm about to tell you, actually predates the story by almost a decade. There was definitely no eureka moment here though, as what I'm referring to is the fact that my parents just lived for music and our house was always full of it. I can't tell you exactly when it started rubbing off on me but I can't have been older than four years old. The fact that I also liked the sound of the music they played, which was usually stuff like Elvis and The Beatles, definitely helped to seal the deal.

Everything was geared towards Saturday night in those days as Mum and Dad could only afford to go out one night a week. Sometimes Dad would have a gig with the skiffle band he played with but more often than not they'd go to a dance some-where. They'd start getting ready at about four o'clock and the volume of the music depended solely on how close they were to leaving the house. It was a gradual thing and used to build up like a good mix. Although I obviously stayed at home, I always used to get swept along by the whole experience and once they'd gone I'd carry on listening.

Had I not been indoctrinated like that – willingly, I should say – I would probably have been a latecomer to music and would never have made a career out of it. I'd have stuck at being a chef most probably, which is what I did for four years after leaving school. I'm still qualified, by the way. Anyway, that's another story.

Something that held me back slightly was a misapprehen-sion that I could only appreciate the English language through reading books. Although desirable, there are obviously other ways of achieving this and one of my routes was through song lyrics. Song lyrics became my dictionary in a way, and I became fasci-nated by them; not only the words themselves and how the lyrics were formed and fitted the music, but the stories and messages they conveyed. As a skill I find it mesmerising and song lyrics are responsible for a large proportion of my vocabulary, such as it is. There's nothing I love more than reading the lyrics to a song I like, coming across a word I don't know and then looking it up.

Each one brings the English language more and more to life and the more I learn the more captivated I become. To coin a popular phrase, it's the gift that keeps on giving.

I forget what the catalyst was for me accepting my dyslexia but I must have had a word with myself or something. I wish I could remember. After that I started to appreciate the positive effects it had had on my life, which allowed me to reappraise the event I'm about to tell you about. Not to mention one or two of the events surrounding it. It's funny how things work out.

What probably prevented me from being affected by it sooner was my character. As well as being quite a cheerful soul I was involved in everything at school, and if the need arose I could talk myself in or out of almost anything. Nothing fazed me. I was also very good at taking the mickey out of myself, which didn't do any harm.

I should have been beaten up a thousand times at school just for being a Chelsea fan (rather than Palace), but somehow I almost always managed to come out unscathed. The trick was to say something derogatory about Chelsea before they did which, to be honest, wasn't difficult in those days as we were bloody awful. Had I been less of a gobshite then, as well as being beaten to a pulp every lunchtime, more questions may have been asked about my performance in class. The usual refrain from my elders and betters when I got things wrong or buggered things up was, 'Don't worry, it's just Paul. He'll be all right.' The thing is, nine times out of ten I was all right, so when a genuine problem arose, nobody noticed. Oddly enough, my character is what made the incident memorable as it robbed me of all that confidence, at least temporarily.

Anyway, here goes.

One day in English, the teacher, who was a bit of a prat and a right miserable bastard, announced to us all that we were going to take it in turns to stand up and read a passage from a book. As soon as it clicked what this entailed, I was engulfed by a tsunami of nerves. Butterflies in your stomach? Have a day off. These were more like bats, mate. What made it worse was that I couldn't understand why the nerves were there. Normally, if a teacher asked me to stand up in class, I'd jump at the chance as it would give me an opportunity to show off and make people laugh. So why not now? Everyone suffers a crisis of confidence from time to time but this was like hitting a wall.

By the time my turn came around I was bricking it, and when I stood up to speak I must have stumbled over every word. The longer these things go on the worse they normally get, but mine couldn't have got any worse. At first glance the words on the page made no sense whatsoever to me and the only one of my senses that appeared to be working was my hearing. As I stood there mumbling my way through the passage, a chorus of sniggers began to creep into my consciousness. I'm not sure if this is my memory playing tricks on me but it seemed to get louder with every word.

Something I'm a lot surer of is the look on my teacher's face. When I finally dared to divert my defective gaze in his direction, he appeared to be seriously embarrassed but also pissed off that I was holding up the proceedings. It was crippling. All I wanted him to do was shoot me a quick grin, tell me not to worry about it and ask me to sit down. I then made the stupid mistake of having a quick look around the classroom. Every single person there was pissing themselves laughing. It was pretty fucking demoralising.

When I finally reached the end of the passage I immediately sat down and just looked at the floor. When every other kid before me had finished reading, the teacher had thanked them by name and then asked the next kid to stand up. In my case he skipped the first bit and went straight to the second. Not that I wanted thanking or anything. I didn't. It just shone an even brighter light on what had just happened. But what had happened?

I remember walking out of the classroom after the lesson in a daze. My locker was to one side of the classroom and after opening my locker door, for no reason really, I just stood there in front of it with my gob wide open. I remember that locker well because a year or so later it was the location for one of the few occasions when my legendary gift of the gab wasn't quite enough to save me from the fact that Crystal Palace were even shitter than Chelsea. I think we beat them in the quarter-finals of the FA Cup and the following day I was set upon by a group of rabid Eagles fans seeking revenge. They got it all right.

The other reason I mentioned this locker is because as I was trying to make sense of things, a classmate of mine, who was a bit of a tosser and whose locker was nearby, wandered up and started taking the piss. 'You can't read, can you?' he said. 'Thirteen years old and you can't read. Fucking hell, you must be thick.'

In the eyes of my English teacher and classmates, that lesson turned me from being a happy-go-lucky mid-table achiever who had a load of mates, hundreds of acquaintances and more than a bit of bottle, into a class dunce and a Billy fucking no mates. Talk about a fall from grace. Also, instead of offering me any kind of help going forward, my teacher just blanked me and didn't even question why or what had happened. My legendary bonhomie had been replaced by insecurity and even shyness. If you'd known me at the time you wouldn't have believed it.

The only class that I progressed in after this and felt comfortable turning up to was PE. With no books or sodding recitals to worry about, all my self-consciousness evaporated. I also had a bucketload of hormones and testosterone washing around inside me so if I hadn't been able to kick a football about or climb a rope a couple of times a week, I might have ended up like a drummer from Spinal Tap and spontaneously combusted. I used to look forward to that lesson a lot more than I used to dread the others, which must have been the old confidence and bonhomie fighting back a bit.

The reason I haven't mentioned the teacher's name is because I can't say for sure that he wasn't in a similar position to me and might have been troubled by the fact that he didn't know what was going on. Had he been teaching today then I'm sure he'd have been clued up on things like dyslexia and his attitude would have been different. I think the problem was also cultural and pupils who were thought to be incapable were often just left on the scrapheap. I hope things have changed and I'm sure they have.

The effect all this had on my general wellbeing was a game of two halves. On one side it made me appreciate the things in life I loved like music and football, but on the other it made the prospect of going to school about as alluring as a club with no PA. As far as my academic career was concerned this was a bit unfortunate as the alternative to me attending school like a good little boy was bunking off and doing the things I loved like a bad one. In the circumstances there was only ever going to be one winner and on the days when I had double English I'd roll out of bed, put on my uniform, tell my parents I was going to school and then bugger off round to my mate's house instead.

At first this was a right touch and had I stuck to the football and music then I might just have got away with it, m'lud. At least for a few weeks. The success of my deception unfortunately got the better of me and resulted in an attack of bravado. At the time, bravado was the last thing I needed chucking into my adolescent emotional mix, and it resulted in me and a couple of likely lads descending on Croydon town centre one afternoon and nicking a load of football shirts. We didn't go out intending to nick the shirts, just as me, Danny Rampling, Nick and Johnny didn't intend to start the reinvention of modern club culture. We just found ourselves in the department store, saw the shirts and then one thing led to another. It was spur-of-the-moment theft as opposed to premeditated. A moment of recklessness. I knew it was wrong but I was looking for an out. And, I was with the wrong crew.

Happily, me and my two mildly malevolent compadres turned out to be as adept at shoplifting as I was at reading and my career in crime can't have lasted longer than about ninety seconds. We were collared by the store detective while trying to do one and although I can't speak for the other two, I very nearly shat my pants. Apart from scrapping with my brother and knocking on a few doors, I'd led a fairly unblemished life so far. Or at least that's how I remember it. My mum might tell you a different story.

'You lot wait in there while I call the police,' growled the store detective while pushing us into a small room. The three of us just looked at each other. I was fucking terrified.

It took the police all of about one minute to deduce that instead of being in the presence of a trio of criminal masterminds, they had in their midst three south London dickheads who couldn't steal cheese from a dead mouse. A bit of hand slapping then ensued, after which we were driven home to our respective homes where I was made to say, 'Sorry, officer, it won't happen again,' before receiving the mother of all rollockings. Fuck, did my dad go for it!

I'm not sure my accomplices were really that bothered about having our collars felt, but I was. To them it had just been a bit of fun whereas to me it had provided a glimpse into a future that I didn't like the look of. As a consequence, I decided to steer well clear of them in future, and of the police. I started going back to school. I might have had trouble reading but I wasn't stupid. No way was I. I also had a decent work ethic and a desire to learn.

My parents were fucking furious with me but at the same time they realised that what had happened was part of something a lot bigger. Sure enough, a few days later I received my results for that year's exams and for English I was bottom of the entire year, and by quite some distance. Dunce, you say? Me?

The first thing my parents did was sit me down for a natter. Not in an accusatory or critical way. As I said, they knew there was something wrong. They were just keen to get to the bottom of it. Their reactions were interesting, though. My dad, who was always a voracious reader, took the news that his eldest boy wasn't much cop at it as a bit of an affront. My old mum, on the other hand, who hardly ever reads books, didn't take it to heart. To her it was just one of those things and not something to fret about.

After that my mum and dad went to talk to the school. Now they'd been called out about it they had no choice but to recognise I had a problem and do something about it. It was nobody's fault but because dyslexia was still a mystery, it was treated as something that had to be cured or overcome as opposed to something you should learn to live with. Hindsight's a wonderful thing but this approach probably did me more harm than good. Had I been encouraged to live with it then life might have been a bit easier. It would certainly have made more bloody sense.

My parents were amazing, though. God, was I lucky. Each of them had two jobs when I was at school and every spare penny they had went on making sure that me and my little brother and sister were OK. I always had a very happy home life though, which is worth its weight in gold. That was all down to them.

I've heard tell that people who lose the use of one of their senses will often compensate by developing a heightened sensitivity of another. Whether this is done intentionally or not I obviously couldn't say, but to somebody who always looks for a positive I find it fascinating. The reason I mention it is because despite not being very good at understanding words on a page, I still had an ability to retain information. What's more, I was damn keen to prove it.

Instead of applying this to my school work and learning a couple of Shakespeare's sonnets or something, which might have been advisable given the circumstances, I decided to learn the football league tables instead. The intention was there.

It took me a few days but after a lot of hard graft and a couple of late ones, I was finally able to read the name of every team in every division from top to bottom. From Aston Villa and Brighton and Hove Albion to Tranmere Rovers and Walsall.

The following Monday I went to school and made a point of reading out every single one of these teams to my form teacher. I sat there with them written out in front of me and read them all aloud. It took about twenty minutes. What my form teacher thought I'm not sure, but my wish is that they were left believing that perhaps Paul Oakenfold wasn't quite as stupid as everyone thought he was. This, more than anything else, helped me to claw back at least some of the self-respect and confidence I'd lost in that lesson.

My attitude towards my dyslexia now is a hell of a lot different to what it was then. I understand it now, I deal with it and I'm not afraid of it. Back then I was. What ultimately saved me was my work ethic and my desire to improve as a human being. This helped me to appreciate that finding something hard doesn't necessarily mean you can't do it, at least to some degree. You've just got to change your approach.

One of my ways of compensating for dyslexia is through travel. I forget when it was, but one day in the distant past I realised that when it comes to educating yourself, experiences are just as important as books. It must be great being well read and educated, but if you're unable to complement all that knowledge and information with some actual experiences, you're only halfway there. In my opinion, each one is the other's best friend. Both my kids have dyslexia – my boy, Roman, isn't quite as bad as me, but my girl, Elsa, is even worse – and I tell them exactly that all the time. It doesn't always have to be far, but the more you travel the more chance you'll have of coming across something or somebody who floats your boat and makes you think, 'Fuck me, I'm glad I came here.' That's a fact.

I'm not sure anybody should ever take advice from a reprobate like me, but if I had to send a message to a young person living with dyslexia, I'd tell them to take a step back, spend a bit of time figuring out what you're good at – and you will find something, believe me – and then grab it by the horns, shake the hell out of it and see what happens. And then, if and when you get bored, go and find something else.

The common denominators in everything I've done since that English lesson are a willingness to go above and beyond in terms of effort, a readiness to adapt and a determination to learn and to improve. You could also throw in a tendency to misbehave, but that's for later on. As I said earlier, if you have dyslexia you can either push yourself to thrive or let it get the better of you. If you have got dyslexia, do me a favour, will you? Give yourself a push. You won't regret it.

CHAPTER 2

Yes, Chef

How many sixteen-year-olds know what they want to do for a living when they leave school? In my experience, not many. Some will obviously stay on in education, but the ones who don't will probably be left scratching their heads. That's exactly what happened to me when I left school, except I was a year younger than that. You already know that I wasn't what you'd call academically inclined, so when the dust finally settled (or should I say when I stopped celebrating!) I had to make a decision – and quick.

I was actually quite lucky in a way because in addition to my parents not threatening me with eviction after I left school, I also had a couple of options open to me career-wise. Better still, one of those options was my dream job which was a professional footballer. It still is my dream job if truth be known, although I might be a bit past it now. Anyway, as opposed to leaving school on a downer and worrying about the future, I was quite chipper really. Life was good.

Funnily enough, I had this conversation with my own son a little while ago, who is also fifteen, but he wasn't having any of it. 'I don't want to talk about this, Papa,' he said. 'I'm too young. What's more, you're stressing me out!' I could have just dropped it I suppose but the father in me pursued the conversation doggedly.

'Look, Roman,' I continued. 'The smarter way is to start thinking now, at least a little bit, about what you're going to do when you leave education. Don't get caught out, mate!' 'Yeah, Papa,' he said now wanting to get rid of me. 'I'll do that. Now leave me alone!' One of the reasons I pursued it was because I never had that conversation with my own father, and despite me not being in a rut when I left school, it would definitely have helped me. He had a wise head on his shoulders my old man, and I looked up to him. I still do, despite him no longer being around.

As I said at the start, I was far more interested in what my dad did in his spare time than at work, which was play music, but I never thought for a moment that you could make a living out of it. Or at least not ordinary people like us. It was something to be enjoyed, and there was absolutely nothing wrong with that. Saying that, my dad was quite a talented musician, so had he ever been given the opportunity to commercialise it in some way, then he might well have given it a go. Who knows?

So, on to those two career options of mine. The first one, which is the one I ended up going for in the end, was becoming a chef. That's right, boys and girls – DJ Paul Oakenfold is also a qualified chef. But not any old chef, I'll have you know. A classically trained chef, no less. It's true. Together with PE, it was one of the only things I excelled at in school, and one of the only lessons I looked forward to. To be fair, I did have a bit of a leg-up courtesy of my grandmother, who was called Alice. She used to be a chef at County Hall cooking for hundreds and hundreds of people, and when I wasn't at school – or should I say when I wasn't trying to avoid going to school – I used to hang out with her. My other kind of passion at the time was photography, and while she cooked for the masses I used to take photos of her. We had a great time and a lot of what she did and said used to rub off, to the point that, when

I eventually made the decision to try and emulate my grandmother and become a chef, I knew a lot more than I realised. Looking back, that decision provided me with a lot more than just a job and a salary. It gave me hope, dreams and ambitions, which had often been in short supply at school. To be honest, that was all I really wanted at the time. Something to work towards.

OK, on to option number two.

Before deciding to become a chef, I'd say 99 per cent of my thoughts, let alone any dreams and ambitions, had something to do with football, and in the months leading up to me leaving school there was a chance, although admittedly a slim one, of me being able to play football professionally, or should I say semi-professionally. The teams I played for regularly back then were the mighty Dulwich Hamlet FC on a Saturday and Pollards Hill on a Sunday. I could play either as a winger or an attacking midfielder, and if you had to equate me to a modern-day footballer, I was like an early version of Eden Hazard. Yeah, sure! I was pretty good though, even though I do say so myself, and what I lacked in skill I more than made up for in effort.

At some point while I was at Dulwich Hamlet, I had a trial for Tooting & Mitcham United who were a semi-professional outfit. They were playing in a division known as the Conference at the time, which was the one below League Three, and they took me on. That's probably when I started to dream about making a living out of the game, but before I could make that a reality I was beaten by – well, reality. What I mean is that while all this was going on, I was given the opportunity to enrol as a trainee chef at Westminster Technical College, which is where the likes of Jamie Oliver and Ainsley Harriott cut their culinary teeth. Believe it or not I had quite a sensible head on my shoulders at that age, and as much as I adored playing football, I knew in my heart of hearts that Tooting & Mitcham United was probably as far as I could go as a footballer. I don't wish to sound disrespectful, but my ambitions were loftier than that and I needed to be involved in a profession where I could keep on progressing. At the time, cooking fitted the bill, so with a heavy heart I decided to quit football altogether and throw myself into the food game. I did for a time consider trying to juggle the two, but it was just impossible. Chefs' hours don't allow them to do many things, least of all play football every Saturday and go training every Wednesday evening.

My first job as a chef, which I got shortly before enrolling at the college, was with the catering company J Lyons and Co, and for the first couple of years I earned the princely sum of £26 a week. You used to get your wages in cash in those days, and I remember opening my very first brown envelope, peering inside and thinking to myself, 'My God, look at all that cash!' I'll tell you what though, I had to work bloody hard for that money and although I look back on that time with a certain amount of fondness, I wouldn't like to have to do it all again. No thanks.

The killer for me was something called a split shift which is the bane of every chef's life. For those of you who aren't aware, a split shift in chef land consists of turning up at 10am, prepping till 3pm, taking a break until 5pm, and then working through to, at the earliest, 11pm. If you take into account the travelling, which for me was about an hour each way, you have the makings of a pretty long day. The killer was that two-hour break in the afternoon. You couldn't go home as you didn't have time, which meant you couldn't really put your feet up. I used to kill the time by going for a walk or if the weather was bad I'd find a café, drink tea and watch the world go by. The point being though that by the time it was 5pm, the last thing you wanted to do was go back and work for another six hours.

The qualifications I was working towards at college were a City and Guilds 7061 and 7062 in French cuisine. They were basically your passport to working in the world's best kitchens and at the time that was my ambition. I wanted to get to the top.

After a year or so I left J Lyons, while continuing to study, and went to work for the Naval and Military Club, which is a private members' club on Piccadilly. You know the kind of thing. Posh, posh, posh. We'd usually cook for between thirty and a hundred people, and they were generally a mixture of retired generals and admirals and members of the Royal Family. It was proper old-school English. I'd work under the sous chef usually and spent six months in each section. While I was there I also got a chance to get involved in some outside catering and ended up working at Wimbledon during the tennis championships where I knocked up about a thousand portions of strawberries and cream. My favourite event though was the British Grand Prix. It was held at Brands Hatch that year and the atmosphere, not to mention the noise, was a lot different to Wimbledon. I loved it.

When I look back on my time as a chef, I appreciate how much I learned, and not just about cooking. It was something far more rounded than that. In fact, you could almost call it an elongated life lesson and it set me up good and proper. The importance of things like discipline, timekeeping, being able to focus, working as part of a team, the chain of command, self-promotion and ambition. I was already quite adept when it came to self-promotion and ambition, but what the job did was turn my ambitions from dreams into reality, or at least a potential reality, and my efforts at self-promotion from being brazen and lacking in humility – like an advert for a January sale, basically – to something a bit quieter, more considered and targeted. And then you have self-worth, of course. Until I became a chef I don't think I'd ever achieved anything. Or at least anything worth mentioning. After all, I was just a kid; a kid who so far hadn't really amounted to very much at all, apart from scoring the odd goal.

When I started learning how to cook, in addition to getting things wrong occasionally, which I did, I also started getting the odd thing right, and when that happened I began to develop a sense of self-worth. With that came a sense of confidence and a sense of empowerment which made me even more ambitious. In my opinion these are some of the most important things a young person needs when they are starting out in life. Perhaps most importantly of all though, being a chef taught me how to communicate with people and at all levels. You can be the brightest person on God's earth, but if you can't communicate with the people around you, then you're going to find it really hard to get on. Fortunately, I was already quite talkative and the environment I worked in taught me how to refine that and put it to good use.

I suppose the downsides to working as a chef at that age were a lack of time, football, girls, fun, alcohol and sleep. My days off were always Sunday and Monday and in those days nobody did anything on a Sunday because nothing was ever open. Mondays were even worse, of course, as everybody was back to work. It was rubbish. Over time this started getting me down and I went from being an ambitious head chef in the making – or even a restaurant owner if my ambitions were to be realised – to a frustrated, bored and increasingly resentful young man.

Over the years I've had several of what I believe are called 'Road to Damascus moments' which have all been life-changing, and the first one took place in my bedroom one Sunday morning. I'd been working my arse off all week, and when I woke up that morning I realised I had nothing to look forward to, at least over the next two days. Also, because I had no outside interests, when

I did meet up with my mates I had bugger all to talk about. Except cooking, of course, which they weren't interested in. I remember thinking to myself, 'This ain't living; this is just existing.' It was what my parents used to call 'the grind' and I made up my mind then to do something else and start living, the moment I'd finished the course. That was actually still many months away, but one thing my parents had taught me – one of many things it has to be said – was the importance of having a trade or something to fall back on if everything goes tits up. The fact that I'd made that decision to leave the industry and try something new was enough to keep me motivated and, sure enough, I passed. Actually, that's not strictly true with regards to the motivation. Sure, the prospect of starting to live a bit was powerful, but there was another element to this. Something in the kitchen. Or should I say, someone.

Since I'd started working as a chef I'd made lots of mates and had met lots of interesting people, but there was one bloke who really stood out and who I gravitated towards. To my shame I'm afraid I can't remember his name, but he was Irish, I remember, and he was a bit of a rebel. I was probably quite similar in that respect but I was a young pretender and this bloke was the real deal. He was a maverick, you might say. Somebody who was respectful but didn't always toe the line. He was the only one I'd ever want to hang out with on the break during a split shift and, if he didn't have anything planned, which he often did to be fair as he seemed to know everyone, we'd hook up. He had an aura about him, if you see what I mean. A presence. I think you remember people like that, especially at that age.

He was one of the first people I told after deciding to leave the industry, and because he was a bit older than me and a lot more experienced, he was able to bring the prospect of change to life. He told me stories about what he'd done before becoming a chef, which seemed to include every profession and destination and I couldn't get enough. Don't get me wrong, this bloke was both dedicated and talented when it came to being a chef. Unlike the others, he just seemed to know exactly what he wanted to do with it and I found everything about him – his manner, his patter and even the way he held himself – quite inspirational.

By far the biggest loss from this period was losing touch with many of my old football friends. Looking back it was inevitable I suppose, but they were people I'd grown up with and had known since I was small. After becoming a chef I went from spending most weeknights and every weekend with these people to a weeknight every so often and one weekend in six. The longer it went on the less we had in common and, subsequently, the less we had to say to each other. It was sad, but there we go. Life goes on. Fortunately, during the latter part of my career as a chef, a new interest began taking up more and more of the limited time I had available, and with that new interest came a new crowd of people. A crowd of people, incidentally, who seemed to keep the same unsociable hours I did, but for different reasons, and who seemed like kindred spirits. The interest, if you haven't already guessed, was music.

CHAPTER 3

Enter Danny

By the time I'd finished the course and had collected my two City and Guilds in French cuisine, I'd decided that my new life and career would lie somewhere within the music industry. I had no idea where exactly, but at least I'd chosen a path, so to speak. I just needed to find out where that path might lead me. To be honest, I didn't mind that. The lack of security, I mean. In fact, I probably preferred it as the last thing I wanted at that time was another job to walk into, or even one to start looking for. I wanted music to be an open book without any restrictions. Then, once I'd had a good look around, I'd start figuring out what I wanted to do and where I wanted to go. Just the prospect of being able to do that, to immerse myself in something that floated my boat and without any expectations, gave me a sense of euphoria that I wouldn't experience again until I was on a dance floor in Ibiza, if you get my drift. Anyway, that's for later.

I left Westminster Technical College with a backup if things went tits up in the form of two qualifications, a few quid in my pocket, but not much, lots of confidence, a good work ethic, a little bit of attitude, a burgeoning group of friends who were all heavily into music, and an ambition to succeed that grew literally by the second. To do what, I wasn't sure, but that was the driving factor.

It's not often you get a chance to make a living doing something you love and enjoy, and because I'd already but committed myself to the music industry – prematurely, some might say – it felt like I was already halfway there. It was time for a bit of trial and error.

This new group of friends of mine were heavily into the jazz funk and soul scene, which for some reason was massive in south London back then. I remember we used to listen to a guy called Robbie Vincent on Radio London who also used to play live at a venue called Tiffany's in Purley. His partners in crime I remember were an established and very popular DJ called Chris Hill and a young upstart named Pete Tong. Whatever happened to him, I wonder? The name definitely rings a bell.

By the mid to late 1970s, that scene had become massive, and I remember attending some of the early all-dayer events they used to hold in venues such as the Top Rank in Reading. They'd play Northern soul in the main room, which I didn't mind, and jazz funk and soul in the smaller one. It was known as Night Owl and they played all sorts of sounds: Lonnie Liston Smith, Roy Ayers and Herbie Hancock. The man in charge of the music at these events was the aforementioned Chris Hill who, as well as being a bit of a character, always compiled an exceptional selection of sounds. The tune I remember most from those early all-dayers is Billy Paul's 'Bring the Family Back'. If you haven't heard that track before, give it a go. It's an incredible tune.

It's fair to say that the two audiences at these all-dayers weren't exactly fans of each other's music, and on the one occasion when Chris Hill decided to try and unite the two crowds it ended in disaster. He began the experiment by organising a conga from our room into the main hall to the Roy Ayers tune, 'Running Away'. I'm not sure we were terribly impressed but the Northern soul crowd certainly weren't, and as the conga, which was comprised mainly of our crowd (although not me), moved slowly and hesitantly into the main hall, a Northern soul fan jumped on to the stage, grabbed Roy Ayers' seven-incher and smashed it to smithereens. 'I've paid two quid to get in here,' he shouted, 'and I'm not listening to this shit!' This diatribe was met with a hail of copper coins that were hurled by my own contingent and, after a frank exchange of words, we went back to our room, never to be seen again. Or at least until the next all-dayer.

The next one I remember took place at Tiffany's, which was a much larger venue, and it attracted about four thousand people. One indelible memory from that event is seeing the enormous wall of speakers that covered one end of the room. It was an incredible sight. They belonged to a guy called Steve Howlett, aka DJ Froggy, and could produce around 12,000 watts of power. DJ Froggy was one of the first DJs in Britain to learn how to mix, a skill that he picked up in New York under the tutelage of one Larry Levan at a legendary club called Paradise Garage. Larry ended up playing a pivotal role in my own DJ'ing career which I'll come on to in a bit. Suffice to say he's an icon in my eyes and was a true pioneer. Incidentally, legend has it that because of his association with Larry Levan, DJ Froggy became the first DJ in the UK to own a pair of Technics SL-1200MK2 turntables. Given what's happened since then that's quite a claim to fame. Anyway, when DJ Froggy, who very sadly passed away at the age of just fifty-seven in 2008, started practising these new skills of his in the UK, it caused quite a stir and before very long, at least with the soul and jazz-funk crowd, it became imperative. The mix was everything.

The beauty about being into this scene, apart from the music, was that it was niche, and because the fan base was so small you had to actively seek each other out. This took me and my fellow jazz-funk and soul lovers all over London, and the DJs we followed were Chris Hill, Robbie Vincent and DJ Froggy, who were like gods, Greg Edwards, who was on Capital Radio, Jeff Young, Chris Brown and the fresh-faced Peter Tong. They were known collectively as the Soul Mafia and the two main clubs we frequented in order to catch them were Frenchies in Camberley and Flicks in Dartford.

The problem we had with Flicks was that the last train back was at 11pm and Robbie Vincent didn't come on until midnight. The first thing we'd try and do was make friends with a couple of locals in the hope that they'd let us crash at theirs, and if that didn't work we'd just crash at the station and wait for the first train. You can do things like that at that age. Incidentally, one of the people we used to hang out with occasionally during my jazz-funk and soul days was Carl Cox who, like Pete, you might just have heard of. Carl lived in the Carshalton area which is about five or six miles from where I was in Thornton Heath. We belonged to different groups, so to speak, but when we came together at clubs we were one. We were … the South London Crew!

Fuelled by my burgeoning love of music, not to mention the art of playing that music to a crowd of like-minded people in a venue of some kind, I began taking an interest in the records themselves, so much so that within a few months I'd started a collection and was properly addicted. Addiction's a strong word I know, but that's the only one I can think of that does my 'condition' justice. No other object (of the non-human variety), brings me as much happiness as vinyl. At the last count I had roughly 30,000 records in my collection and it grows on a weekly basis. The last record I bought was a copy of *Pills 'n' Thrills and Bellyaches* by the Happy Mondays which me and Steve Osborne produced for Tony Wilson's Factory Records. There's a chapter or two about that later on and certain substances, not to mention a certain amount of bad behaviour, may or may not be involved. I bought the record during a visit to HMV in Maidstone which is where my mum lives. Even now, when I walk into a record shop, I always get a bit of a thrill because I know for a fact that there'll be stuff in there I want to hear yet didn't even know existed. I always walk out with at least one new disc under my arm, sometimes more, and the experience itself always makes me feel on top of the world. It doesn't take much.

The first record shops that fed my new addiction all those years ago were Groove Records on Greek Street in Soho, The Record Shack in Ladbroke Grove, and City Sounds in Holborn. In the late 1970s most of the tunes I wanted to listen to, which was usually stuff I'd heard members of the Soul Mafia playing either live or on the radio, were album tracks as opposed to singles, so it was an expensive business. The ones I remember buying first, at least during my soul years, were records by Lonnie Liston Smith, George Duke and Bobbi Humphrey. The very first record I ever bought, which was many years earlier, was 'Get It On' by T. Rex. What a tune that is.

The two main characters in this new group of friends of mine were Trevor Fung, a DJ who I'd first met on a coach heading to a soul night in Slough one night, and who later became one of my main inspirations to start DJ'ing, and Danny Diamond. I'll come on to Trevor later, but for the time being let me concentrate on Danny. Danny is six feet tall, blond and flamboyant. He's a couple of years younger than me, and has more front than Southend Pier. To be honest I didn't really like him at first, which apparently was the norm when people met him. They often found him arrogant and cocky, but once you got to know Danny you realised that he's actually a really nice guy.

The reason I eventually gravitated to Danny was because he has an aura about him that makes you think that with him by your side you can take on the world and win. The closest I'd ever come to meeting somebody like that was probably the Irish guy I mentioned at college, but Danny was on a different level to him. I've done things and been places with Danny that I'd never dream of doing or going with other people. Never in a million years. We were sparring partners. Partners in crime. He's an inspirational facilitator is Danny. Somebody who won't take no for an answer and who does things off the cuff, often without considering the consequences. To be fair, that hasn't always worked out for him over the years, but there was a time in each of our lives when everything we touched seemed to turn to gold and although we've had our ups and downs over the years, he's still one of the most amazing human beings I've ever met.

One of the high points of working as a chef, apart from developing my love of music, going to the odd soul night and meeting people like Trevor and Danny, was my annual holiday which, for the last two or three years I was there, took the form of a two-week adventure with Danny, and I mean an adventure! Each year, a few weeks before, we'd meet up and decide where we wanted to go and we'd always try and pick somewhere as far away as possible, at least for our budget. My only extravagance at the time was vinyl so everything else went into what I used to call 'the adventure pot'.

The first place we visited together was Hong Kong followed immediately by Beijing, or Peking, as it was then known. We thought Hong Kong was going to be the most exciting place on earth, probably based on watching movies and things, but when we got there we weren't all that impressed. The flight in was extraordinary, I remember that. It's about 15 miles out now, but back then the airport at Hong Kong was in the centre of the city and as you came in to land you could see pretty much every-thing. It's one of the most densely populated cities on the planet and as the plane descended you could actually see thousands and thousands of people just going about their business. I remember seeing a woman doing her washing when we came in to land and she didn't even bat an eyelid at this enormous bloody aeroplane flying past her. I remember thinking, 'Wow! That's cool.' It was also one of the most dangerous airports in the world at the time as the pilots would have to fly into the centre of the city where all the skyscrapers are, turn in what in aeronautical terms must have been a ridiculously tight space, and then fly in over all these people and finally land. While the locals were all going about their business you'd have planes full of tourists like me a few hundred feet in the air absolutely shitting themselves. It was mad!

One of the first things we did on arriving in Hong Kong was try and find an opium den, as you do. Two teenage Londoners in Hong Kong for the first time, trying to get off their tits. What could possibly go wrong? We'd had the idea of going to an opium den after watching a movie but I can't remember which one. We assumed they'd be everywhere though, but after two or three hours of searching we couldn't find one. I remember us scratching our heads wondering where we'd gone wrong. It's a tiny place and we'd been everywhere. Most people in Hong Kong speak English but we figured you could hardly walk up to a complete stranger in the street and ask where the nearest opium den was. We were just naive, I suppose. Adventurous. Brave, even. But very naive.

After a couple of days we came to the conclusion that Hong Kong looks great, but is actually quite boring; especially for a couple of teenage thrill seekers like us. I can't believe we got bored there so quickly though, but we did. We couldn't shop because it was too expensive and as impressive as the skyline is, once you've seen it a couple of times it tends to lose its attraction. The clubs too, as well as being bloody expensive, weren't really up to much so, as opposed to moping around and wasting our holiday, we decided to cut our losses and move on.

After weighing everything up – plane fares and accommodation, etc. – we decided to try and kick-start our adventure in Beijing, which, as I said, was then known as Peking. Even then the city was enormous and with legendary places such as the Great Wall of China just a train ride away, we figured we were on to a winner. Because the flights were so cheap – actually, everything was compared to Hong Kong – we decided to buy a camera each and do the full-on tourist thing. Why not?

When we arrived in Beijing the first thing that hit us were the amount of bikes there. There were literally millions. Far more than there were cars. It was like Amsterdam times a hundred. One of the reasons I wanted to go there was because of Peking duck, believe it or not. Yeah, I know that sounds a bit rubbish. I was a chef though (who liked Peking duck), and I got it into my head that, as I chef, I should try and have some Peking duck in the city where it originated and after which it was named. It was a big moment. We had some not long after landing and unfortunately it tasted exactly the same as the Peking duck I'd had in Chinatown. I was gutted! Anyway, on with the adventure.

One of the first places we visited after finding a hotel was the Forbidden City. If you've never been, the Forbidden City is a series of palaces right in the centre of Beijing that are surrounded by acres and acres of very opulent gardens. It completely blew our minds to be honest. We were in a country that, even to us youngsters, had a kind of mythical quality to it and a culture that was completely different to our own. That was probably what we found most interesting, apart from the sights, of course. And the panda bears. They and the Great Wall of China were top of our list of things to see.

The only slight issue we had with being in Beijing was the language barrier. It's different now but back then nobody spoke English, and I mean nobody. This meant we had to make sure that we always stayed within the tourism circle, if you like. Beijing's so vast, you see, so if you got lost and didn't have the address of your accommodation to hand – remember, there were no mobile phones back then – you'd be screwed. I got talking to a tourist guide one day and he told me some right horror stories. Some people had been lost for days apparently and others kidnapped and even killed. I'm not sure whether he was just trying to scare us or not, but if he was it worked!

The place that made by far the biggest impression on me while we were there was the very aptly named Great Wall of China. It's obviously an impressive structure but for some reason I was absolutely mesmerised by it and it sent my inner tourist into overdrive. My camera, which had been used periodically since arriving, was now a permanent fixture around my neck and for reasons that are still unknown to me, I began taking photographs of the wall from just about every conceivable angle. I was obsessed! It was only when we got home and had the photos developed that I realised what I'd done. It was ridiculous. I'd literally become a wall bore. I remember sitting down with my parents and showing them all these photos and after about the fiftieth they just said, 'Enough! Show us a photo of a panda or something Paul, for God's sake!'

In addition to an impressive collection of photographs of what is basically a gigantic brick wall, I arrived back in the UK from China with a desire to visit and experience as many countries and cultures as is humanly possible. It was like an all-encompassing atomic wanderlust. I'd always been fairly adventurous but this was different. I was a different person.

In terms of where this came from I'd hazard a guess that it was from my paternal grandfather. He spent the majority of his adult life travelling and would arrive in a country, immerse himself in its culture and geography, learn some of the language and then find a job within the tourism industry. It sounds incredibly easy and uncomplicated, but I suppose it was in those days. What I got from my mother's side of the family, and my mum in particular, was the belief that if you get off your backside and put the hours in you can achieve pretty much anything you want. So, I got the travel and the music from my dad's side, the attitude and belief from my mum's, and the work ethic from both. I'm a lucky boy.

Prior to becoming a chef and then taking my holidays with Danny, I'd been on a family holiday every year since I was small, and they were some of the happiest times of my life. Although they didn't earn much money, Mum and Dad always managed to scrape enough together to take me and my brother and sister away for a week or two and we always had a blast. It was usually somewhere like Butlin's or Pontins in the early days, but then as I got older we started venturing further afield. I remember we went to Spain one year and when my mum and dad told us we were going, I almost exploded with excitement. Abroad? On an aeroplane? To Spain? Us? You've got to be bloody joking! Travel and music are my lifeblood really.

What I wasn't that interested in back then, even after I left college, were things like girls, alcohol and drugs. In fact, I didn't even try drugs until I was twenty-seven and hardly ever drank. Strange, isn't it? I did have the odd girlfriend in my teens and twenties but nothing very serious. I don't know. They just didn't really interest me at the time, whereas music, travel and experiencing new things (that weren't girls, alcohol or drugs) just did. That would all begin to change as I got older, of course, but the truth is that throughout the majority of what you'd call my formative years, all three of those things played second fiddle to the former.

ENTER DANNY

My second adventure with Danny was to Brazil where we took in Rio de Janeiro and the Amazon. What we'd taken away from our maiden journey to China was that you can have two adventures in two weeks, and after choosing Rio as our initial destination, which we assumed would be all beaches and bars, we thought the Amazon would give us a nice contrast. And we were right.

Part of the fun of travelling is planning where you're going to go and what you're going to do and see and, just like Hong Kong, we had a vision of Rio that had probably been formed more from what we'd seen on celluloid than in any books or brochures, or from any imparted first-hand experiences. What we had in our heads was basically part of a James Bond movie, except instead of having one good-looking hero who makes husbands and boyfriends jealous, can kill a man just by looking at him and is irresistible to women, you had two – me and Danny.

Just looking at the departures board at the airport where it said RIO DE JANEIRO made the hair on the back of my neck stand on end. Like Beijing, it had an almost mythical quality to it and I couldn't wait to start exploring. Neither of us could. Although it didn't quite live up to expectations, we had a lot more fun in Rio than we did in Hong Kong. The beaches are obviously legendary, as is the music scene. Next up, the Amazon.

The Amazon wasn't just a contrast to Rio, it was a contrast to everywhere I'd ever been before, or have been since, to be fair. We had about six days there in all, but as opposed to finding out what we were going to be doing there we just read a brief description, which told us bugger all really, and decided to give it a go. I suppose that was part of the attraction in a way. We considered ourselves explorers more than tourists, and what self-respecting explorer reads a brochure about where they're going to be going beforehand? No, we wanted some surprises.

Rio, while exceeding expectations in a visual sense, still didn't float our boats to any great degree when it came to nightlife. Having been there many times since – I've even played at the legendary Maracanã Stadium while supporting Madonna – I'm well aware of the fact that Rio de Janeiro boasts one of the most vibrant club scenes anywhere on earth, but for whatever reason we just didn't click into it while we were there. To be honest that didn't really matter though as the touristy side of things – Sugar Loaf Mountain and Christ the Redeemer, etc. – kept us well busy and we left the city wanting more.

I remember setting off on the long journey from the airport into the Amazon jungle. 'Hang on a second,' I thought to myself. 'Where are we going to sleep?' 'Excuse me,' I said to the guide. 'Where are we going to be sleeping?' I'm honestly not sure what I was expecting the guide to say, but when he said to me, 'We'll all be sleeping in hammocks,' I almost fell off my seat. 'Why hammocks?' I asked. 'I'll explain when we get there,' said the guide. 'You'll understand though when I show you.' He didn't need to show me. I realised as soon as we got there. Because of what lives on the jungle floor – insects and animals of all shapes and sizes with differing amounts of deadliness, basically – had we been daft enough to sleep there we'd either have been bitten to shreds, poisoned or eaten alive. Or all three! Fortunately, I found the hammocks quite comfortable, although what prevented me from sleeping for more than a few hours a night were the noises. My God, the noises! You go to bed when the sun goes down basically as there's nothing to do and get up when the sun rises, so it's a long old night. I don't know what the ratio is but I'll wager that there are far more creatures that come out at night in the Amazon jungle than come out during the day, and boy do they make themselves heard. You're about two feet off the ground in these hammocks and in addition to all the noises that come from around you there's a constant stream of noises coming from underneath you. They're the ones that used to shit me up. I'd lie there in my hammock and all of a sudden I'd hear something scurrying across the jungle floor in my direction. I couldn't see a thing so would just close my eyes and pray that it wasn't hungry and/or poisonous. Sometimes these creatures would stop when it sounded like they were upon you. They were probably just curious as to what was hanging above them but it was terrifying. If I was ever daft enough to do something like *I'm a Celebrity... Get Me Out of Here*, I'd probably get flashbacks and have to go home.

On the morning after our first night in the jungle we went canoeing up a river, which was interesting. It must have been a tributary of the Amazon as it wasn't that big and the canoes were tiny. Again, this scared me half to death because, as with the hammock, I had no idea what was underneath me. Actually, that's not true. I knew exactly what was beneath me – crocodiles and piranhas! Fortunately, crocodiles are nocturnal animals so were probably fast asleep. Not so the piranhas. They feed during the day and every time a ripple appeared on the surface of the water or something jumped out of it I convinced myself that we were under attack. Apparently piranhas only attack humans if they're bleeding as they can smell the blood. Had they attacked on smelling fear I'd have been a dead man.

On the second evening the man in charge suggested that we go and find some crocodiles. It was either that or remain terrified in our hammocks so we agreed. As we got into our canoes I realised what we'd agreed to. It felt like turkeys voting for Christmas! The man leading us was a real character and after a few minutes he turned around to us and said, 'Would you like to see a baby crocodile close up?' 'Yes please,' shouted some idiot behind me. Before I could say anything the guide put his hand into the water, pulled out a baby crocodile which he had hold of by the snout, turned around again, held it out and started waving it literally in front of my face.

Although a baby, this thing was at least a metre long and it wasn't happy. 'For fuck's sake don't drop it,' I said, trying to hide my fear by laughing a bit. Just then my canoe started to rock a bit, probably because I was nervous, and the more it rocked the more fearful I became and the more fearful I became the more it rocked. The parents of the crocodile he'd pulled out of the river wouldn't have been far away and after a few seconds I was at panic stations. 'Don't worry,' said the guide after releasing the crocodile and steadying my canoe. 'It's OK. Here, look at this.' Just then he shone his torch up the river and there in front of us were about fifty pairs of eyes all scattered about and looking in our direction. 'Are they all crocodiles?' I asked the guide. 'That's right,' he said. 'They're called black caimans and they can grow to about five metres in length.' 'I do wish you hadn't told me that,' I said to him. I was being serious too.

The following year, which was the year I decided to ditch cooking and college and immerse myself in music, we sat down at the usual time to decide where to go on our trip. 'OK,' I said. 'So we've done Asia for two weeks, and we've done South America. Where to next?' 'How about New York?' Danny said. 'I've got a cousin who lives there. We can stay with him.' The moment he said New York my head started spinning and my heart started beating like a drum. Or should I say like a drum machine. New York? Of course! Not only was it the Mecca of the music industry, or at least the kind of music that Danny and I enjoyed listening to, but it had the best nightclubs in the world, bar none. This was going to be immense.

CHAPTER 4

New York Baby!

I didn't know it then but this trip to New York would end up rubber-stamping my decision to enter the music industry. Before leaving I'd written a letter to every record company in the UK offering my services and each one had either turned me down or just not replied. Most people would have been left despondent by such a unanimously negative response, but for some reason I wasn't. We were going to New York and I had it in my head that while we were there I would find my path somehow, come back, and make myself indispensable to at least one big player within the industry. Yeah, I know it was a lot to ask in two weeks, but you've gotta think big.

From the moment we landed at JFK I felt energised. It had a buzz to it, the like of which I'd never even come close to experiencing before. This would have been about 1981 and New York was actually a bit of a shithole, in that it was dirty, full of reprobates and stank to high heaven. That didn't matter though. Not to me. In fact, that was part of its character. New York is what it is and it doesn't give a shit what anybody thinks. It's as if it says to you, 'Look, mate, if you don't like it, piss off, but this place ain't changing for no one.' In an American accent, of course.

In contrast to Hong Kong and Rio, New York was exactly like it was in the movies, which is one of the many things that made me fall in love with it. I'd visited places that had lived up to expectations before, and have done since, but not in such a stark and interesting way. In that respect New York stands alone in my experience. It's a unique place.

Danny's cousin's apartment was in West Harlem on West 131st, and for the two weeks we were there we had to sleep on the floor. Not that we cared very much. We hadn't gone there to sleep. By now my musical taste, or at least the stuff I listened to most frequently, had shifted from jazz funk and soul to hip hop, which merely added to my excitement at being in New York as it was where it all began – and, it was still home to its chief protagonists.

Things had started to shift in the direction of hip hop about a year previously, much to the annoyance of some of my soul friends and even one or two of my work colleagues. By that time, in an attempt to relieve the monotony of working in a kitchen once in a while, as well as fund my now dangerously expensive record-buying habit, I'd taken a couple of part-time jobs. The first one was helping Trevor Fung sell clothes on a market stall on Petticoat Lane. That was OK, but I was far more of an indoors kind of person and before long I managed to get myself some hours at a menswear shop called Woodhouse which was on Oxford Street opposite Selfridges. There were usually two of us working the shop floor when I was there – me and a young upstart named Nicky Holloway. Although I still listened to it, Nicky was a big jazz-funker who loved his soul, and when I started working at Woodhouse he had control of the store's tape machine. This meant that when a customer came in they'd be greeted by the sounds of someone like Herbie Hancock, when what they should have been greeted by, in my opinion, was a blast of Grandmaster Flash.

While Nicky was serving a customer I'd wander over to the stereo and swap tapes, and as soon as he realised what I'd done he'd throw me a big scowl. This was war, it seemed. Over the weeks and months we'd spend the entire morning, or however long we were there, battling to get control of the stereo and whoever wasn't getting their own way would stand on their side of the room with their arms folded throwing big evils. Over time a truce was called, and on realising that our musical tastes actually weren't too dissimilar – not to mention the fact that we were both heavily into collecting vinyl – we became mates. In fact, as many of you reading this will know, Nicky was one of the three people who accompanied me to Ibiza on that fabled trip in '87.

Although it had originated sometime in the early 1970s, by the time Danny and I arrived in New York for the first time hip hop was just coming into its own, so although it was unintentional our timing was perfect. Grandmaster Flash and the Furious Five, Houdini, Kurtis Blow. It was the most exciting thing to happen to the music industry in years and culturally it was turning New York on its head. The introduction of hip hop back in the UK had been piecemeal at best so far, in the sense that we'd been treated to just a fraction of the music, knew little about its history, and next to nothing about its culture, apart from what kind of clothes you were supposed to wear. You can imagine then the effect that arriving in its epicentre had on me.

One of the first things I remember seeing after leaving the apartment for the first time was a b-boy walking down the sidewalk with a boom box on his shoulder listening to Afrika Bambaataa. Fuck me! Did I want to be that guy. Later that day I began discovering some of the radio stations in the city that were playing hip hop such as Kiss FM, WBLS and KTU. It was new and it was dangerous. It was, as I said earlier, New York just like you see in the movies. I'd never been so close to the roots of an actual culture before. You could hear it, see it, smell it, feel it, taste it. I'm mixing my musical genres here, but to coin the title of an extremely well-known song, my senses were working overtime. And I haven't even mentioned the breakdancing yet, have I? It was all just incredible. By the end of the two weeks, New York and hip hop had taken a tight hold of me, to the extent that although we had to go home, I knew that, for me at least, it wouldn't be for very long.

The first thing I did on my return was to call in a few favours job-wise so I could save up some extra money. Fortunately, New York was quite cheap at the time and with Danny's cousin rather bizarrely agreeing to let me stay with him again, I knew that, with a following wind and a curtailment of my record-buying habits, I could be over there pretty soon. When I told Danny of my intentions he immediately told me his. 'If you're going back, so am I,' he said. 'We've started this together, so let's see it through together.' You'll pardon the pun boys and girls but that was like hip hop to my ears. We really were like partners in crime, Danny and I. Brothers, even. It made perfect sense.

We planned our return to New York exactly as we used to plan our holidays, as in we met up in a pub somewhere, chucked around some ideas and just booked it. The main difference this time, apart from the fact that we were going for three months as opposed to two weeks and would also need a visa each, was that this trip would have a bearing on the rest of my life, I just knew it. That two-week holiday had brought my future, or at least the future I wanted for myself, a little bit closer to becoming a reality, in that it had given me an insight into how music can help to create, not just a fan base with some merchandise, but an actual culture. Until now that's exactly what I'd been really – a fan – but after experiencing the hip-hop phenomenon in New York first-hand for a couple of weeks, not to mention the music scene in general which seemed to be far more vibrant and real than the scene in the UK at the time, I felt invested. It was like having a foot on the first rung of the ladder.

Arriving in New York as two young men on a mission as opposed to just tourists was a very different experience, and I must admit that the reality of our situation brought us down to earth a bit. Or should I say it levelled us off. We'd been on a high ever since arriving the first time and by the time we landed the second time we'd kind of persuaded ourselves that the only thing we had to worry about was what part of Lexington we wanted to live in and what colour we wanted our Rolls-Royce. The reality was different, but it was no less exciting.

The apartment we were living in – on the floor still – was three floors up in a very ugly brownstone building, and in addition to having some black metal bars adorning the door and windows, it had a sizeable contingent of cockroaches. There were also rats every-where on the street. The neighbourhood itself was mainly Puerto Rican and Dominican so hardly anyone spoke English. It was also pretty rough and there was always a police siren or two to be heard and even the odd gunshot. Yet again, and with all of the above, we didn't really give a shit. Danny's cousin wasn't charging us any rent, which was kind of him, or should I say daft, and he also fed us a lot of the time. This would have to change once we'd got jobs but for the first few weeks we were sorted. The only thing we had to worry about really was spending money, but as I said, it was dead cheap. Transport wasn't a problem as everyone used to jump the turnstiles on the subway and so New York really was ours for the taking.

What amused me the most about New York, at least in the first couple of weeks, was the television. As well as having adverts every two minutes, which I found fascinating at first because they were nearly all dreadful and then just annoying, the programming often went from the sublime, or the slightly less rubbish, to the ridiculous. I'll give you an example. One night Danny and I had been out somewhere and we'd had a few drinks. I still wasn't what you'd call a regular drinker but I was finding my feet, as was Danny. When we got back to the apartment we switched on the TV and were treated to an episode of *The Love Boat*. Most things can seem better after you've had a few drinks but we must have had a skinful as I remember us laughing our tits off. After *The Love Boat* was a programme called *Midnight Blue*, a sexually themed chat show on the Manhattan Cable Television channel that was presented by a man in his birthday suit. All the adverts for this show were for brothels and escorts. It was mad. After an hour of that it felt like we must have been drinking absinthe! It was New York all over.

The first sort of dilemma we faced there was how to get into nightclubs. As frequenting them was high up on our to-do list, if we couldn't gain entry it would be a disaster. Each club obviously had its own door policy and so it was a case of turning up and just trying our luck. We went to Danceteria (where Mark Kamins signed Madonna), Bond's, Roxy, Fun House (where John 'Jellybean' Benitez was behind the decks), Save the Robots in the East Village, Studio 54 and, of course, the underground extravaganza, Paradise Garage, which was home to the aforementioned DJ'ing legend, Larry Levan.

Because of all the stories we'd heard in the UK, Mr Levan had achieved an almost godlike status in our eyes and Paradise Garage was the first nightclub on our list. Unlike many of the other clubs we visited, we didn't actually encounter any problems entering Paradise Garage which probably lulled us into a false sense of security. We were soon brought down to earth though.

A lot of the clubs on our list were frequented by either black, Hispanic or gay crowds – sometimes all three – so a couple of straight white English guys were not really 'on the list', if you get my drift. There were several occasions while we were in New York when I felt a bit out of place, but I never had any trouble. The majority of the kids at my school had been black and a lot of my friends were. It's just something that never occurred to me. I remember going to a concert by The Jones Girls one night in New York months later and I was literally the only white person in the venue. I got a few funny stares from a few people but that was it. I didn't care and for the most part, neither did anyone else.

At Paradise Garage the crowd was mainly gay, male and either black or Hispanic. The club, which was basically a disused garage (the clue's in the name) was situated at 84 King Street which is in Soho and about three blocks from the Hudson River. We arrived there on that first occasion at about 2am and queued up in front of the two enormous garage doors which made up a large proportion of the building's forecourt. Even today, I always get a little bit of a thrill going into a nightclub; a mixture of excitement and anticipation. It's not always very powerful, but it's there, washing around inside me. Paradise Garage was like having a hundred shots of that simultaneously, and if you consider how many nightclubs I've been to over the years – I couldn't even hazard a guess as to how many – it still stands alone.

One of the two garage doors, which were bolted shut, had a smaller door within it which was where the punters entered. Every time it was opened the music escaped momentarily, infusing the waiting hordes with a shot of that special brew I just mentioned. Because of the make-up of the crowd we didn't really fancy our chances much. We'd rehearsed a few plea lines just in case, but we were expecting the door staff to take one look at us, have a bit of a laugh and then send us on our way.

There must have been about fifty people already in the queue when we arrived, all black or Hispanic, and only about half had been allowed in. When it was finally our turn, instead of being told to do one, like we'd been expecting, we were waved in without a word or even a second look. We might have been quite young and naive, but Danny and I were smart enough to realise that in situations like that you don't give people an opportunity to change their minds, so we just put our heads down, walked through the steel interior door and headed towards the metal detector.

'What the fucking hell happened there?' I whispered to Danny.

'No idea, mate,' he said grinning his head off. 'We're in though!'

Although we'd heard plenty of stories about Paradise Garage it had all been about the music, so we had no idea what to expect when it came to the layout, etc. The room itself was surprisingly small and probably held no more than about three or four hundred people. It was also boiling hot and all four walls had been painted jet black. It was a real sweatbox. The crowd were going insane when we arrived, and on averting our gaze upwards we saw the reason why. There, in a booth high above the dance floor (it should have been on a cloud really) was Larry Levan, often referred to as the Jimi Hendrix of Dance Music. I remember walking on to the dance floor, which brought me a bit closer, and just standing there looking upwards. It was almost spiritual, although I probably looked like a bit of a weirdo. In fact, I must have, as after a couple of minutes a black guy came up to me, tapped me on the shoulder and shouted in my ear, 'Hey, man, if you ain't dancing, get off the floor!' He had a point.

Having entered the club unchallenged, we'd now regained some of our legendary confidence, and so instead of just standing there gawping at Larry's booth we decided to go and say hello. Back then you could actually do things like that, and when we climbed the stairway to heaven and poked our heads around the door, there were already five or six people there, including Larry.

On realising they had company everybody nodded in our direction and then just carried on their conversations. 'Wow!' I thought. 'We're in again!' After a few minutes we began shuffling in Larry's direction so we could watch him in action, but without getting too close. Had somebody told us before we went out that night that we'd end up watching Larry Levan spin from just a few yards away I'd have just laughed. We both would've. That's exactly what was happening though. We were in a club that today is cited as being a prototype for the modern dance club watching a man who is referred to as the Jimi Hendrix of Dance Music. We watched, we listened, we learned, we marvelled. What a night!

Larry's strength was his arrangement, as in knowing what record to play and when. His mixing was great, but in the days before house music, which had rigid beats per minute, it was often difficult to mix records together. If this was the case Larry would often do something unexpected – something brilliant. My favourite example happened on that first visit while Danny and I were downstairs on the dance floor. A record ended and when it did Larry left a gap. It was pitch-black and everyone on the dance floor gradually came to a halt. Suddenly, emerging out of the darkness and the silence, we heard the sound of a train somewhere in the distance. As the sound got louder and louder, a spotlight suddenly lit up which made it seem like a train was charging towards us. Then, as the noise reached its crescendo, Larry dropped in 'Don't Make Me Wait' by Peech Boys. The place just exploded. What a fucking reaction! I just stood there again, looking up at Larry open-mouthed. What the hell had I just witnessed? It was my Sermon on the Mount.

One of the other most important lessons I learned from Larry Levan was how to break a record. Or at least he gave me an idea of how to do so. This came into its own when I had my residency at Cream, by which time I already had my own record label, Perfecto. If Larry liked a new tune he'd sometimes play it two or three times in a set, and if it didn't go down well the first time around he'd spin it again at a different time the next night. A lot of these tunes he played were promos and if I liked them, which I often did, I'd head down to a shop called Vinyl Mania the next day to see if I could get a copy. Sometimes Larry would have an exclusive on these tracks which meant it wouldn't be available for months, and in that situation I'd go straight to the record label and start begging. It didn't always work but sometimes I had some luck. What Larry created by doing all this was a desire to seek out and procure hitherto unheard pieces of music, and when I started up at Cream I did exactly the same thing. Or should I say I commercialised it. I'd have a list at Cream of twenty tracks on the Perfecto label that weren't yet available but that I thought, given the right foothold, might well catch on. Before playing them at the club I'd go down to 3 Beat Records in Liverpool and give them a box of promos for each one. It was entirely up to them what they did with them but I'd imagine they'd have sold them. The majority of people who'd go looking for these tracks once I'd played them would be fellow DJs so they'd head off down to 3 Beat Records, 3 Beat Records would sell them a copy of one of the promos and make a couple of quid, and the record would then be played in front of a brand new crowd of people. Bingo! The biggest success we had by employing this now obsolete method of breaking a record was a tune called 'Bullet in the Gun' which sold a couple of hundred thousand units. That was all down to Larry.

For the next few months, Danny and I went to Paradise Garage every Saturday night. The place didn't really get going until about 3 or 4am and we'd roll out about midday. Nine times out of ten we'd end up falling asleep on the train home and wouldn't wake up until we reached the end of the line. We didn't care though. Not one bit.

OK, here's an interesting aside for you. Given what went on to happen in Ibiza a few years later, perhaps the most comically ironic example of our naivety in New York was the fact that we couldn't work out for the life of us how everyone at Paradise Garage managed to stay awake all night without drinking any alcohol. We didn't see anyone taking coke or anything so what on earth could have been going on? We later found out that not all of these places had alcohol licences and in order to keep the party going they'd lace massive bowls of punch with MDMA powder.

I used to think like a lot of people that MDMA powder, and later ecstasy, came out of somewhere like Amsterdam, and it was only when I visited Dallas, of all places, back in the early 1990s that I began to question it. I was over there with Mike Pickering, Graeme Park and Dave Haslam for what became known as the United States of the Haçienda Tour. Boy oh boy, did we have some fun. It was out of this world.

This is when the Manchester sound was massive and believe it or not the good people of Dallas used to think I was a Manc. 'Have a day off will you,' I used to say to them. 'I'm not a Manc, I'm a flaming cockney!' They were still none the wiser. Anyway, that was the first place I saw MDMA powder being used openly as opposed to ecstasy and the reason for that, so I was told, was because it was being prescribed by doctors at the time, either to treat certain psychological issues or marital ones. Yes, you read that correctly. In Texas in the early 1990s doctors were prescribing couples who were going through a bad patch with MDMA! 'Off you go then. You'll have a lovely time on that. Everything's gonna be rosy.' And it probably was, for a few hours. What on earth were they thinking? Eventually the authorities cottoned on and it was banned.

OK, what about these other clubs in New York?

Well, in order to maintain the right kind of atmosphere, some of these legendary venues used to employ a little bit of what you might call 'positive discrimination' on the door, which often made the clubs themselves feel more like private parties or private members' clubs. The late Steve Rubell at Studio 54 was the worst for this. He used to like his crowds to be as starry as possible (regular patrons at Studio 54 included David Bowie, Mick Jagger, Freddie Mercury, Woody Allen, Elton John, Sylvester Stallone, Robin Williams and Dolly Parton, to name but a very few) which posed a problem for Danny and me. Or should I say, it presented us with a challenge. We couldn't give a shit about the celebrities who were going there, but what we did give a shit about was the music, not to mention the people who were spinning it. We just had to get in. After several times of trying – and failing – to circumnavigate Studio 54's uber-elitist door policy, we finally came up with an idea.

'Let's pretend we're press,' I said to Danny one day. 'I can be from the *NME* and you can be from *Melody Maker*.'

This was ironic really as both the *NME* and *Melody Maker* absolutely hated the kind of music we listened to, but that was kind of the point really. It was like cocking them a snook. Let's use the buggers to our advantage. Fortunately, Danny thought this idea had potential so we set about making a false ID badge each. I wish I still had mine. It was bloody rubbish! That said, it certainly did the trick when it came to blagging our way into nightclubs and it sent us both on a bit of an adventure.

The first place we used our IDs was at Studio 54 and they worked like an absolute dream. If I was Moses when it came to verbal dexterity of the persuasive variety, then Danny was God himself and within seconds of rolling up there we had them eating out of our hands. Drinks, VIP areas, access to the DJ. You name it, we had it, and it was all courtesy of a little bit of front, a little bit of luck most probably, and a couple of crudely made false IDs that wouldn't have got you into a pub gig in London.

After quite literally pulling the wool over the eyes of New York's nightclub fraternity for a few weeks, we decided to see if our IDs – not forgetting our considerable charm, of course – would have the same effect on New York's live music community. I forget who the first band or artist was who we went to see (I think it could have been either Bobby Womack, The Jones Girls or Maze) but after ringing up the venue where they were going to be playing and making the manager aware that two of the UK's most influential and powerful music journalists were in town for a few days, and were keen on seeing whichever artist or band happened to be playing that evening, we were thanked for getting in touch and told that two tickets would be waiting for us at the ticket office.

It felt too good to be true at first (perhaps they'd rumbled us and it was a trap?) but when we turned up at the venue, there they were – two tickets. What used to compensate for our shitty IDs were our English accents and depending on how the person we were speaking to reacted we'd either say as little as possible and just move on or we'd have a chat and see what else we could blag. Some people were all over us like a rash – 'Oh my God, your accent is AMAZING! Are you sure you're not Australian?' – and others were dead cagey. Ultimately though, the same thing would happen every time, as in it didn't matter where the hell we were going, we'd always get in.

As our confidence inevitably grew in this situation so did the ridiculousness of our requests, and the next thing I knew we were queueing to collect tickets to go and see Bob Marley. It was about to get worse though, or better. After collecting the tickets, one of Bob's people came to see us and asked if we'd like to interview Bob after the gig. I was a bit gobstruck to be honest but Danny wasn't. 'Aww, we'd love to,' he said. 'Thanks very much.' After arranging a time with Bob's assistant we went to see the gig, which was awesome. 'What are you going to ask him?' I said to Danny. 'I don't know,' he said. 'I'll think of something.' Although we both enjoyed Bob Marley's music, neither of us were reggae fans.

After the gig we went to the bar as planned and about half an hour later in walks Bob. Danny is about six feet tall and his feet are at least a size eleven. He's also a bit clumsy, or he was then, and as he went to greet Bob Marley he ended up tripping him up. How it happened exactly I have no idea, but I remember whispering to Danny, 'Good start, mate. Good start!' Luckily for us Bob seemed to be quite a laid-back sort of fellow (ahem) and he just laughed it off.

'So, Bob,' began Danny once he'd sat down. 'You like your music then, do you?'

As opening questions go to one of the most influential artists on the planet, that was an absolute blinder.

'Yes, yes. Very much,' said Bob looking slightly bemused. 'Music is my life basically.'

'Good answer,' said Danny. Next question. 'How long did it take you to write "Walking on Sunshine"?'

'That was Eddy Grant you prick,' I said, digging him in the ribs.

'I know!' blagged Danny. 'I was just kidding.'

He wasn't kidding.

I don't know how the hell he did it but Danny managed to complete a thirty-minute interview with Bob Marley without getting beaten up by his security guards. It really was an incredible effort. Honestly, he knew more about the bloody Archers than he did about reggae, or its most famous protagonist. He truly was the Blag-meister General!

It was in New York that I had my second 'Road to Damascus' moment. Funnily enough, it wasn't too dissimilar to the one I had back home, in the sense that it was a warning about what might happen if I wasn't careful. It was a cold and very miserable morning in February and I was on the subway. I forget where I was going exactly but I'd have been on my way to hustle for some work. Have you ever sat on a subway train or a Tube train during the winter months? It's a different atmosphere to spring or summer. I suppose it's the same everywhere, but if you want to gauge the mood of a city in just a few minutes, take a ride on one of them during rush hour. You'll pick it up immediately.

This February morning I was sitting there when all of a sudden I noticed a bloke sitting opposite. He was probably in his mid-sixties and although he was staring at a newspaper, I could tell he wasn't reading it. He looked lost, to be honest. Like he'd given up the will to live. I looked at the person next to him and then at everyone else in the carriage and they were all exactly the same. There were no mobile phones and nothing worth looking at out of the windows. God, it was depressing. I looked back at the man sitting opposite and I thought to myself, 'If I don't keep an eye on things and make my dreams come true, I could become just like you one day.' Taking the same journey day after day, week after week. To be fair, I had no idea what that man's situation was and for all I know he could have been the happiest man on earth. The situation, however, spoke to me and at first it scared me half to death. It was a fear of having to do the same thing every day for the rest of my life and just for a moment I was shit scared.

Don't get me wrong, we all need a little bit of routine in our lives, but it's one of the few things I find difficult to cope with to any great degree and when presented with it as being part of everyday life – real or not – which is what happened on the subway, I tend to go a bit funny. Even to this day I usually reject routine which means my life is a little bit chaotic, which I love. Not in a disorganised way; I'm very organised. It's just here and there. Sometimes I'll look at my diary and see, for instance, Germany Monday, studio Tuesday, day off Wednesday, back to LA Thursday, gig in Austin Friday. That kind of thing really lifts my heart.

After six months or so, the honeymoon started coming to an end with regards to our financial and living arrangements and we had to get ourselves sorted. So far, New York had been a blast and had exceeded just about every expectation we'd had. We were ready to take the next step though. Ready for a challenge. I also had to start thinking a bit more about what I was going to do in the industry I'd chosen as 'phoney music journalist and first-division blagger' wasn't going to get me to the top of the chain and help me attain world domination. The main problem we had in this department was that we were obviously on a tourist visa so we weren't supposed to be working. In fact, we were actually supposed to have left the country by now. Luckily, one of Danny's many cousins came to the rescue yet again. This one worked for the investment bankers Morgan Stanley and suggested that we both work as couriers, although Danny had other ideas. I didn't need papers as it was cash in hand. All I really needed were a pair of legs – check – a rudimentary knowledge of New York – check – and a decent pair of trainers – check.

In addition to some much-needed cash, this opportunity gave me an idea, an idea I hoped would enable me to finally get a foot on the first rung of the music industry ladder, or at least help me to prepare the groundwork. You see, if I was going to be getting paid for dropping parcels off at all these companies around Manhattan, what was to stop me from dropping in at the record companies and asking to speak to the club promotions manager. I could tell them I was a DJ from the UK who was in town for a couple of weeks and ask them if they had any promos for me. Back then, that's often how a DJ would get hold of things like promos as there was no social media and no email. You literally had to doorstep a record company, if you had the balls, and they'd either say voila, here you go, or tell you to bugger off.

After just a few days I got this off to a fine art and would change my patter accordingly, depending on what was going on. 'Hi, my name's Paul and I'm a DJ from London. I was at the Bob Marley gig last night with the guys from *NME* and I thought I'd drop by and ask if you had any promos for me?' Once again, the English accent was a big help and was even more effective face to face than it had been over the phone when we'd been blagging tickets. Thanks to film characters like my hero, James Bond, the English accent (even a cockney one like mine) makes some Americans go weak at the knees, or it used to, and my hit rate for getting to speak to the right people and blagging free promos must have been in the mid-nineties. There was always the occasional one who seemed to either hate us Limeys or was just naturally suspicious, and when that was the case I'd bid them good day and make my exit, sharpish. These days you'd never get away with such a blag as the courier company would be able to track you, so you wouldn't last more than a day. Also, with the advent of Google, etc., the people at the record companies would be able to look you up. It was definitely a con of its time.

The actual aim of this exercise, apart from collecting as much free vinyl as I possibly could, was obviously to network and to eventually create myself a job. That may sound a bit daft to some people but that really was the plan. There was nothing I could think of or even knew about within the music industry that was a natural fit for my talents, so I had to think outside the record box. What is it they say – necessity is the mother of invention? Well, that's exactly what I was doing.

While I was doing this, Danny had enrolled himself on a bartending course at Columbia University and seemed to be having a great time; so much so that after a few weeks I decided to join him. I still carried on couriering and conning people out of boxes of vinyl, but because the course was part-time I managed to fit it in. This is probably when I started to develop a proper taste for alcohol, and it's easy to see why. There were about twenty people in the class and we each had to write down the measures for a cocktail, mix them, and then drink just a very small amount, or enough to know what it tasted like. Danny and I situated ourselves at the very back of the class like a couple of naughty schoolboys and instead of taking a sip like the rest of the class, we'd always down the lot. We used to learn how to make seven or eight cocktails in a class and I don't remember one occasion when we didn't fall out of the building absolutely hammered. We passed the course though, somehow, and I still have the certificate somewhere. In fact, for many years after that I used to tell people that I was a graduate from Columbia University and a few years ago it won me $1,000. I was talking to this American geezer and he didn't believe me.

'There's no way you graduated from Columbia,' he said condescendingly. 'That's a top university.'

'Don't be fooled by the accent,' I said to him. 'I passed with flying colours, mate.'

This bloke was with his girlfriend and in order to try and impress her he then bet me $1,000.

'Prove it,' he said smiling at his girlfriend. 'I bet you can't.'

'OK, then,' I said. 'You get your money on the table and the next time I see you I'll do just that.'

At the time I wasn't quite sure where the certificate was and when I eventually found it I was well pleased. This bloke, whose girlfriend is signed to my label, had been so rude and so disrespectful. I wanted revenge, and I wanted it now. As soon as I found the certificate I was on this bloke's back. 'You get yourself down to my place,' I said to him. 'I've got something to show you.' You should have seen the look on his face when I showed him the certificate. He was gutted. And he was also $1,000 poorer!

Just to prove to you how adept Danny and I had become at pulling the wool over people's eyes and getting our feet in the right doors, Danny even managed to blag his way to becoming a ski instructor for a while. Could he ski? He might have done it on holiday once or twice, but that was it. As I said, the man was just a behemoth.

As the months went by my record collection grew at about the same rate as my liver, but so did my list of contacts. Instead of just popping in for vinyl at the record companies I'd start popping in just for a chat, and slowly but surely the job that I intended to create for myself began to take shape. Once again I had to custom-ise my patter for the situation and the idea I had was quite simple. 'I'll tell you what,' I said to the record companies. 'Why don't I bring over some promos from the UK, and if you like the artists, you can sign them.' As I said, it was a very simple idea really – a middleman for English and American record companies. A facilitator.

I'd already applied for jobs at every single record company in the UK, and although I hadn't had any luck I'd made contacts at quite a few. I also knew people who knew people, so I had a good chance of making it work, or at least getting hold of some UK promos. Sure enough, after a few times of asking, they started to trickle through from the UK, either from record companies or from friends. A single by Haircut 100 was one of the first discs to arrive, although it didn't make many waves. Shortly after that a record by The Human League turned up which seemed a bit more saleable. 'Check this out,' I said to them all. 'These guys are going to be massive.' Little did I know that The Human League had just signed a worldwide deal with Virgin Records! I had to talk my way out of that one.

One of the first people I got to know well within the music industry in New York was Chuck Chillout, who was part of DJ Red Alert's crew. DJ Red Alert was the doyen of hip hop radio in New York and used to broadcast on 98.7 Kiss FM. Since landing there, in addition to immersing myself in hip hop, I'd become mildly obsessed with breakdancing. Not participating – God no! – but I loved the whole b-boy style thing.

One of the other facets of hip hop that fascinated me was DJ'ing, so scratching and cutting basically. It was obviously a contrast in both style and music to the people I'd been listening to and watching such as Larry Levan and Tony Humphries and it opened things up even more. Could DJ'ing be something I could get into? I was beginning to think that way. There was definitely a DJ within me trying to get out, even then.

Chuck Chillout took me to the Bronx one day and had I had the benefit of hindsight, I might well have made my excuses. I'd heard all the rumours about how dangerous it could be in the Bronx and that white guys shouldn't venture there alone at certain times, but when I arrived I realised that that had all been underplayed. The sense of danger there was almost palpable. It was as if war was about to break out. Luckily for me, I was with Chuck and he made sure I was OK. We ended up going to his place where he gave me a masterclass in scratching. That was some evening and I remember leaving his pad with a head absolutely full of dreams.

The first record company executives I became friendly with over there were Cory Robbins and Steve Plotnicki at Profile Records who hadn't been on the scene very long but who had already signed the likes of Dr Jeckyll & Mr Hyde and Run-DMC. To this day the label specialises in hip hop mainly, although they do deviate. This gave me an idea at the time as I figured that if I could find a British act for Cory and Steve to sign, I could then approach them about becoming the label's official European scout. And so it came to pass. The act they ended up signing on my recommendation was Boys Don't Cry who ended up having a big hit over there in 1985, although ironically not in the UK, with a song called 'I Wanna Be a Cowboy'. Although the hit came sometime later, I now officially had a foot on the first rung of the music industry ladder. All the blagging and bullshit had paid off. I was on my way.

By the time we were ready to leave New York I was a very different person to the one who'd arrived there two and a half years earlier. That's right, we were slightly late leaving. If you had to equate it to something conventional, I'd say it was my version of attending university, or at the very least doing something like the Knowledge. Actually, that's probably more accurate as I'd been to hundreds if not thousands of different places, had met a multitude of different people, had experienced all kinds of different things, and had learned more about the industry that I now belonged to than I could have done in a hundred years in London. I'm not bad-mouthing the place of my birth, by the way. The fact of the matter is though that in terms of dance music, club culture and hip hop, New York was in a different universe to London and that definitely gave me a big, big advantage. Yes, I was new to it all, but I was also ahead of the game and knew many things that my friends and colleagues in the UK did not.

When it finally came to us leaving the country, it's fair to say that our arses were squeaking more than somewhat. We'd outstayed our welcome by over two years and had heard all kinds of horror stories about how the authorities, who were notoriously hard on illegals, dealt with people like us. The last time I'd broken the law had been in Croydon when I'd nicked those football shirts.

Back then I felt like the Artful Dodger. Now I was like Al Capone, or at least that's what my imagination had cast me as. What would I get, ten years?

What they used to do in those days was make you fill in a form when you arrived in the USA, attach part of that form to your passport, keep the other part on file, and then match the two up when you left – job done. Unfortunately, that wasn't going to work for us as on checking our documentation they'd realise that we'd overstayed our welcome and we'd be sent straight to the local penitentiary.

By the time we arrived at the airport we were bricking it and the only excuse we'd managed to muster was that we'd lost the pieces of paper that were attached to our passports. 'But it's your responsibility to produce that, sir,' said the female immigration control officer who was about as friendly as a malnourished T. rex. 'But I didn't know that,' I said pleadingly. 'Look,' I continued. 'I came here a couple of weeks ago and lost the piece of paper. What can I tell you? I'm sorry.' Nothing was on computers in those days and I have no doubt that the lengths she'd have had to go through in order to investigate my case properly had a bearing on what she said next. 'OK, move along please, sir,' she said. 'Have a pleasant flight.' I didn't need asking twice and luckily Danny had a similar experience. Without looking back we headed for the gate and prayed that they didn't have a change of heart. If I'd been caught I wouldn't have been allowed back into the USA for God knows how long, if ever! Given the fact that I've now lived there for almost two decades and have a passport, I think I was quite fortunate, don't you?

CHAPTER 5

Irons in Plenty of Fires

The label that Boys Don't Cry had been signed to in the UK were called Champion Records and they were one of my first ports of call when I arrived back. After my mum and dad, of course. They were still living in Thornton Heath and with no place of my own they allowed me to move back in. Boy, did I have some stories to tell them – I didn't tell them everything though! Some of what went on in New York had to stay in New York, if you see what I mean. The thing I wanted to talk about most when I came back was hip hop (not to Mum and Dad though) and I couldn't wait to spread the word.

Champion Records were based in Harlesden in north London, and although I had plenty of contacts over in New York, they were the only record label I'd had any dealings with in the UK. I say 'they'. Champion Records actually had a staff of one at the time, a man called Mel Medalie. Although he'd only set up the label quite recently he'd been in the industry a long time, and if memory serves me correctly he'd cut his teeth working with glam rock bands.

When I first went to see Mel I was like a dog with two dicks. As far as I was concerned I'd discovered oil and I wanted him to know that. I wanted everyone to know. Luckily, Mel believed what I told him and put his faith in me. Mel's very good at recognising new talent, whether that be an artist or some geezer from south London who reckons he's found the next big thing. A case in point is when I contacted Mel, told him I was working for Profile Records (which I actually wasn't at the time), and asked him to send me some promos. Unlike many of the other labels, he actually did send some, and look what happened. He's never been afraid to take a chance has Mel, and has always had an eye, and an ear, for what works. I never got paid a bean for that deal involving Boys Don't Cry, by the way. It was an act of altruism, of which I ended up being the main benefactor.

I left Mel's office that day having agreed to become his assistant and to this day it's one of the best decisions I ever made. It was like a crash course in how to run a record label single-handedly, which is basically what Mel had been doing. I did the press, the marketing, plugged the records, sent out the promos and went to the clubs. I did the lot. I was also working with Mel, of course, who had an enormous amount of experience and who filled in all the gaps. My office, such as it was, was a box room at Mel's place. I had a desk, a telephone and a little sofa bed at the back. Sometimes I'd end up kipping there if I was working late. It was great. I was now immersed in music twenty-four hours a day. I had two jobs now: A&R scout and assistant to the MD at Champion Records, and European scout for Profile Records.

Actually, I've forgotten something here. I had three.

Before I came back to the UK I had an idea that, if it worked, would provide me with a nice little income while at the same time help me continue building my network. The idea was to create a record pool similar to one that Frankie Knuckles had established in the States called Def Mix. In the UK, if a record company wanted to plug something they'd send it directly to a list of DJs, whereas in America they'd send five hundred copies to a record pool instead. The DJs over there would pay a subscription for access to that pool and away you go. Purely from a saturation point of view it was a much better idea, but it also gave me an idea too. I thought, I can go back to England, get all the best DJs in all the best clubs – whether they be gay, black, white or straight – to pay me a subscription and I'll supply them with everything that's hot in the USA, courtesy of all my contacts. It took a while to get off the ground but ended up working like a dream. The money was obviously welcome but it forced me to introduce myself to every DJ out there.

In January every year Mel would take me to Midem, a huge event held in Cannes where key players from the music industry congregate to, among other things, listen to and license one another's records. It's like a music version of the Cannes Film Festival I suppose, just less public. And less pretentious. When Mel first told me we were going to Midem my head almost went bang. I thought, 'My God, I've arrived!'

We always used to stay at the Martinez Hotel which was a five-star establishment. Proper posh. I'd have a room and Mel would have a suite. Throughout the week, in addition to us visiting all the stands in the halls and eating and drinking our own body weight in lobster and champagne, just to be sociable, a steady stream of A&R people would pass through Mel's suite and try and flog us some tunes. Mel, who must be in his seventies now, was always a bit of a foodie and if any of these A&R people turned up in the afternoon – so after lunch, basically – I would listen to the music and look after business while Mel had a kip on his bed. To be fair, listening to the music and deciding what to go for was a big part of my job. Dance music and hip hop, etc. – modern music, in other words – were not Mel's speciality, so I was what you might call the ears of the outfit. Had I played Mel something that sounded like Slade or The Sweet he'd have been up and at 'em, but those sorts of tunes were a little bit thin on the ground.

Without wanting to blow my own trumpet too much, although I may be about to, because of what I'd picked up in New York, and because of the people I was still speaking to over there, I was still well ahead of the game when it came to things like house music and hip hop. Like hip hop, house music was just beginning to filter through from the States at this time, but still at a snail's pace. Even so, many of the majors, or at least the ones that had a bit of foresight, were now creating their own dance departments so if Champion were going to capitalise, it had to be now. Enter Mr Willard Carroll Smith II and Mr Jeffrey Allen Townes, collectively aka DJ Jazzy Jeff & the Fresh Prince.

I forget when, but sometime after starting at Champion I was sent a tune from the States called 'Girls Ain't Nothing But Trouble' by an unknown Philadelphia duo called DJ Jazzy Jeff & the Fresh Prince. The song was built around a sample from the theme tune to a 1960s television programme called *I Dream of Jeannie* and I told Mel we should sign them. The boys were unknowns on both sides of the Atlantic so it wasn't going to cost him much. Anyway, fortunately Mel agreed and we went ahead. When it came to us releasing the tune I'd had some second thoughts and so went to speak to Mel.

'What's up?' he said. 'The track sounds absolutely fine to me.'

'The mix isn't right,' I said. 'Don't ask me why, I just know.'

I really did have no idea why it sounded wrong, but it did. It was instinctive.

Mine and Mel's relationship had always been based on a mutual trust, but without either of us ever having to go into any detail or find out why. This was a case in point as had he pressed me for an answer, I wouldn't have been able to give him one. Not at that moment. If I'd worked for a major record company I wouldn't have dared to say anything. And even if I had, I'd probably have been swept aside. 'What the hell do you know?' I trusted my gut instinct though, and luckily so did Mel.

'OK, we'll have to hire a producer in to remix it,' I said to him.

'No we won't,' said Mel. 'That'll cost us a fortune. Why don't you do it?'

'Me? But I've got no experience in the studio. I'm not capable.'

I was a confident soul as you know, but working in a studio was still pretty alien to me and I thought he must have been on something.

'I don't mean on your own you wally,' said Mel. 'Look, you're the one who says it needs remixing. I'll give you an engineer. Just tell him what you want.'

Without going into too much detail, we brought in a DJ called Mastermind Herbie who could also produce and engineer and after a few hours working with him I came to the conclusion that, as well as being too long, we needed to get to the hook of the song, as in the sample and the chorus, a little bit quicker. The drums were also wrong in my opinion – they weren't continuous – so once the length of the song and the hook had been sorted out, we set about reprogramming them and turning them into a loop. Many years later when I was producing the Happy Mondays on their album *Pills 'n' Thrills and Bellyaches*, I wanted to use hip-hop rhythms and spent hours playing hip-hop records to their drummer, Gary Whelan. He picked it all up and they sounded fantastic with acoustic drums. It really worked.

I obviously have no idea how the record might have fared had I not remixed it, but when it was finally released in the UK, as the Paul Oakenfold remix, it charted almost immediately. Mel went off his head when he found out, but in a good way. 'Girls Ain't Nothing But Trouble' was in danger of becoming Champion's first-ever hit record. It was an exciting time for us.

In order to maintain momentum and try to ensure that the record became a hit, we decided to bring Jazzy Jeff and the Fresh Prince over to the UK to do a load of promotion. 'OK, but somebody will have to come over to the States and get them,' said their manager. 'I'll go,' I said. Any excuse to get on a plane. I must have spent about two weeks with the boys altogether and all they wanted to eat while they were over here – surprise, surprise – was McDonald's. To be fair, English food was crap at the time (apart from fish and chips and they weren't having any of that) so it was probably the lesser of two evils.

I looked after Run-DMC a bit later and they were exactly the same when it came to food. In terms of character, however, they were poles apart, the main difference being that with Run-DMC I had to prove that I was the right man for the job. I was a white guy, and in those days the vast majority of people who produced and listened to hip hop were black. To three old-school hip-hop guys like Joseph, Darryl and Jason, having a white guy taking care of them on a promotional tour wasn't cool, at least at first. None of that ever mattered to me as I knew my hip hop, which is how I won them over. Jazzy Jeff and the Fresh Prince were a lot more laid-back and the only thing they cared about, apart from McDonald's, was having a good time.

During Jazzy Jeff and the Fresh Prince's promotional tour we got them on loads of different TV shows, including the mighty *Top of the Pops*. In those days that was still the show to do and if you managed to get a slot, barring a PR disaster, you were guaranteed at least a minor hit. In addition to that and the other TV shows we must have done about thirty radio interviews, God knows how many magazines and at least ten nightclub appearances. The upshot of all this was, as well as having a laugh for a couple of weeks, we had a nice little Top 10 hit on our hands which made everyone very happy indeed.

Their material was lighter and more commercial than old-school hip hop and the mainstream radio stations and television programmes responded accordingly. It was summer music. Will Smith though – that man just oozes charisma. He was always going to be big, which is exactly why we signed him. Funnily enough, although I've seen Jazzy Jeff on numerous occasions since then through my antics as a DJ, I haven't seen hide nor hair of Willard Carroll Smith II since waving him off at the airport.

The only mistake we made with the whole Jazzy Jeff and the Fresh Prince thing, which eventually turned into a whopper, was only signing them on a one-record deal. The moment that record became a hit in the UK, in came the majors and before we knew it we'd lost them to Jive Records. I was so pissed off when I found out. Not just because of the lost opportunities, although that did turn out to be a bone of contention when they started getting big. It was because of all the groundwork we'd put in. All that energy and hard work. Nobody had done anything dishonest or untoward, despite how we felt. We'd just dropped a bollock, plain and simple.

Anyway, I learned two lessons from that episode. First, never take these things personally (even if it does become personal or is, it isn't worth bothering with), and secondly, always keep one eye on the future. Our biggest mistake was loading all of our efforts and attentions on to that first record without even thinking about what might come after. It was a schoolboy error really and one that I had to try and ensure would never happen again.

The next act that Mel and I tried to sign to Champion were Salt-N-Pepa. While over in New York I'd got to know their producer, a guy called Hurby 'Luv Bug' Azor, and we'd stayed in touch. He called me about a song they'd done called 'The Show Stoppa (Is Stupid Fresh)' and they were ready to make things happen. The first thing I had to do was talk to Mel about an advance. The majors were all into it now and so we couldn't expect to pay peanuts. We had to offer big money, and more. The label who seemed to be most interested in Salt-N-Pepa, apart from us, were London Records, whose new A&R man was Pete Tong. Financially, we didn't stand a chance against them, so although I think we might have made them an early offer, we pulled out soon after. Exactly the same thing happened with Run-DMC. Had we had the money we'd have been the best men for the job, but we didn't. They too went to London. Funnily enough, London Records were the very first label I signed to as an artist, although it wasn't Pete Tong who did the deal. He was long gone by then.

London became the first big label to actually get a grip on hip hop, and because of what had happened with Jazzy Jeff and the Fresh Prince, when it came to looking after the artists they called me. I suppose this was the next best thing to signing them long term and I was happy to oblige. It was a job and Pete and I had a good relationship. We had a lot in common musically, of course, and we often thought along the same lines. It wouldn't be the last time our paths crossed either, as you'll soon find out.

While all this was going on, I'd happily been maintaining my relationship with Profile Records, who'd now asked me to be their official UK representative as opposed to just a scout, not to mention my growing list of contacts over there. As a result, I was contacted one day by a promo company called Rush Release who'd recently started working with a newly formed American label called Def Jam. Def Jam's owners, Rick Rubin and Russell Simmons, had launched the label in 1984 and their maiden release had been LL Cool J's 'I Need A Beat'. Two years on and they now had a roster featuring up-and-coming artists such as the Beastie Boys, Public Enemy, Jay-Z and DMX. They were nobodies in the UK at the time, admittedly, but in the USA they were making it big. The potential was massive.

The reason I was contacted by Rush Release was because Def Jam's UK distributor, CBS, were having problems planning the promotional tours in the UK for some of Def Jam's acts and they needed help. A showdown had been arranged involving everyone concerned at CBS's offices and they wanted me to attend.

Before the showdown Rick and Russell from Def Jam had really put CBS through their paces, both in terms of what they expected, what they wanted to achieve and how they expected CBS to achieve it. The upshot of their conversations so far had been that it wasn't going to be a walk in the park and the people at CBS were understandably nervous. Def Jam definitely wanted things to be done their way, and when it came to negotiations they'd been able to motivate, manipulate and terrorise, all at the same time. It was like a hungry and annoyed Jack Russell nipping at the heels of a very anxious Great Dane.

In addition to advising them on a few things, such as how the tours might work and who we might contact (remember, hip hop was still a bit of an unknown quantity to the majors in the UK), I was basically the meeting's mediator. A special envoy, like Kofi Annan, brought in to bridge the yawning gap between old-school hip hop and the British corporate music industry. It was a tough job, but at the end of the day somebody had to do it.

Joking aside, what we actually had to achieve at that meeting, apart from ensuring that everyone remained on good terms, was a map of exactly how we'd promote Def Jam's acts in the UK, which in turn led to my continued involvement. After all, somebody had to take care of the acts while they were over here and liaise with the press and the venues, etc. Who better than me? In order for this to work, however, I first had to speak to Mel. Since starting to work for him I'd acquired numerous other jobs and I had to be honest with him. Yes, I wanted to have my cake and eat it, but only because I was sure I was up to the job. Or jobs, should I say.

It wasn't just CBS and Def Jam though. Other people had been in touch such as Mr Tong at London. He'd recently signed Run-DMC who were on Profile in the States, and as Profile's UK representative I was the go-to man. What was I launching here, a crèche for hip-hop artists? Not surprisingly, Mel gave me his blessing to carry on with my extracurricular activities and I certainly made the most of it.

One of the first Def Jam acts to arrive from the good old US of A were the mind-blowingly incredible Beastie Boys. As with my friends Jazzy Jeff and the Fresh Prince, I went out of my way to be the perfect host and was looking forward to showing them my country, although I did hope that they might be willing to deviate from McDonald's occasionally.

The biggest problem we faced with the emergence of hip hop in the UK was the reaction from the press. At the end of the day, bad news and bad behaviour sell newspapers, and after having been starved of that on a musical front by the New Romantics for several years, they were hungry for a headline or two. Unfortunately, their malnourishment had rendered them desperate – or even more desperate than usual – and before they'd even got off the plane the Beastie Boys became a target.

OK, let's just forget about all the negative crap for a second and concentrate on the positives. The Beastie Boys were coming over to the UK to promote *Licensed to Ill*, which had already sold a shitload of copies in the USA and would go on to sell about

20 million worldwide. I was going to be responsible for organising not only the promotional tour of that record in the UK, but ensuring the band's continued happiness and wellbeing while they were in the UK. It was a disaster waiting to happen.

What you have to remember with the Beastie Boys is that everything they did, both in the studio and live, was pretty groundbreaking at the time. That said, what they were ultimately trying to achieve was simple, certainly when it came to their live shows. You had three white blokes, on a stage, playing hip hop, who wanted to throw a ginormous fucking party. End of. Forget punk. That was no party. That was just a spitting convention with a few punch-ups thrown in. This, although not exactly cuddly, was nothing less than a physical celebration of rudeness, bad behaviour and hip hop. What's more, the people of Britain – me included – absolutely loved it.

As with my two friends from Philadelphia, the three boys from New York City were a good bunch, and although they'd already experienced a certain amount of success over there, they hadn't let it go to their heads. If I had to describe the Beastie Boys' maiden tour of the UK in two words it would be 'wonderfully riotous'. Never in my life, both before and since then, have I been involved in such a glorious orgy of musical bad behaviour. Their press launch, for instance, which took place at the Diorama in London, started off as a vaguely civilised affair featuring the band and the good people of the British press and quickly descended into abject mayhem. Somebody had ordered several trays of vol-au-vents (not me), and after a period of good behaviour involving a string of inane questions, somebody got bored and started using said vol-au-vents as weapons. As food fights go, and I promise you this was neither rehearsed nor planned, it was monumental, although it did nothing to quell the press's preconceptions.

What the press became guilty of was confusing a bit of high jinks and bad behaviour – deliberately I think – which is all the Beastie Boys were guilty of, and their fans, with what the punk movement had sought to achieve a decade earlier, which was to piss off and intimidate the establishment. What probably legitimised that reaction, at least to a certain extent, was the theft of several thousand VW logo badges. Once that started to happen the hacks became creative, falsely accusing the band of a number of very serious crimes including assaulting a young boy in a wheelchair outside the Brixton Academy and mocking a group of terminally ill leukaemia patients, which was supposed to have happened at the Montreux Festival in Switzerland some weeks earlier. All of this was absolute bullshit by the way, but that didn't stop the MP Peter Bruinvels, who was a strong supporter of Section 28 and wanted a return of capital punishment, from forwarding a motion in the Houses of Parliament asking for the band to be deported. What a tosser. Had he ever seen the band live? Of course he hadn't. Actually, I wish he had seen them live as that might have finished him off.

Looking after the Beastie Boys gave me the first of my two appearances on the front cover of *The Sun* – so far. Or at least appearances for something I'm associated with. The headline for this one was something along the lines of 'BEASTIE BOYS CHAOS AT LONDON CONCERT', which again was a load of rubbish. Granted, the shows could often become quite raucous, but they were no worse than your average heavy metal gig. A few cans would be thrown at the stage, but that was it really. If it had been the Monsters of Rock Festival, for instance, it would have been bottles of piss. As I said before, you had three geezers playing hip hop who just wanted to throw a party.

By the end of the tour the band had been demonised so much by the press that just being a fan of theirs made you almost notorious. This created a very different vibe and as the tour drew to an end the atmosphere changed, both on and off the stage. During the last gig in Liverpool, a hail of beer cans were launched at the stage, forcing the band to eventually leave. Afterwards Ad-Rock, aka Adam Horovitz, was charged with GBH after allegedly having thrown one of the beer cans back at a female fan. A succession of death threats followed and it took him over a year, and about five trips back to the UK, to clear his name.

On the plus side, *Licensed to Ill* became one of the biggest albums of 1986 and went on to sell almost a million copies in the UK in its first two months of release. All things considered, the press attention, although unfair and very frustrating at times, definitely had a bearing on that number. You know what they say, any publicity is good publicity. That MP though. What a dickhead.

CHAPTER 6

The Project Club

About this time Trevor Fung and I started something called The Project Club. It was basically a Friday night party which we held at a venue called Ziggy's on Streatham High Street. Together with Danny, we'd already tried something similar to this on a more ad hoc basis called Fun House which we'd named after Jellybean's club in New York. I remember we made some graffiti banners for Fun House and we used to stick them all over the venue. That was supposed to give the proceedings a kind of New York feel, although I'm not sure it worked. Kids from all over London used to come down and breakdance on some lino that we put down while they did their thing and I'd be in charge of the music. To be fair to us, Fun House was probably the closest thing London had to a hip-hop club at the time. In fact, a lot of people who came down there had never even seen breakdancing before. We even had a 4 July party. My God, I'd almost forgotten about that. I bet we all used to speak with American accents too. In fact I'm sure we did. It was all a bit crude and amateurish, but so what? We had fun. In the Fun House.

Although it had only been an occasional thing, Fun House did quite well so we decided to notch things up a bit, hence us starting The Project Club. The only person we knew who owned a PA big enough for the venue was Carl Cox, so we asked him to come on board. I could be wrong but I'm pretty sure that I was the one who ended up buying Carl – who after a lot of hard work has managed to forge a modest living as a DJ – his first ever turntables. How about that? I can't remember the exact details but he'd been after some turntables for a while, and because he couldn't afford them I offered to pay. If memory serves me correctly I bought him a pair of Technics SL-1200s and he paid me back every penny. He later became the warm-up DJ at The Project Club, so a star was quite literally born. I'd almost forgotten about that. It's not a bad claim to fame.

The Project Club became quite popular, not least because, via my contacts with Def Jam, etc., I was able to line up some pretty hot acts. One night LL Cool J had been playing at The Lyceum in town, and after leaving the stage at midnight we drove him down to Streatham and by 1am he was entertaining us. We also got the Beastie Boys, who performed on a later visit to the UK, Run-DMC and Marshall Jefferson. They all played The Project Club. Another coup was managing to get Darryl Pandy and Farley 'Jackmaster' Funk to perform at The Project Club. They were over here promoting a new house tune called 'Love Can't Turn Around' and guess who'd been charged with driving them around? What an experience that was. Darryl was gay, very camp and about 18 stone. He was also pretty outrageous, and while I was at the wheel he'd either be singing, screaming or kicking off his slippers on the back seat. He'd always spot some white boys in the crowd who he liked the look of and make a beeline for them. And they'd have no idea he was gay, of course. None whatsoever. They ended up playing The Project Club the day after their appearance on *Top of the Pops* had been broadcast, so there was a big crowd and a real buzz. Darryl went down really, really well. So well, in fact, that part way through his performance he decided to try and crowd-surf, but after leaning back he fell into the audience. It was like Moses and the Red Sea – you should have seen the looks on their faces. Abject fear!

Given the success we'd had so far with the hip-hop acts, not to mention my association with Def Jam, I suggested to CBS that we should throw a party, but not just any old party. One thing we hadn't done so far in the UK was have an event that showcased the best that hip hop had to offer – artists, break-dancers, the lot. Also, instead of just inviting the great and the good to this event, which is what usually happened when you put on something high profile, we'd invite all the people who actually gave a damn about hip hop. The DJs, the breakers, the rappers, the fans. Anyone and everyone who actually cared about it and/or had a vested interest had to be there. Or at least as many as we could fit into Mayfair's Embassy Club.

Parties like this used to happen in New York all the time and it was an essential part of the culture. Danny and I had even been to a few and they'd been amazing. We'd already imported the music and the moves, so why not the merriment? It made sense. Fortunately, both CBS and Def Jam absolutely loved the idea and so I went ahead and booked it. Who did we have there? Or should I say, who didn't we have. Run-DMC, Grandmaster Flash, LL Cool J, Kurtis Blow. It was a good night.

A little while later I came up with another idea, this time involving the Beastie Boys. It was to take place at the Hundred Club which is on Oxford Street, and the idea was that no press or media should be invited. When I suggested this to CBS they thought I'd gone mad. 'Hang on,' I said. 'Just hear me out. Once the press get wind of this, and they will, they'll be desperate to get in.' What we ended up doing was issuing the press with red wristbands, but when they arrived we just turned them away. 'Sorry, there's just no room,' we said. I remember suggesting this to the label and once again they went berserk. 'You can't do that,' they shouted. 'We'll get slaughtered!' 'Not if we're convincing,' I said. 'As long as we make them believe that we've had to turn them away because the band are just too damn popular, we'll be fine.' And that's exactly what happened. We obviously had a few whingers but the buzz that this created was just off the frigging scale. When you can't get in somewhere and everyone's telling you how great it is, that freaks you the hell out. Am I right? If you make it easy for people – they come, they dance, they leave – then nobody's going to be that bothered about coming back. People want what they can't have. It's human nature. You have to create desire.

I remember the first and second times that Danny and I tried getting into Studio 54 in New York. The first time we tried we wore suits. We looked like a right couple of numpties and when we got to the door they just laughed at us. 'On your way to work, boys,' they joked. It was a fair comment. We looked like a couple of bank tellers. As well as changing our attire, we decided that we might have appeared a bit nervous on that first attempt, so in order to loosen ourselves up a bit we had a drink or two first. Actually, we had about six each, and by the time we arrived at the door we were plastered. 'On your way, boys,' they said, waving us away. You see what I mean by creating that desire though. They had something that we wanted and we were prepared to do almost anything in order to get it. In this case, the Beastie Boys had a big tour coming up, much bigger than the first one, and when that finally went ahead the level of anticipation from the press was unprecedented. You can't beat a bit of grass-roots promotion. That was what I was good at. And I loved it.

While all this was going on, Danny was still in the loop. He too was heavily into hip hop and we were revelling in the fact that a culture that we'd helped to champion in the UK was starting to catch on. One of our favourite aspects of the culture, apart from the music and the clothing, was breakdancing, and almost by accident we ended up helping to form – and subsequently ended up managing – a crew of up-and-coming breakdancers. It all happened after Danny and I became friends with a crew called Mastermind in Harlesden. Mastermind consisted of four DJs on eight turntables and their leader was a guy called Herbie. In terms of hip-hop DJ'ing ability, he was the closest thing I'd seen in the UK to the likes of Chuck Chillout. He really was an excellent turntablist.

Anyway, Herbie and all his mates had been devouring every aspect of hip hop since it first came to light, so when Danny and I told them that we'd seen the likes of the Rock Steady Crew first-hand, they were fascinated. One thing led to another and before you could say, 'Hey you, the Rock Steady Crew,' they'd formed their own. They were a little bit wobbly at first, but what they lacked in aptitude they more than made up for in endeavour. They also looked the part, and boy did they put the work in. They were so into it. The only thing they were missing now was a manager.

After a while Danny and I decided to offer them our services, and after having a chat with Herbie we decided to name the crew the London All-Star Breakers. The interest from the press was immediate. Hip hop was reaching its peak in the UK and despite some negative connotations regarding the music, breakdancing was seen as being something positive – a way of getting kids to do something active.

To cut a long story short, because the reaction to the crew had been so positive we decided to think big and, thanks to a bit of sponsorship, we ended up entering the London All-Star

Breakers into the coveted World Breakdancing Championships in New York. I was like, 'Guys, we're going to New York City!' We obviously didn't stand a chance of winning, but so what? It was all about the taking part.

The championships, which were sponsored by Swatch (remember them?) took place at The Roxy and featured giants such as the aforementioned Rock Steady Crew and the New York City Breakers. And who did we end up battling against? The Rock Steady Crew. If I could have bottled just a fraction of the happiness and positive energy emanating from the London All-Star Breakers at that time, it'd keep us all smiling for a decade. It was a bold move, but it paid off.

When we arrived home the press were all over us and it appeared that everyone between the ages of five and twenty-five in the UK wanted to breakdance. Or at least have a go at it. By far the most high profile approach we received on our return was from the BBC. They wanted us to appear on their flagship kids' show *Blue Peter*, alongside the presenters Simon Groom and Janet Ellis. They wanted a demonstration, basically, and while the crew all did their thing I explained to Simon and Janet what was happening. I know what you're about to ask, and yes I did get a *Blue Peter* badge. It's probably at my mum's somewhere.

Incidentally, I did actually try my hand at breakdancing several times, but I just couldn't get the hang of it. It also unnerved me a bit. Going in for a tackle while playing football's one thing, but if you're doing a windmill spinning on your head, something bad's going to go down, man. Nah, I'm good, thanks. I prefer having my feet on the ground, at least some of the time. What an experience though.

As if remixing, plugging, marketing, managing, not break-dancing, A&Ring and preventing the likes of the Beastie Boys being locked up weren't enough, I even managed to fit a bit of DJ'ing into my schedule about this time. A man called Gordon Mac was about to start a radio station called Kiss FM from his house in Peckham and wanted a hip-hop DJ for his roster. I had next to no experience as a DJ at the time, but what I did have were the records, fresh from New York, which is why Gordon hired me. I'd play the new Beastie Boys before anyone over here had heard it, and the new Run-DMC. I had the lot. It was the same when I was at the Ministry of Sound and Cream. I always had the right records.

When it came to Kiss FM, I also provided a logo for the station, which came courtesy of a 98.7 Kiss FM car sticker that I'd brought back from New York. You know what they say, imitation is the sincerest form of flattery. This wasn't an imitation though, it was an exact copy! It didn't matter though. Kiss FM London was a pirate station, an illegal entity, so it kind of fitted the bill. I remember the station got raided a couple of times. That made me wary because if you were the one on air, the police would confiscate your records. They were like my children. Take me, but don't take my records!

Although I tried my best, it's safe to say that radio DJ'ing wasn't really my thing. I don't know whether it's a shyness that resulted from having dyslexia, but in addition to not being good with the written word, as in reading, I'm also not too hot with the spoken word either, and I used to dread having to speak into the mic. I was OK when the mic was off, but as soon as that red light lit up I'd go to pieces. One day I left the mic on by mistake while a record was playing and I spoke through the entire thing. It was an inadvertent mash-up, you might say, but not a very good one. A few years later I was approached by Radio 1 about doing a weekly show (Kiss FM was only monthly) but turned them down flat. I hadn't been scarred for life exactly (I later became a resident DJ on Pete Tong's Essential Mix, which I enjoyed, and currently have a show on U2's station in America, SiriusXM) but I know where my strengths are, and talking publicly, whether in person or on air, definitely isn't one of them. It's a case of less is more with me.

By early 1987 my love of hip hop was starting to wane, mainly because I didn't like the way it had been evolving. The first school of hip hop, which is the one that got me hooked, had included the likes of LL Cool J, Run-DMC, Houdini, Kurtis Blow and Grandmaster Flash. On the whole the messages in their music had been positive and that had always been one of the attractions. After that you had the likes of Public Enemy, whose central message was about the fight for power. I didn't mind that so much but by the time gangster rap came along with the likes of Snoop, 2Pac, Eazy-E and N.W.A., I really had lost interest. The change was also filtering into nightclubs, even over here, and shootings were becoming commonplace. That wasn't for me I'm afraid. Not at all. I'm a lover, not a fighter, and I like my music to follow the same direction. As somebody who never likes to stay in the same place for too long, either geograph-ically, musically or culturally, this was actually a blessing in disguise. The question is, where would I go next?

The answer to that question was house music. My love affair with hip hop had been all-encompassing, and while that was happening this new sound from Chicago had been taking the States by storm and making inroads into Europe and the UK. I'm talking like house was completely new to me; it wasn't. It just hadn't had my full attention yet, although I had already dabbled, so to speak.

Hailing from Chicago, the genre of house music takes its name from a nightclub called The Warehouse where the legend that is Frankie Knuckles was the main man. He was friends with Larry Levan and landed the job after Larry, who was a New Yorker through and through, turned it down because he couldn't bear to leave. Frankie's initial offering at The Warehouse was a hearty mixture of old-school classics and Euro sounds as well as a new sound that came courtesy of two emerging Chicago labels, Trax and DJ International. By 1985, the tracks by the two local labels had become Frankie's bread and butter, and some sounds had even begun finding their way to the UK. One of these tunes, 'Jack the Groove' by an American duo called Raze, really caught my ear. The sound was so fresh. It completely blew my mind. After playing it to Mel I told him that we should sign the duo now and fortunately he agreed. It's hard to overestimate the effect that these early house tunes had on me. They had this kind of sparse minimalist vibe to them. 'Jack the Groove' wasn't especially fast – about 118 beats per minute – but that's where things were going. Mega tunes such as MARRS' 'Pump up the Volume', which was slightly slower than 'Jack the Groove', were just around the corner and would bring with them a new kind of energy to the dance floor.

We released 'Jack the Groove' just a few weeks after 'Love Can't Turn Around', which was another early house tune, and both of them became Top 20 hits. As well as selling well in the shops, which was great, house music was also taking the dance floors by storm. And all this with hardly any radio support. Underground records, from any genre, weren't supposed to have this kind of effect on the mainstream. The trend was being well and truly bucked.

Because of the amount of house tracks that Champion were releasing at the time – we'd started putting out compilations, twelve-inchers and all sorts of things – we began to attract the attention of the two record labels in Chicago who were basically responsible for all this, namely Trax and DJ International. We received a telephone call from each of them completely out of the blue, and within a week they were over here, as large as life. We had Rocky from DJ International followed by Larry from Trax. I'll never forget Rocky's visit. He literally walked into Mel's office with an enormous suitcase, plonked it on his desk, opened it and said, 'There you go, guys. What do you want to buy? Come on, take your pick.' There must have been about five hundred records and tapes in there, some of which, it turned out, they didn't even own! He was a proper chancer was Rocky. Larry was exactly the same, in that he had with him a treasure trove of music and could have sold a black cat to a witch. Just getting through it all took me weeks and we bought and released an awful lot of music.

Our activity in the genre of house music is what initially put me in touch with Pete Tong over at London. Sure, he'd end up nicking all the hip-hop acts I wanted to sign, the bastard, but before that we had some 'house keeping' to attend to (sorry!). You see, without us even realising it, Champion Records had become the label most associated with house music, and so when Pete wanted some assistance promoting Steve 'Silk' Hurley's future chart and dance-floor hit, 'Jack Your Body', he came to me. The brief from Pete was to work on some club promotion for the track and from the moment I heard it I knew it was going to be big. Sure enough, 'Jack Your Body' hit the number one spot in the UK at the start of 1987 and young Pete must have received a big slap on the back.

Not long after 'Jack Your Body' became a success, Mel and I had a parting of the ways. In his eyes I was juggling far too many plates, and although I disagreed with his assessment – the more plates the merrier as far as I was concerned – I could kind of understand where he was coming from. Not that he wanted me to leave. He didn't. That was my idea.

Without wanting to sound too arrogant or big-headed, I think I'd outgrown Champion Records. It's a theory that, in my eyes, was being proved on almost an hourly basis just by the sheer amount of offers I was receiving and the amount of work I was doing. The thing is, unlike Mel, I was loving every second of it.

Without realising it he probably needed to move on as much as I did. We'd had fun and we'd had a certain amount of success. It had run its course though, as these things often do.

Unfortunately, when it came to me telling Mel that it was time to leave, he ended up losing his temper and showing me the door. It's a pity really as I'd learnt so much from him. In fact, knowing what I know now, had I had the luxury of being able to map out my own career before starting out, I'd definitely have put an apprenticeship with Mel at Champion Records in there, no worries, if only for the memory of him lying on his massive bed at the Martinez Hotel in Cannes snoring his head off while I sat there entertaining people and listening to music. He's a good bloke is Mel and I'll always be very grateful to him.

CHAPTER 7

Behind the Decks

I think it's about time I told you how I got into DJ'ing, as it's about now that things started getting serious. For as long as I can remember, I'd always had a desire to express myself through music, and the older I got the more frustrated I became. My dad had been a musician in his younger days and I'd seen first-hand how much joy that used to bring him. It was in me too, somewhere. I couldn't sing – at all – and the only instrument I'd ever been any good at as a kid was the piano.

As enjoyable as that could be sometimes, it still didn't give me the joy or the outlet I was looking for. I'm not sure why. Perhaps it was because piano lessons were something I was made to do? I did try a bit of guitar and bass when I was older, but I neither had the aptitude nor the interest. I thought about putting a band together at one point, with me as the keyboard player, but quickly realised that having an extra three or four people to consider probably wouldn't be for me.

Years later I ended up signing a few bands to my record label, Perfecto, and that hunch of mine was confirmed. If you get the dynamic right then perfect, but in my experience, nine times out of ten you'll have passive members in a band and you'll have active members and in that kind of environment I wouldn't have been able to deal with the passive members very well. In fact, as an A&R man and record label owner, there have been times when I've had more enthusiasm for their music than the bands I've signed and been working with. That's frustrating, I can tell you. I did try and find some musicians who had the same kind of drive, enthusiasm and outlook as I did once or twice but in the end I gave up. I figured that, even if I did find the right musicians, would I really want to work exclusively with them? I mean, why put all your eggs into one musical basket? This, I think, is why I always found DJs and DJ'ing so fascinating. Just the thought of taking all the music I liked and wanted to listen to, regardless of genre, and then mixing it all together and creating a soundscape used to make me salivate, and still does. It was a life without boundaries. Surely that's what everybody's looking for?

By the time all this started making sense, my old mate Trevor Fung was DJ'ing at a place called Rumours in Covent Garden. Rumours wasn't a nightclub. It was a cocktail bar with a small dance floor in the corner. Even so, it was one of the places to be seen at the time and London trendies such as Steve Strange and Rusty Egan used to hang out there. Trevor used to play jazz funk and soul mainly, and after finishing his set at midnight, me, him and Danny would all go up to a club called The Embassy.

I forget when exactly but at some point during this period I bought myself a pair of turntables. The aim, however, wasn't to start emulating Trevor. I hadn't thought that far ahead. All I wanted to do initially was what I said earlier – take all the music I loved, mix it all together, create a few soundscapes and just enjoy myself. I was a bedroom DJ, but a very happy one.

One day Trevor came down sick and so he couldn't do his set. I'm not sure if it was he who recommended me, but at some point during that day I received a telephone call from the manager at Rumours asking me if I'd be able to fill in. I was always there, you see, hanging out with Trevor. Had Rumours been an actual nightclub then I wouldn't have said yes, nor do I think they would have asked me. Although it was integral to what made the place popular, people didn't go to Rumours just to listen to the music, so the pressure was kind of off. As long as I put a good set together and didn't start playing the Sex Pistols I was going to be OK.

The DJ booth at Rumours was just to the left of the main doors which meant you could see exactly who was coming in and out. I remember sitting there on that first night wondering who'd come in next. Would it be a load of girls? Would it be Steve and Rusty? Would it be a celebrity? It was exciting. I made sure my set list was different to Trevor's as although I was filling in for him I wanted to do my own thing. It was time to ring in the changes, even if it was just for one night.

Because it was a bar and not a nightclub you could basically play anything you wanted and I took advantage of that big time. I went from the Isley Brothers to The Human League, The Human League to Houdini, Houdini to Visage, Visage to Bob Marley, Bob Marley to Duran Duran. I also chucked in a few promos, although I forget by who. The chance to be able to play just a tiny fraction of my vinyl collection to a live audience was a privilege and I walked away from Rumours that night hoping very much that it would be something I could repeat.

While Trevor was at Rumours, Steve Strange and Rusty Egan, who'd been running clubs together in London since the late 1970s, opened a club on Great Queen Street in Covent Garden called Blitz. Just like Steve Rubell at Studio 54, Steve Strange, who was in charge of the door at Blitz, went to great lengths to ensure that the people entering his club were exactly to his taste. Unlike Steve Rubell, however, he didn't judge the would-be clubbers on how famous they were. Well, not always. To Steve Strange, it was what you were wearing that really mattered and it didn't matter who you were, if you didn't meet Steve Strange's strict sartorial standards you were sent packing. One of his most famous refusals was Mick Jagger who turned up to Blitz one evening with his entourage wearing a baseball jacket and a pair of trainers. You can imagine the conversation, can't you? 'Sorry, Mr Jagger. You're not coming in looking like that.' 'What do you mean? Come on, man. I want a drink!' 'No, I'm sorry. Kindly leave the queue.' Steve Strange could be a hard bugger when he wanted to be and if he said no, it was no.

Through his work at Rumours, Steve and Rusty eventually offered Trevor an occasional Tuesday night slot at Blitz and, of course, he said yes. I ended up filling in for Trevor again at Rumours, but on a more regular basis, and eventually I was also offered a spot by Steve and Rusty. Since opening their doors at Blitz, Rusty and Steve had become regulars at Rumours and they must have heard me play. It was a big thing getting a gig with those two as they were at the forefront of the London club scene. Later on they started running a night at The Lyceum called Playground which had as its centrepiece a 30-foot high television wall. I remember seeing that for the very first time and thinking, 'What the hell is that thing?' I just stood there staring at it. It didn't always work for Rusty and Steve and towards the end of their reign it was a bit hit and miss. In their pomp though, they were big time.

What really began to hit home at this time, which had first popped into my head while watching and listening to Larry Levan, was, once again, the significance of the arrangement. If me and five other DJs were each handed the same ten songs to play at the same nightclub, what would separate us? It's how you put those ten songs together. That's what sets you apart. The more I got to play in front of an audience the more I appreciated that fact and it became a kind of obsession with me. It still is in a way. It's like alchemy to us DJs. The holy grail. What you have to remember though is that it's impossible to get it right every time, and if you do judge things incorrectly, learn from it.

A big advantage for me in those early days at places like Blitz was that I was never the main attraction, so the only real pressure I felt was pressure I put on myself. In fact, there was more pressure put on me by the people at Blitz to wear make-up than anything else! That's what they were all wearing at the time – boys and girls. It was never really my thing though to be honest. I understood it, and I appreciated it. It just wasn't for me. Another important lesson I learned around this time was that if you wanted to be the main DJ, the best way to go about it was to start your own club. I admit, it sounds pretty fanciful, but that's exactly what we did. We started Fun House, of course, where I basically played music to accompany breakdancers, and then there was The Project Club, where I was more of a promoter. I didn't really come into my own as a DJ until we started clubs like Spectrum, Future and Land of Oz. All that ties in with what they call the second summer of love. We've a bit to go though before then, starting off with a nice little trip to Ibiza.

CHAPTER 8

We're Going to Ibiza

After leaving Mel's employment, in addition to all the other stuff, I started doing more work with the promo company, Rush Release. Of all the pies I had fingers in, A&R was my favourite and it had been ever since I'd started doing it. I'm a people person at the end of the day, a people person who adores music, loves to travel, and enjoys watching and helping people succeed. Mix into that a few nightclubs, some DJs, a pay cheque at the end of the week and a lot of pretty girls, and you have before you what I still consider to be one of the best jobs you could ever wish for. It's something I was literally born to do.

After a while Rush Release decided to launch their own record label, and in addition to me continuing my promotional duties with them they asked me if I'd like to run it. The label was only small and wouldn't take up too much of my time so I agreed. In fact, I bit their hand off. One of the first acts we signed was Divine, the larger-than-life American actor, singer and drag queen who, as well as making it big in the 1970s thanks mainly to the transgressive cult films of John Waters, had recently had some chart success on both sides of the Atlantic, and even more success in the clubs, with a cover version of the Frankie Valli and the Four Seasons song, 'Walk Like a Man'.

To be honest, I didn't really know much about Divine when we signed him. I'd never seen a John Waters film before and the music that Divine had been producing so far hadn't been on my radar. All I really knew prior to us getting together was that he was a 22-stone transvestite who had been Andy Warhol's best buddy in the 1970s and who'd had one or two hits both here and in the States.

As well as releasing a couple of singles with Divine, neither of which troubled the charts too much but did quite well in the clubs, we also went into partnership with Record Shack, a gay record label based in Soho. This had me working with people like Eartha Kitt and Sinitta. Gay icons, basically. It was a lot of fun. Not exactly my scene, but a lot of fun.

I'll never forget the first time I met Divine. I suppose I'd been expecting him to turn up in character but he was dressed in a very smart suit and was very polite and quiet. He was shy, almost, but at the same time business-like. It was a nice surprise really as had he lived and breathed the persona that made him famous twenty-four hours a day I'm not sure I'd have coped.

As me and Divine got to know each other, little bits of that persona began to spill out occasionally which made our relation-ship more interesting. He could obviously be pretty outrageous when he wanted to be and took great pleasure in trying to shock me. His stage persona was obviously just that – outrageous – and although it used to make an appearance every now and then, the contrast between Harris Milstead from Maryland, which is who he actually was, and the drag queen who'd become an icon and had entertained millions, was striking.

Funnily enough, I was watching a documentary about Adele the other night at my mum's house and it was exactly the same with her. When you see her being interviewed she's this brash girl from

Tottenham who's a bit scatty and as soon as she walks onstage she becomes a kind of goddess. I'm always fascinated by people who are able to change character like that. It must really take some doing. I witnessed this again when I went on tour with U2 and it was then that I truly appreciated how important a persona can be. Nobody wanted to see Bono as Paul Hewson, the husband and father from Ireland. They wanted to see either The Fly, which was the first persona he adopted for the *Zooropa* tour, or MacPhisto, which was the persona he adopted for the Zoo TV tour.

The closest I ever get to having to adopt a persona is when I'm doing a gig and I'm jet-lagged. The people in the audience don't wanna know if I've only had three hours of sleep and don't know where the hell I am. Nobody gives a fuck. In that situation I have to pull myself together as best I can, have a little drink, which in my case would be a shot of tequila (or two), and give the people what they want. Doing that night after night though? I wouldn't last five minutes.

It was while I was looking after Divine that I got my first taste of Ibiza. This would have been in 1986, so the year before the visit that would help to make me famous. Or should I say, infamous. Yes, I probably should. We were over there on a promotional tour. Divine had been booked to appear at the legendary Ku Club, which before then had been called Pikes and is now called Privilege. He appeared every year, and when I found out we were going I was like a kid at Christmas.

The Ibiza we know today is very different to the Ibiza of the 1970s and early to mid-1980s, and it was also very different to the majority of other Spanish resorts at the time. Most Brits went to places like Majorca or the Costas back then. Ibiza, however, had a unique vibe to it which had as much to do with its history and its people as it did anything else.

Apparently, a group of hippies had settled there sometime in the 1930s and it had morphed into a hideaway for outsiders, bohemians and fun seekers. By the time I first arrived there with Divine, not a lot had changed. Certainly with regards to the kind of faces the island attracted. The only difference was the addition of a few celebrities. Ibiza wasn't anyway near as commercial as some of the other Balearic Islands which made peace and quiet and even anonymity much more achievable.

An old actor called Terry-Thomas was one of the first British celebrities to make the island his home, followed by another you may have heard of called Denholm Elliott. Luckily, the lack of infrastructure there coupled with the fact that it was still full of free spirits prevented the island from turning into a precursor to Malaga. There's nothing wrong with Malaga, by the way. I'm just more of an Ibiza man.

Although it didn't have anywhere near the reputation it has today, Ibiza was still known as being a bit of a party island and the hub of that activity was the aforementioned Ku Club. Known as Privilege since about 1995, the Ku Club, which was owned and run by a legendary figure called Tony Pike, was one of the biggest nightclubs in the world at the time and could comfortably hold about 10,000 people. The video for 'Club Tropicana' by Wham was filmed there and regulars at the club included the likes of Grace Jones, Duran Duran and Freddie Mercury. Just like Studio 54 it was very starry, and in its heyday would have given that place a run for its money. Soon after it became known as Privilege, the guys from Manumission moved in and they stayed there until 2007. I've played there myself a few times – 1995 was the first occasion – and although it's all a bit sketchy, I'm pretty sure my set was broadcast on Pete Tong's Essential Mix.

My one abiding memory of this trip is watching Divine take to the stage for the first time. The club was absolutely heaving and what struck me was how mixed the crowd were. It was a good vibe. I'm not actually sure what I was expecting when Divine was finally introduced. I'd never been to see a drag queen before but I had a feeling it was going to be special – and different. I wasn't disappointed. When the DJ screamed out Divine's name, there was a pause of about five seconds and then all of a sudden a baby elephant came trotting on to the stage with Divine on its back. The entire place just erupted and I'll tell you what, he put on one hell of a show. He really was one talented guy.

OK, it's time to bring in the main event.

Have you heard the one about the four guys from south London who went to Ibiza for two weeks, were taken on a musical journey by a DJ called Alfredo while off their heads on a new wonder drug and then returned home armed with modern dance music? If you're reading this book you must have at least an inkling of what I'm referring to. If not, well, you might be in for a shock.

If I spend any more than a moment or two pondering the true global consequences of that trip, I start to get a headache. I really do. It's been credited with launching all sorts of cultures and subcultures over the years, from the rave scene to acid house. It certainly changed a few things. In some cases, not before time.

My own short headline for what happened is that we ended up reinventing club culture. Found a vibe we were into, recreated it back in the UK with some different music and – Bob's your uncle. There's your new club culture. Did we think it would catch on like it did? Probably not. At least not at first. We were too smashed for a start.

If you went to a mainstream run-of-the-mill nightclub in the mid-1980s, providing you could get past the bouncers who ranged from moody and menacing to mildly violent, you'd find a few guys chatting at the bar, some girls dancing around their handbags on the dance floor and a so-called DJ stuck in the corner somewhere. It was a sad state of affairs. Nobody would be focusing on either the DJ or the music and the atmosphere would be about as effervescent as a dead dog. They may as well have just played tapes.

For most of the evening these charlatans would knock out nothing but chart hits, interspersed with some inane chat. As the girls danced, the blokes would stand around leering at them in the hope that they might pull one in time for the erection section. Remember that? Things would get busy about fifteen minutes before that resulting in the club being split right down the middle. You'd have the haves on the dance floor with their tongues down each other's throats and the have-nots looking enviously on. It was always 'Lady in Red' by Chris de Burgh or 'True' by Spandau bloody Ballet. I feel sick just thinking about it. Regardless of whether you managed to pull or not, what a depressing way to end a night. Nightclubs in those days were just cattle markets. Try and pull, and if you can't pull, get pissed. Whoop-de-fucking doo.

Post '87 the focus shifted, not just from what people wanted from the experience of visiting a club, which was music they could dance to played by somebody who didn't look and sound like a creep, but also the direction they faced on the dance floor. Instead of standing around in little circles, everyone started facing the DJ. What a seed change that was. Most importantly though, everybody danced.

In this respect, the definition of the word DJ changed almost overnight. They went from being gaudily dressed throwbacks who couldn't mix a fucking drink to people you thought were cool. The old guard used to play a chart hit, talk on the mic, play a chart hit, talk on the mic. Radio 2 in a nightclub, basically. The new breed of DJ had nothing in common with this lot. They were just clubbers, the same as you, and nobody gave a shit what they sounded like. Their voice – or the only voice that mattered – was the music. End of.

The touchpaper for this story of mine was lit when I decided it would be a great idea to celebrate my twenty-fourth birthday, in Ibiza, with some mates, getting smashed. Simple. The year was 1987 and work-wise things were pretty much the same. A&R and promotion were still my bread and butter, and as well as doing a bit of DJ'ing here and there I was still collecting vinyl like a squirrel collects nuts.

One of the main things that had changed in my life were that my two partners in crime, Danny and Trevor, had flown the nest. Or should I say they'd moved to Ibiza for the season, which was somewhere they knew well, to have some fun. Because of this, when it came to planning my birthday party it seemed prudent to pay them a visit. I just needed to decide who to go with. Top of the list was my old mate, and one-time shop-floor adversary, Nicky Holloway. I'd been doing quite a lot of promotional work for Nicky who was running a few clubs and we got on really well. He'd also been going to Ibiza on holiday for donkey's years so it made sense. The other bloke I invited was Johnny Walker, a fellow budding DJ who I'd known for quite a while. Initially it was just going to be the three of us, but then Nicky Holloway rang me one day and asked if he could bring a friend. 'Sure,' I said. 'Who is he?' 'He's called Danny Rampling,' said Nicky. 'He's a painter and decorator.'

What better way for a young man to celebrate his birthday than travelling to a beautiful Mediterranean island in the company of his mates and misbehaving for fourteen days? I must admit, life was pretty darn good at the time.

Before leaving for Ibiza I came across a feature in *The Face* magazine about Ibiza's nightlife and I must say it got me quite excited. The front cover headline read, 'Holiday Babylon', and much of the article concentrated on the shenanigans at the Ku Club which I'd experienced and a couple of other venues. In reference to the Wham video having been filmed there they said, 'At £157 for a fortnight, anyone can purchase a chance to visit Wham's mythical Club Tropicana.'

I'm not sure the drinks were free.

'The aptly named Club Amnesia,' it went on, 'doesn't even open until 5.30 in the morning, and it would be impolite to leave before 8am.' I didn't know it then but, of all the venues mentioned in the article, the one that would become most pivotal to the story was Amnesia.

I remember reading the article at home and thinking, 'What the actual fuck?' The pubs still closed in the afternoon in the UK and everyone was in bed by eleven. Surely this was the promised land? And we were going for a fortnight!

Danny Diamond and Trevor had started going over to Ibiza the year before and Trevor had managed to land himself a job running a small bar called, funnily enough, The Project Club. Situated on the way to Café del Mar from the centre of San Antonio, it was small but perfectly formed and can't have held more than fifty or sixty people. The overspill on to the street could take that number to a good couple of hundred so it was a popular little spot. I wasn't quite sure what Danny had been doing over there, but you can guarantee he won't have been idle. I know he'd been helping Trevor run the club a bit, but knowing Danny he'd have been moonlighting as a hang-gliding instructor or the man from Milk Tray. Danny circa 1987 would have made Del Boy look shy and retiring.

As soon as we got off the plane in Ibiza I could tell that the mood on the island had shifted. I couldn't put my finger on it but something had definitely changed. The people who were arriving there – young fun seekers mainly, but not many from the UK – seemed really, really up for it, as if there was something amazing waiting for them. Danny and Trevor had mentioned a new drug that they'd all been taking over there the last time I saw them but I didn't make the connection. How could I?

I began joining the dots the moment I set eyes on Trevor and Danny. They seemed – how can I put it – a little bit more laid-back than they had been the last time. Actually, they were fucking horizontal! They also appeared to be in an almost constant state of mild euphoria, which was different. I remember chatting to them after we'd landed and it was like talking to a couple of hippies. Their weight was slightly disconcerting. Although they'd never been fat they'd never exactly been skinny either. None of us had. I thought, 'What the hell's going on here?' Danny and Trevor introduced us to some of their new friends a bit later, people like the DJ Nancy Noise who became a good friend, and they were all in exactly the same state. It was just weird.

After quizzing them a bit it turned out that they'd all been taking a new drug called ecstasy virtually every single day since arriving, and as opposed to eating two or three meals a day, they'd been eating about two or three a week. Despite being slightly startled by their appearance and character, I was intrigued. Partly because everybody seemed to be on such a high all the time, and because I didn't like feeling left out!

I could be wrong, and if I am I'm sure that somebody out there will take great pleasure in putting me right, but until then I'm almost certain that the strongest drug I'd ever taken was a puff of marijuana. I'd knitted myself a nice pair of drinking trousers by this point, but when it came to anything illegal, I was a bit of a slow starter. Not because I was against it or anything. I was still a bit naive in some ways and it just hadn't arrived in my life yet.

As far as I know, Danny Diamond was the one who'd been procuring the new wonder drug (Danny knew everyone and could have got you an elephant if you'd asked for it) and not long after arriving at the bar he handed me and the boys a bag of samples each, which was nice of him. Not one of us had ever taken ecstasy before, and when we took the bags from him it was as if he'd handed us a bag of rat poison or something. Or at least at first. We just needed to get used to the idea.

After heading back to our villa and getting changed, we donned our glad rags, put a few pesetas in our pockets, not to mention the bag of fun that Danny had handed us, and descended on San Antonio for what we hoped would be a jolly first evening. There was definitely an air of caution about the group, mixed with a large dollop of anticipation. To that end, the conversation had been based mainly around the suggestion that we'd each try the drug once and that would be it. The rest of the holiday would be dedicated to beer, music, sun, having a good laugh and quite possibly some girls. It was a distraction if nothing else and one that the four of us were keen to get out of the way. The question was, who would end up going first?

The first place we went to on that first night was a bar called Nightlife. I'm not sure how we ended up there but it wasn't our thing at all. It was beery, full of wankers and the music was shit. There must have been a promise of a free drink or something, or a group of girls. It was like that scene from *The Inbetweeners* movie when they're lured into that shit club. Looking at things positively, we were on the first night of a two-week holiday in Ibiza, had enough pesetas for beer and a bit of food, and the forecast for the foreseeable future was hot, hot, hot. Oh yes, and we also had a massive bag of Es in our pockets. What on earth could possibly go wrong?

With the venue being a bit of a let-down, we were forced to take action and in mine and Danny Rampling's case that meant popping a pill. Nicky and Johnny were still being cautious – Nicky especially – so instead of following suit they just stood there nervously like a couple of virgins outside a brothel. Me and Danny Rampling, on the other hand, were ready for action. Or should I say lift-off! To be honest we had little or no idea of what was going to happen, although Danny Diamond and Trevor had tried to go into detail about the effects. How do you imagine extreme euphoria though if you've never experienced it?

Fortunately there were some other people in the place who were obviously under the influence and by the looks of things they were having a nice time. 'Sod it,' I thought. 'I'm going to pop one.' Danny Rampling did the same and after about twenty minutes we were still standing there like a couple of lemons. Just then I went to say something to him, probably about the fact that they weren't working, but before I could get the words out I noticed something strange. His eyes were closed and he was smiling like he was just remembering a foursome he'd had with Charlie's Angels. He was also starting to dance like somebody who'd only recently discovered their sense of rhythm.

'Are you feeling it?' he asked after opening his eyes for a second and gazing adoringly in my direction.

'Nah, not yet. You obviously are, though. What's it like?'

'Fucking amazing, mate!' he said before closing his eyes again and rejoining Charlie's Angels.

As far as I could tell, Nicky and Johnny still hadn't imbibed and what was happening to Danny Rampling seemed to terrify and excite them in equal measure. I was going to say something to them along the lines of, 'Come on, lads, get involved,' but before I could do so something started happening. I was feeling hot all of a sudden. Clammy. To be honest I wasn't very keen on the experience and at first I thought that I must have taken a bad pill. I was about to report this turn of events to Mr Euphoria who was to the right of me when – BANG! It fucking hit me.

'You're up then,' said Danny Rampling sporting a grin that went about an inch beyond his ears.

'Too fucking right I am,' I said, starting to move a bit. 'Shit, man, this is amazing!'

The thing that had intrigued me the most about taking ecstasy, which had resulted from Trevor and Danny Diamond telling me about their own experiences, had been the effect it had on music, or should I say the effect it had on your listening experience. According to them it changed everything – in a good way – and I couldn't wait to find out.

My God, they were right. I have no idea what the hell we were listening to, although it wasn't dance music, but as soon as I started coming up it was front and centre of my consciousness. What's more, it sounded absolutely amazing.

Reassured by mine and Danny Rampling's experiences, Nicky and Johnny must have decided to pop theirs as before too long all four of us were dancing away like madmen. We were on it! What's more, what had been the world's shittest bar half an hour ago had now metamorphosed into Shangri-La with a PA system. The euphoria had well and truly taken hold.

Incidentally, out of all four of us merrymakers, the one who appeared to be enjoying himself the most that night was the one who'd expressed the most concern – Mr Holloway. He was riding off into the sunset and what's more, he wasn't looking back.

At some point during the evening one of us remembered that Danny Diamond and Trevor had recommended that we float off down to a club called Amnesia. Float being the operative word! In the first two or three hours after having taken the pills, we must have made about a hundred new friends and had distributed more hugs than you could wave a stick at. The euphoria had taken hold. As far as Danny and Trevor were concerned, taking E and visiting Amnesia were synonymous with each other, and once again they'd gone to great lengths in order to try and bring it all to life.

Amnesia's history began in the mid-1970s when a young man named Antonio Escohotado signed a lease for the venue, turned it into a nightclub and called it The Workshop of Forgetfulness, which was catchy. The idea behind the club, so they said, was for people from all backgrounds to be able to come together, have some fun and forget about everyday life. Soon after opening, Antonio changed the name of his club to Amnesia which, as well as capturing the original idea of forgetting all your problems, was catchier and a bit more concise.

When house music was first liberated from the clubs of Chicago in the early 1980s, one of the first places it resonated was Ibiza, and one of the island's first champions of the music was Alfredo, Amnesia's resident DJ. According to the man himself, who I eventually got to know quite well, Alfredo had fled Argentina after the military coup of 1976 and after spending a few years in Spain had ended up in Ibiza. Once again, the genius behind what Alfredo did at the club was his arrangement, and after surviving two or three difficult seasons at the club (his mix of disco, house, pop and even some rock and indie was a bit rich for some people at first) his magic finally started making sense to the faithful, and by the time we arrived he was already a legend. He'd mix up Bob Marley with Tears For Fears, Donna Summer with Depeche Mode. Even Kate Bush and Queen, FFS. Half the records he played we wouldn't have touched with a barge pole at home, yet in that sort of environment, and with the help of our new-found narcotic friends, it made sense. Seriously, it just worked!

Unlike the effects of the drug, which we just couldn't get our heads around before taking it, the picture that Danny and Trevor painted about Amnesia and Alfredo had had us chomping at the bit and we couldn't wait to get there.

We must have rocked up at Amnesia at about four o'clock in the morning on that first night, which is when the fun really began. The two things that first caught my eye at the club were the open-air dance floor – something I'd never seen before – and the clientele. They were very cosmopolitan and ranged from about eighteen to fifty. That alone blew my mind. It seemed that all of life was there. What's more, everyone was smiling. It was the antithesis to those mainstream nightclubs I mentioned earlier. And potentially the antidote.

The first thing we did after having a mooch around was take to the dance floor and pop another pill. Alfredo was in full flow so while he weaved his magic behind the decks, we allowed yet another new utopia to take shape in front of our eyes. This one was special, though. We were dancing under the stars.

At one point I went for a wander and saw a pool with some people jumping in. There were swings either side of it so for a few minutes I sat in one and just watched them. It was fucking nuts!

For me, up until this point, it had always been about the music. But then I took this pill and it was like, 'Oh my God, what have we here?' I've always liked sharing things so when I find something I love – whether it's a record, a film or an experience – I want to share it with other people. This, though, was really special. I wanted to bottle it and take it to every country and every club on the planet.

Later that day the party started again at the villa we were renting. Danny Rampling and Nicky, who'd also experienced an overwhelming urge to share, decided to write a letter to a friend of theirs in America urging them to come and experience Ibiza. The reason I remember this so vividly is because we were all holding hands around the swimming pool at the time listening to a tune called 'Moments in Love' by The Art of Noise. Had somebody – anybody – suggested to me prior to our trip that we'd spend a whole afternoon holding hands by a swimming pool, writing letters and listening to The Art of Noise, I'd have reported them to the authorities and had them sectioned.

But it wasn't just the pills or even the venue that made the experience so revelatory. It was Alfredo's music policy. One track that captured the spirit of the holiday was 'Why Why Why' by an indie rock band from London called The Woodentops. Alfredo played a 150bpm live version as the last song one night and everybody went mental. I just stood there with my chin on the floor. He was playing a tune by a little-known indie rock band as his last record of the night. What had I been taking, ecstasy or acid? Come to think of it, what had I been taking? That was some trip, man. The whole place went off.

Ending a set was also Alfredo's *pièce de résistance*. The rest of his sets were always brilliant, but knowing how to end a set is a real skill and Alfredo had it off to a tee. It's not just about the crescendo by the way, or the last song. It's about leading up to that moment which makes you think in terms of structure and entire sets, as opposed to individual songs. It's especially prevalent when you have a residency, as once they get used to you the crowd will start expecting certain things. It's probably no coincidence but whenever I'm asked who my favourite DJs are, the two names that spring to mind are Alfredo and Larry Levan, and for that very reason.

We spent one afternoon trying to think of a comparison to Amnesia and the closest we came to was Paradise Garage. I'd obviously been there dozens of times, most recently with Nicky on a trip during which we went to Gwen Guthrie's birthday party which was at the club. Timmy Regisford was spinning and it was a great night. Just like Amnesia, the music had been all over the place and now we knew exactly what had been helping things along. The atmosphere though was different to Amnesia. The clientele were still black or Hispanic gay men and in addition to having those blacked-out walls I told you about, it was quite enclosed. It was a lot more intense than Amnesia. A different vibe.

Something I remember very vividly after the first night in Ibiza was how much I was looking forward to the next one. It was like Christmas times ten and I don't think I've ever looked forward to anything as much, either before or since. The evening before had been life-changing and when something like that happens, you want it to happen again as quickly as possible.

In between frequenting Amnesia and holding hands around the swimming pool, we did manage to sample more of what Ibiza had to offer after dark. Café del Mar and Es Paradis were our preferred pre-Amnesia hang-outs and then, after leaving Amnesia, we'd go to Manhattan's, which was the underground club. There was another one we went to called Glory's, but that was more your *NME* style of music, bands like The Cure, Simple Minds and U2. We left Pacha alone as it wasn't really up to much then.

Providing you got the vibe of the island and you weren't just looking for another Majorca, Ibiza could be all things to all people. If you wanted heavy and frenzied you could find it easily, and if you wanted chilled, it'd be just around the corner. On future visits we used to go up into the hills to see friends only to find a hundred people running around off their heads. Thing is, because of the infrastructure, or lack of it, it was often difficult to get back. You'd be up there for days sometimes. Not that anybody cared much.

The music policy, coupled with the ambiance and the drugs we were taking, affected us all in different ways. Nicky and Johnny, for instance, were heavily into soul. Hearing Alfredo play Kool Moe Dee and the Beastie Boys, and watching the crowd respond, changed them. It changed them big time. It was different for Danny Rampling as he hadn't yet got behind the decks. To him, everything was just raw and exciting. To me it was different again. My taste in music was more varied than the others and in my eyes the magic came from Alfredo. Trevor and I had tried mixing things up at Fun House and The Project Club once or twice but it hadn't worked. Not so Alfredo. I remember vividly standing there in Amnesia on that first night thinking, 'This is fucking amazing! How's he getting that reaction?' It was obviously a bit of everything: the venue, the atmosphere, the drugs and the choice of music.

The next logical step on hearing the music Alfredo was spinning was to track down the vinyl. Easier said than done. This was made difficult by the fact that it was all so eclectic and Alfredo had accumulated the collection over several years and from a variety of sources. Specialists, mainly, in a number of different countries. In this case I obviously had an advantage as I'd been sourcing my own vinyl since the year dot and knew the game inside out. Tracking down rare vinyl can be a frustrating business, but when it turns up it's the best feeling ever. No need for any helpers there.

The trick, when it came to achieving this, was to get as close to Alfredo as possible. As a vinyl enthusiast himself he welcomed my interest, and by the end of the holiday I was handing him vinyl that I'd come across in record shops on the island. "Ere, Alfredo, mate. What do you reckon to this?' The prospect of handing somebody like Alfredo a record that he might deem worthy of gracing one of his sets was massive – the ultimate accolade. It stirred something in me and again, the only thing I could compare it to was what I'd seen at Paradise Garage with the great Larry Levan. Although I wasn't yet a professional DJ – well, not full-time – I was slowly starting to realise that actually, this really could be for me.

Apart from the above, by far the best thing to come out of that first trip to Ibiza were all the new friends I made. Danny Diamond's network of friends and contacts over there was already extraordinary, and a lot of the people he introduced me to are friends to this day. The aforementioned Nancy Noise, who went by the name of Nancy Turner at the time (we gave her the name Nancy Noise when she started DJ'ing), works for me at my label, Perfecto Records. Like Danny, she'd been going to Ibiza and Amnesia since 1985 or '86 and had already started collecting the vinyl that Alfredo had been playing.

By the end of the holiday we were all absolutely knackered, as you'd expect. Knackered, but enlightened. I don't know how many hours sleep we'd had, but it can't have been more than about three or four hours a night. Or should I say three or four hours a day! Sleep, after all, was for sleepy people, and we hadn't really felt like it. What kept us awake and interested had been an intoxicating infusion of music, drugs and people, the like of which not one of us had ever come into contact with before. This, as I said earlier, was life-changing.

We arrived back in London about three weeks before the closing party in September and my first thought on landing at the airport was, 'Fuck it. I want to go back!' As daft as that sounds I knew that it was actually a possibility, and after umming and ahhing for a couple of days, Nicky and I decided to retrace our steps. After arranging some accommodation we ended up booking a ticket each, and about two and a half weeks later we were back in San Antonio.

Trying to recreate a vibe like Alfredo's obviously isn't easy. Trying to recreate several moments in time, however, which is basically what me and Nicky were trying to do by running straight back to the scene of the crime, and especially so soon afterwards, is almost impossible, even with some little helpers.

Sure enough, about an hour after arriving at Amnesia on our first night and popping a pill each, the heavens opened and the mother of all thunderstorms began. About five minutes later the electricity went off and didn't come on again. Somebody shouted, 'Has anybody got fifty pence for the meter?' We ended up sitting outside Star Café for a few hours telling anyone who'd listen, or even just appeared to be listening, about how absolutely fucking amazing Ibiza was. Wasted or not, that became the norm for us. We were like ambassadors for the island, and in particular its nightlife. The one thing I did before we left again was to make sure that Alfredo and I stayed in touch. I wasn't sure how, when or why exactly, but given the ideas that were now running around my head I had a feeling that our paths might cross again, and not necessarily in Ibiza.

CHAPTER 9

The Reunions

By the time Danny Diamond and Trevor arrived back in the UK in November, I'd managed to find every single record that Alfredo had played that summer (that's right, I did actually make a note of them all), plus quite a few others that I felt might complement the collection. I wasn't quite sure what I was going to do with them yet (recreating the Amnesia vibe in south London at the start of winter with a recession around the corner wasn't going to be easy), but that was all we had for now – the Balearic Beat, as it was known. All that was missing was the sunshine, the cosmopolitan crowd, the beautiful and unique venue, Ibiza's laissez-faire environment and the pills.

Thanks to Danny and Trevor, I became aware of the fact that, in addition to them two, there was in fact an entire community of people who'd been working, and playing, out in Ibiza for the season who had just arrived home, and who would no doubt be experiencing certain withdrawal symptoms, not least for the bloody weather! There was nothing we could do about that, but what we could try and do was recreate at least some of the elements of the vibe they were missing and to that end we decided to test the water with what became known as an Ibiza reunion party.

Trevor, Danny and I were still running The Project Club in Streatham every Friday night (or at least we were when we were in the country), with Carl Cox on sound who was now also the warm-up DJ, and we'd had the idea of holding the reunion party after that. We'd been playing a lot of rare groove at the club until then, but since arriving back from Ibiza we'd been like, 'From now on we're going to be mixing in a bit of Balearic Beat.' A lot of people didn't like the change but we didn't care. 'If you don't like it,' we said to them, 'go somewhere else.' We were so focused. We knew we'd found something special.

Although there were no mobile phones or emails back then, everyone had managed to stay in touch since arriving back from Ibiza, so getting the word out regarding the reunion party wasn't a problem. One thing we didn't know was how many of them would turn up. Everyone said yes on the phone or whatever, but that's a lot different to actually turning up. We just had to try it and see. We knew at least a hundred people who were definites and figured that any more would be a bonus.

After ushering out the usual crowd at 2am on the night in question, we then opened the side doors and ushered in the Ibiza guinea pigs. They were supplemented by some like-minded pals of ours, not to mention some of the earlier crowd who'd got wind of what was happening. Fortunately, they didn't mouth off about it (which could have been disastrous given the fact we didn't have a licence beyond 2am) and just hung around for a few minutes before joining the throng.

By the time we'd let them all in the place was rammed, and I'm pretty sure every single person who said yes – or yes please – turned up. Some of them were coming from as far afield as Sheffield, Leeds and Manchester, which made it even more incredible. It was time to begin the experiment. Despite it being illegal, the desire to put something on far outweighed the danger. If anything, it probably added to it.

Instead of playing it safe and copying one of Alfredo's sets, one or two of which I'd actually recorded, I decided to play it by ear and see where the mood took us. I ended up playing Thrashing Doves, Elkin, Nitzer Ebb and Nelson. It all went down a storm. I do believe some little white pills might have made their way across the Mediterranean for the event, or from Holland. I'm not sure where Danny got them from. I remember saying to him before the party, 'You know what's got to happen, Danny, don't you?' 'Just you leave it to me,' he said. You never asked any questions with Danny. It was best not to. You just let him get on with it. By three o'clock in the morning, Balearic Beat and the spirit of Ibiza had, for the first time, officially gone international and the party carried on until seven o'clock in the morning. The changes had been well and truly rung.

By the time we started chucking everyone out, in addition to sporting a colossal grin on my face, my head was spinning with dreams of taking this new vibe we'd discovered, and now imported, mainstream. Were they dreams or was it now an ambition? We'd certainly recaptured the vibe so why not do it again?

One thing that first reunion party taught me was that it isn't where you are that really matters when it comes to having a blast, it's who you're with. OK, so we didn't have any stars to dance under at the party (that we could actually see, that is) and there were no fountains and no swings to be seen. We had the music though, and we had the people. All of the people. When Nicky and I had been back to Ibiza for the end of season party, it hadn't been anywhere near as good as the holiday itself. Why? Because we hadn't had the music or the people, which are what created the vibe. OK, and the drugs. Let's not forget them. That scene wouldn't be prevalent forever though and the two constant components we rely on to create any kind of vibe have always been and always will be the people and the music. Everything else is a bonus.

All that aside, at the end of the day we'd held one reunion party for a very captive and predictably receptive audience. Preaching to the converted, basically. The introduction of Balearic Beat to The Project Club had been a bit mixed thus far, so at the end of the day what we were putting our faith in was still a bit of an unknown quantity. If we were going to try and go mainstream with it we'd need balls as big as planets. Bring it on. I was so up for it.

Many years later I did a residency in Las Vegas which I'll go into detail about later, and in the weeks and months leading up to it, and after, to be fair, I experienced quite a backlash, both from fellow DJs and the industry. 'What are you doing that for? People only go there to retire,' some said. I was really slagged off for it by some people. I was pilloried.

As with Ibiza and the Balearic Beat, I'd spotted an opportunity that others hadn't and instead of trying to second-guess what the public's reaction might be, I decided to give it a go. Was it a nailed-on success? Absolutely not. In fact, if you consider what the main tourist demographics are in a resort like Las Vegas compared to those in most mainstream nightclubs, you'd probably think I was barmy. Every single big human attraction prior to me in Las Vegas, and we're going back all the way here, had been a crooner, a magician or, latterly, a pop or rock star. It could have been a seriously big mistake. And this wasn't just a promoter hiring me. It was own thing. My own production.

OK, cards on the table time. As much as I loved, and had faith in the Balearic Beat, the game changer with regards to helping to redefine club culture was always going to be ecstasy. At least to start with. I mean, how else were you going to get the people of

Britain to visit a club on a Monday or Tuesday night in February? Once they were there you could play any music they wanted. Ecstasy was the grease, social and musical. It was the enabler.

The next thing that had to change, and I'd picked this up at several places over the past couple of years, but in particular at Amnesia and Paradise Garage, was obviously the importance of the DJ. Regardless of what kind of music you were into, dancing in small groups was still very much the order of the day at clubs in the UK, and in order to generate any kind of actual vibe it had to change.

What we were trying to create was a feeling of unison, I suppose, which was the antithesis of what existed. A coming together of like-minded people who were all in the same euphoric state listening to the same euphoric music. My first experience of this, as in 'we're all in this together', had been the first night at Amnesia. The significance of it, however, as in the difference between that and everything I'd experienced previously, didn't hit me until I'd been there for about an hour. All of a sudden I realised that, as well as staring in the direction of Alfredo who I could see clearly behind the decks, everyone else was doing exactly the same thing. We were all – in it – together.

I'd actually given out instructions to a couple of mates of mine at The Project Club who, after trying to explain it, didn't get what I was talking about. 'Right then,' I said. 'Take what Danny handed you, focus on the DJ and the music, and in thirty minutes you'll get it.' And they did. Every time.

The next thing that had to change in our clubland revolution was the look. Gaudy Don Johnson suits with flecks on them and shiny shoes were still the in thing for blokes in mainstream clubs and had to be banished for all eternity. It would take a few months, but by the spring of 1988 the clubbing attire of choice for your average Londoner had become baggy trousers and Converse trainers. This, incidentally, was not influenced by Ibiza or New York. In Ibiza most people got dolled up to go clubbing as they were on holiday, and in New York it was a real mixture. Baggy trousers and Converse trainers was actually what the boys and girls who worked in Ibiza used to wear and it caught on.

The other thing that had to change was the door policy. Getting into a club had always been about what you were wearing and what you looked like, whereas going forward it had to be about your attitude and how you held yourself. Looking like a twat and posing at The Wag Club was about to become a thing of the past. Boy, were we doing the world a favour.

By the Friday after that first reunion party almost everybody was wearing baggy trousers and Converse trainers. And, instead of standing around chatting or whatever, they all danced. I remember Carl Cox rocking up to one of the early parties and wondering what the hell was going on. 'Everyone's going crazy!' he said. It changed everything.

Incidentally, one extremely pivotal night during the post Ibiza Project Room period was when various members of two of London's most notorious sets of football hooligans – the Millwall firm and the West Ham firm – turned up to the club at the same time. Neither knew that each other was in the building at first, but it was only a matter of time. Somebody made us aware of this fact and instead of trying to chuck them out, which would have been suicide, we had to think of some other way. In the end Danny went out there, befriended them all one by one and persuaded them to take a pill each. This happened just in the nick of time as in addition to having spied each other, insults were being exchanged, not to mention threats. I had a bird's-eye view of all this as I was in the DJ booth, and within twenty minutes of Danny's mercy dash they were all shaking hands, hugging each other and no doubt extolling the virtues of each other's teams. 'I've always admired Bobby Moore. Wonderful player!' In any another environment they'd have knocked seven kinds of shit out of each other, but for a few hours a temporary armistice was called, thanks to Danny.

We did have setbacks – such as getting raided by the police. That was interesting. I'm pretty sure it was either the fourth or fifth reunion party and some prick had parked their car across the delivery entrance of a supermarket across the road. At some point the police started sniffing round and while trying to locate the owner of the car they came across us – 200 teens and twenty-somethings wearing baggy trousers and Converse trainers, all under the influence and going off our flaming heads. Paradise Garage and Amnesia might well have opened their doors in the wee small hours, but this was Streatham. As we didn't have a licence that was it as far as The Project Club was concerned. No matter. It was time to move up West.

CHAPTER 10

Here's to the Future

By now I'd become what I suppose you could call a professional DJ, despite still having fingers in a lot of other pies. The reason that had happened, in addition to me just loving it, was because I was still the one with all the records. Nobody else played the stuff I did because nobody else had it. It was my calling card. My USP. There's no such thing as a definitive record collection (unless you have every record that's ever been released, of course) and in order to keep things interesting for the punters, and for myself, I had to keep listening and looking. To that end I'd spend most of my waking hours in places like Rough Trade Records in Ladbroke Grove. It's like somebody who's good with words. Because I'm dyslexic my vocabulary isn't as extensive as I'd like it to be, and there's nothing I love more than conversing with people who have a good command of the English language. Not only do they have all the words at their disposal but, just as importantly, they know exactly how and when to use them. I can't do that with words but I can do that with music, so although me and these people don't always speak the same language, we do exactly the same thing.

After the police had very kindly helped us make the decision to move up West, we set about looking for a venue, and in the winter of 1987 we moved into a place called The Sound Shaft which was attached to a much bigger club called Heaven. Many of you reading this will have been to Heaven at least once. It's on Villiers Street underneath Charing Cross Station and has been around since the late 1970s.

The night we went for at The Sound Shaft was Thursday, partly because it was almost the start of the weekend, but also because in the main club they ran something called Delirium that played nothing but house music. We'd been to Delirium a few times and figured they'd be a good match, especially as we'd be playing a bit of house music ourselves.

After several long discussions we decided to call our new club Future, basically in recognition of the possibilities that lay ahead. All we had to do now was find the £300 hire fee. I'm not sure how given everything we were up to, but Danny and I didn't actually have that much money at the time and we had to rely on our mates paying a fiver on the door each to get the full amount. The moment we had it, one of us ran next door and gave it to the manager of Heaven, a lovely man called David Inches.

The club itself was perfect for our needs. It held about 120 people so if you got eighty or ninety it looked fine, and if you got a hundred or more you'd have a party on your hands. It was also dark and had an underground feel to it, similar to Paradise Garage. Musically, I wanted the club to find its own way and that had to happen organically. It had to suit the environment and until we were all in there together, I wasn't quite sure how it would play out. There was a lot of nervous energy at first. A lot of anticipation. The sensibility had to be Balearic Beat but there was a lot of music underneath that umbrella.

Within a couple of weeks we'd found our feet and the club had found its sound. Rap, rock, dance and indie were the main themes – pretty much everything then – with a slight emphasis on

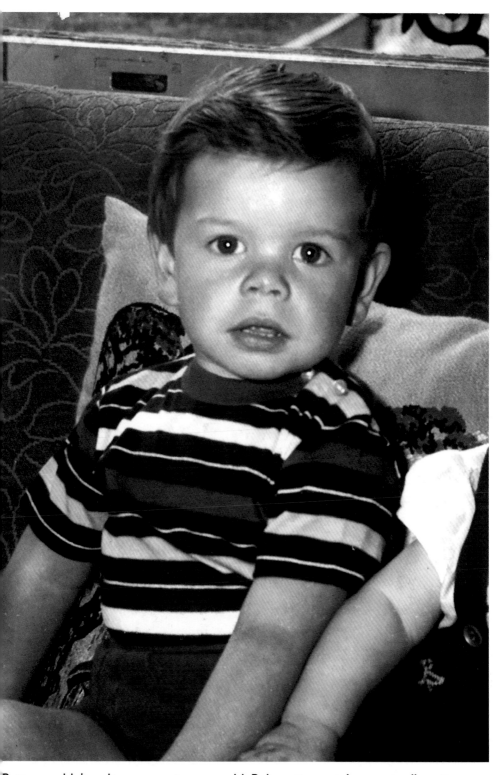

Butter wouldn't melt – me as a two year old. Believe it or not, I was actually quite well behaved!

Top: Me and my gorgeous sister Linda standing next to some dodgy wallpaper sometime in the mid-1970s.

Above: Me in Trafalgar Square in the mid-1970s. This must have been one of the few occasions when I went up West but didn't end up in a club.

If it hadn't been for all that DJing stuff, who knows? Here I am training to be a chef up West somewhere. My God it was hard work!

I know everybody talks about Ibiza, but this is where the journey really began. My first trip to New York way back in the early 1980s.

Left: My first real effort as a producer and definitely the most eventful. The Mondays were off their heads!

Left: Boy, I wish I'd produced this one! Watching the Beastie Boys become massive was a game-changer for me. I wanted what they had.

My fabled trip to my beloved Stamford Bridge where I signed my contract with Cream in 1996. I told you the shirt was like a beach towel.

Top: I've got mixed feelings about Glastonbury and have probably had a better time off the stage than on!

Above: At Home nightclub in Sydney where I once had a brief residency. I love the Aussies. They're always up for it.

Plying my trade somewhere in London circa 1999, and using vinyl! Playing live is the only thing I've ever been addicted to.

indie. I'd also found a new warm-up DJ in the form of the afore-mentioned Nancy Noise. As well as being an avid vinyl collector like me, and a disciple of Alfredo's, she fully appreciated, perhaps more than anybody else at the time, the importance of the arrange-ment. It was a good match. In fact, the only thing that really sepa-rated Nancy and me musically was the fact that I'd be prepared to deviate from my set if needs be whereas Nancy wouldn't. She was very set in her ways like that and as soon as she'd played her final record that would be that. I did try and encourage Nancy to go off piste sometimes or lengthen her set a bit but she wouldn't. One day I decided to encourage her a bit, and as she lined up her final record, instead of making my way to the booth like I usually did, I decided to go for a wander. Just for a few minutes. Nancy went absolutely off her nut the first time I did it, but it did the trick. She was taken out of her comfort zone, had to improvise and rose to the challenge. I only just lived to tell the tale.

Within a couple of months the club had really found its feet and in addition to our regular clientele we also began to attract more than our fair share of celebrities. This hadn't been the inten-tion but word must have got around. I remember The Cure coming in one night. That was interesting. I used to play them quite a lot and it felt like they'd come to check up on me. Play 'Love Cats' now or we'll do you! Don't get me wrong, the club was never starry. These were rare occurrences. It gave us something to talk about though.

Never ones to rest on our laurels for very long, after a few months of success and enjoyment we decided to approach David Inches about moving to the main club. I remember the conversa-tions we had about this clearly, and in hindsight we must have been mad. What the hell were we thinking? You see, the main club wasn't just a bit bigger than The Sound Shaft, it was over ten times bigger.

Ten times! Didn't I just mention something about organic growth? To be fair, that had been about the club finding its feet, which it now had. In order to take it further we had to be bold. Fifteen hundred people a week though. That was going to be a big, big ask.

Had our new night in the main club been on either a Friday or a Saturday then our arses would still have squeaked like a lorry-load of mice, but it wasn't. As it was, I'm afraid neither of those were available. 'The only night I've got in the main club is Monday,' said David Inches when we approached him. 'Monday?' we said to him. 'But nobody goes clubbing on a Monday.' 'Take it or leave it, boys,' said David. 'It's the only one we've got.'

The first thing we did after seeing David was conduct a straw poll among our friends to see how many people thought it was doable. 'What do you think?' we asked them. 'Can we get fifteen hundred people to come out on a Monday night, regardless of the weather, and go to a club until two o'clock in the morning?' One of two things happened when we posed that question: either they laughed at us, which was disappointing, or they'd just stand there looking like they'd shat their pants. Either way, it wasn't the reaction we'd been hoping for, although in hindsight it should have been the one we'd been expecting. I mean, come on. We were just being ridiculous.

'OK, you're on,' we said to David. 'We'll take Monday.' 'Really?' he said, happy but surprised. 'OK, good luck, boys.'

We didn't need luck. We needed a fucking miracle! And our heads testing.

It was awful timing, but the moment we did the deal with David, all kinds of scenarios started playing out in my head, all of which I vocalised to Danny. 'What if we only get a couple of hundred people,' I said. 'A, it'll look shit, and B, we'll lose a bloody fortune! How many did we have at Future last week?'

'About a hundred and ten.'

'Fuuuucking hell!'

As scared and apprehensive as we undoubtedly were, our belief in what we'd discovered and what we were nurturing and developing was unshakable, and deep down I knew we'd done the right thing. Every friend of ours and club promoter we knew had told us otherwise, but we were adamant. All we had to do now was prove it.

We ended up calling our new nightclub Spectrum (can't remember why) and the early clientele was primarily made up of the Future crowd. They'd been willing to migrate to a new venue, and a new night of the week, thank goodness, and were excited about what we were doing. Some of the throng from the early Ibiza reunion parties turned up too in addition to as many mates and contacts as we could muster.

Without wanting to blow our own trumpets too much, although I'm going to, as a clubbing experience Spectrum was off the fucking scale. It wasn't just a case of replicating what we'd done with Future but in a bigger venue. Shit, no! Spectrum was a spectacle. The spectacle. For a start we had the biggest and best sound system in London, not to mention the best light and laser show. We also had the best clothing and merchandise, thanks to a clever Geordie called Dave Little. He designed a psychedelic logo for Spectrum known as 'the all-seeing eye' that still adorns T-shirts to this day. We must have sold thousands over the years. They were everywhere. No other club dared go for that kind of psychedelic vibe, although they soon followed suit. Dave also designed a 50-foot long mural for us which we put on one of the walls. It was immense!

When it came to the music, as well as me and Nancy we had guest DJs such as Mike Pickering and Graeme Park from the

Haçienda. They came down from Manchester to do a battle of the DJs once against me and Colin Hudd. I forget who won. I bet they did. You know what Mancs are like, pushy buggers. We also went off the wall a bit sometimes and one night we had a Japanese guitarist called Kenji playing. He went down well, as it goes. There were no boundaries at Spectrum. Everybody listened to everything.

Despite all of the above the early crowd numbers for Spectrum were disappointing. We initially had a co-promoter, Gary Haisman, who ended up coining the popular catchphrases 'Acieeed' and 'It's All Gone Pete Tong', but he pulled out after a few weeks leaving me and Danny to brave it alone. It was a scary time, man, let me tell you. The nights themselves cost a packet to put on and looming large at the top of our extensive list of outgo-ings was the rent. I forget how much it was exactly but after six or seven weeks we were about £12,000 in arrears.

Our saviour was David Inches, no two ways about it. Fortunately, as opposed to leaving us to it, he watched us like a hawk and although it was slow, after a while he could see that things were starting to turn around. If he'd just sat in his office and listened to our pleas week in week out – 'We'll have it with you next week, David, we promise' – he'd have lost patience and we'd have been out on our ears, but he didn't. He, just like our slowly growing audience, was fascinated and intrigued by what we were all trying to achieve and from a business point of view he could obviously see the potential. After all, the better we did, the better they did. We were relying on word of mouth, however, and although the message was getting out there, the people listening were taking some persuading. Think about it though. If somebody came up to you and said, 'Do you want to come to a club this Monday night, stay out until half past two in the morning and then go to work at nine,' you'd tell them to bugger off, wouldn't you? I'm assuming most of you would.

You know what they say, all good things come to them who wait, and on week eight things really began to change. I remember popping out for half an hour early doors and when I came back the queue to get in was around the corner. Until now, that had never happened before, and when I saw them all standing there I was flabbergasted. That night we almost broke even and the week after, we did. This meant our debt to David and Heaven, which was owned by Richard Branson's Virgin Group at the time, hopefully wouldn't get any bigger. Week ten was just astonishing – a full house – and on the following Tuesday morning when the world had woken up again, we were able to pop around to David's office with a bag of cash and give him at least a down payment on what we owed. And a big thank you. If it hadn't been for his patience and encouragement we'd never have made it.

From then on we were truly off and running. Every week we did something different – on and off the stage – and with that came a demand from the public to keep on pushing the boundaries. The KLF, who'd only formed the year before, did their first ever live performance at Spectrum. How about that? I'm not sure how it came about but I'd been playing their track 'What Time Is Love?' for a while – in fact, it had become a bit of an anthem really – and they ended up performing it live for us.

From a DJ'ing point of view, I was in my element. The occasion and the atmosphere demanded that I keep changing things around, and the more successful the club became the more daring and experimental I became behind the decks. To all intents and purposes this was a residency for me, so remembering what I'd learned from the likes of Larry and Alfredo, I set about choosing a couple of signatures: the opening track of my set, and the closing track of the night. These, once I'd selected them, would remain *in situ* so would have to capture the imaginations of the faithful.

The opener to my set became a piece called 'Flesh' by the Belgian electronic band, A Split Second. A musician and scholar called Richard Norris, who wrote an almost forensic authorised biography on me a few years ago (which has helped jog my memory many times for this book) – and, through his extensive research probably knew more about me than I did at the time – summed it up perfectly when he described 'Flesh' as being 'an expansive Belgian new-beat tune that has all the cinematic sheen and atmosphere of many later trance anthems that Oakenfold would command from the Spectrum booth'. Couldn't have put it better myself, Richard old chap. I really couldn't though. That's absolutely on the nail.

Next up was the final record of the evening – the crescendo. That choice was a little bit harder to come to and I ummed and ahhed about it for quite a while. In the end I took a chance and settled on a piece of music by the German composer Richard Wagner, which had been used on the soundtrack to a movie I liked called *Excalibur*. The very idea of using a piece of classical music to close a set in a nightclub was both dangerous, bombastic and very OTT, which in my mind summed up Spectrum to a tee. It's what we were. Not everybody took to the idea though. In fact, a fellow promoter of mine, who will have to remain nameless, came up to me one night in the club and accused me of playing – get this – the music of the devil! 'That was in *The Omen*,' they said. 'Fuck off!' I replied. 'It was in *Excalibur*, which is a different thing altogether.' It was intense all right – that was the point – but I didn't see any buildings falling down or anyone crossing themselves. I ask you!

Carrying on with the classical theme, something I started doing mid-set at Spectrum, which was a homage to Larry Levan and his trick with the train, was to plunge the club into darkness suddenly and play the finale to the '1812 Overture' by Tchaikovsky – cannons and all! Finishing a set with a piece of classical music was one thing, but sticking one right in mid-set and without any warning was another thing altogether. I trusted the crowd to get it though, and get it they most certainly did. Seriously, if you want to take a shindig up a level or two, try it.

There are actually three rooms at Heaven: the main room on the ground floor, which probably accounts for about 75 per cent of the club, a much smaller room upstairs, and an even smaller room at the back of the ground floor which is often usually used as a VIP area. Once we'd got the music in the main room nailed down, we turned our attentions to the other two. Upstairs we went for the Boy's Own crew, consisting of Terry Farley, Andrew Weatherall, Cymon Eckel and Steven Hall. I remember seeing them all at The Project Club for the first time. They were into that rare-groove look with baggy trousers and floppy hats. Just getting the Boy's Own crew to turn up to The Project Club had been a coup for us and they'd supported us ever since. It was time to give something back.

We decided to turn the back room on the ground floor into a chill-out space, but with a difference. Instead of allowing just anybody in there we made it DJs only. It was the only 'exclusive' part of the nightclub really, and the person we put in charge of the music was Alex Paterson (then calling himself LX Dee) from The Orb. I'm not sure if he'd actually started The Orb at the time, but it's obviously what made him famous. He'd been a mate of mine for a while had Alex and, like me, his approach to music was open and experimental. His brief for the room was to not let anybody dance, which I suppose might have been slightly counter-intuitive. It was certainly a challenge. We figured that if DJs were going to congregate there, the last thing they'd want to do is walk into a thumping room full of sweat and energy. It was a chill-out room for DJs, basically, and in order to create the mood he wanted Alex would often play noises instead of songs.

Spectrum eventually became so popular that we'd have fifteen hundred people inside the club and five hundred people outside waiting to get in – on a Monday. That was unheard of in London. It was just crazy.

The only kind of people we didn't really want at Spectrum, apart from arseholes and troublemakers, were celebrities. There was no door policy banning them or anything. 'Sorry, Mr Bowie, but you're far too iconic for this place.' God, no. The whole starry thing didn't really fit with the vibe we were trying to create. Also, if you have a load of celebrities turning up to your club every week and word gets around, the spotlight will start shining on them. Despite this, as time went on the inevitable happened and they began turning up. We had Grace Jones, David Bowie, Liza Minnelli, Simon Le Bon, George Michael. The thing is, they were only there because they wanted to observe, whereas what we wanted were people who were into it. And I mean really into it. People like that were the foundation of the club and so anybody who deviated from it made us nervous. Because I was always in the booth, I don't remember meeting any celebs at Spectrum. Danny or whoever used to run in and say, 'Guess what, I've just seen George Michael upstairs!'

One of the most bizarre things to happen as a result of us starting Spectrum was a single called 'We Call It Acieeed', which ended up going to number one in about twenty countries. It all happened when a producer called Danny D (not Danny Diamond) visited the club one night. Our former co-promoter, Gary Haisman, was on the dance floor shouting his now familiar catchphrase, 'Acieeed!' and Danny D heard it and thought, I'll make a record out of that, and he did. It was a massive tune and made him and Gary famous. I wish to hell I'd thought of it. From our point of view, the fact that things like this were happening as a direct result of what we'd started (Spectrum is also mentioned in the lyrics to 'We Call It Acieeed') was a big thing and it added to the legend.

I suppose it was inevitable, but after a while the Spectrum brand and vibe began to escape the confines of Heaven and made its way, first of all, to Manchester and to a club called Legends. Because of our friendship with the people at the Haçienda – and because a large contingent from Manchester were already making the journey down to Spectrum in London every week – this made sense, and the people we dispatched to make it happen up there were Trevor Fung and Colin Hudd. After that we took the club to Birmingham, which was also Trevor and Colin, and then toured it around the country. We were a prototype for what the likes of Ministry, Cream and Godskitchen ended up doing years later.

Believe it or not, some of the last people to take notice of what we were doing at Spectrum were the press, or at least the newspapers. Youth culture magazines such as *The Face* and *i-D* had been running features on us for ages, but it was only towards the end of 1988 when the red tops caught up. Given the fact that what we'd created wasn't exactly mainstream, they were always going to be looking for an angle that ensured their readers would end up hating us, and it didn't take much to find one. The first tabloid to have a go at us were *The Sun* and the angle, although it turned out to be a red herring really, was the fact that we were selling Es at the club for a fiver. 'Scandal of the £5 drug trip to Heaven,' was the unsurprisingly unimaginative headline. The reason it was a red herring was because the people – or person – who they were really gunning for was the club's owner, Richard Branson. He, not me, was the target for their ire.

Some so-called journalism though. Talk about not doing your homework. Because of the term, 'acid house', which had originated in clubs like Spectrum, they assumed that the drug we'd been taking had been acid. 'LSD,' they wrote learnedly – 'a favourite with seventies dropouts – is now popular with yuppies.' Really? I thought yuppies were all on cocaine? When describing the antics of the Spectrum faithful they went full-on pious and said, 'Junkies flaunt their craving by wearing T-shirts sold at the club bearing messages like, "Can you feel it?" and "Drop acid, not bombs". The youngsters, mainly in their mid-twenties, try to escape the pressure of work by getting high on acid every weekend.' Hang on, Spectrum was on a Monday!

I don't know if it's the same these days as I haven't lived there for a while, but back in the 1980s the British tabloid press were famous for that kind of spurious, holier-than-thou righteous indignation bollocks. It was designed, quite evidently, to polarise the young and old and more often than not it had the desired effect. Downstairs at the breakfast table you'd have parents tutting away like good 'uns and upstairs you'd have their teenage sons and daughters thinking, 'Drugs in a club? Kids having fun? I want some of that!' Anyway, it didn't do us any harm, as in the club. In fact, it literally gave us a new lease of life and we should have sent the good people of *The Sun* a thank-you letter.

This all came about because Mr Branson, who'd always been very cool with us, was warned by the authorities that unless he took some action his licence might be at stake. The following Monday he came down to Spectrum for a look around and after taking everything in – the sights and sounds and smells – he asked us for a word. He knew what was happening. He'd seen it all before. 'Look, boys,' he said. 'I admire what you're doing here. I really do. It's great. The thing is, I have to be seen to be doing something, and so here's the plan. As opposed to closing you down, which is what the authorities would like me to do, why don't you take a month off, come back, and then relaunch under a different name?' That seemed fair to us.

We closed the doors at Spectrum for the final time in October 1988 and opened our doors again about five weeks later. The original name for the new club was Phantasia and we even got Dave Little to design a new logo for it. Unfortunately, this incarnation only lasted about a month as the press got it into their heads that we'd named the club after a new kind of drug. That was bollocks though. We hadn't. In the end we settled on the name Land of Oz which seemed to represent, not just what we wanted the club to be, which was something theatrical and out there, but what the customer wanted too. 'Follow the yellow brick road in here, my friend. You'll have a great time!'

What Land of Oz did was take Spectrum's 'theatre if madness', which is what the concept had been named by some people, to another level. If I'm being brutally honest, this version was perhaps slightly pretentious in some ways, but at the end of the day it was all new. We were experimenting. Using our imaginations. We also used the stage in the main room a lot more with Oz, which was huge. I mean, why not? One week we turned it into a castle. I forget where we got the scenery from but it looked amazing, like something out of a film. Another week we decided to have ghosts flying from one side of the stage to another. I wish I could remember who made the ghosts. One of us did. We used really thin chicken wire to transport them from here to there, and when the lights were down and the night was in full flow it looked fantastic. I know it sounds a bit shit but I promise you, it wasn't.

What we had with Land of Oz that we didn't have at Spectrum, apart from imaginations that had been expanded somewhat by things like ecstasy, was money. That enabled us to make the ideas we were having a reality and we had a lot of fun in the process. Glitter explosions, snowstorms, giant insects. It was fun, not to mention a privilege. I mean, how many young people do you know who get to indulge their creative sides like that? We didn't just think about things, we actually did them. It's been the story of my life really. We were like kids in a sweet shop.

With regards to the music, or at least the music on the main floor, my main ports of call were ambient music, which was just starting to appear, or big anthemic house tunes, the kind of stuff that, if you weren't quite ready for it, could make you fall flat on your arse.

It was about this time that Danny and I began to drift apart. This was hard as we'd been inseparable for a long time and had shared so much. We'd done the Amazon, Hong Kong, Rio and the Great Wall of China. We'd taken on New York together – and won! We'd discovered a new club culture over in Ibiza and imported it to the UK. We'd put everything on the line more than once and had always had each other's backs.

Danny had always been the fixer, so to speak, and until now I'd never really given that a second thought. Things just appeared, if you see what I mean. 'Danny, we need this.' 'OK, give me a day, I'll sort it.' He's a force of nature and always has been. By now he had a flat in Covent Garden, a woman on each arm. He had the lot. It was glamorous all right, but it was all becoming very, very dark. He was also taking a lot of drugs – cocaine, mainly – and it was pulling him in. I did try speaking to Danny about this but he was having none of it. As far as he was concerned there wasn't a problem. He had money, contacts, mates, girls, and a share in a successful club. Life was golden in his eyes. To me though, it was becoming a problem, not only because of the change in Danny's personality, which was now very up and down, but because one of the main people behind one of the most successful clubs in London, if not the country, was a known drug dealer. That, in the light of all the negative press that drugs, and especially ecstasy were generating at the time, was not a good look. The thing is, Danny was and is much more than that. As well as being the fixer he also had a lot of very good ideas and had always been very much a part of the creative process. To that end, he was just as responsible for the birth of acid house as anybody.

With regards to our relationship, it all came to a head one day when we ended up having the mother of all arguments. The last time this had happened to me was with Mel, but this was on a different scale. Danny was like a brother to me, and me to him. It was devastating really, but what could you do? It had been on the cards for months.

With regards to Danny's activities this also came to a head one day when he had a run-in with some gangsters he'd been dealing with. They ended up spraying ammonia in his face which partially blinded him. I remember going to see him in hospital. What a mess! He was still in denial though and seemed more worried about saving his reputation than his health or even his eyesight. It was a messy business and although our relationship suffered, we managed to remain on speaking terms – just.

After coming out of hospital Danny eventually saw the light and hightailed it to LA where he set about trying to recreate what we'd created over here, if you get my drift. There was nobody better equipped for the job. You know what they say, you can't keep a good man down. The man's genuinely unstoppable though. After that he ended up travelling to Goa in India which is when our paths crossed again. Does Goa ring any bells? I have a feeling it might do.

CHAPTER 11

Mr Remixer

Given everything that had happened, it was inevitable that the whole club thing would eventually come to an end, and when that finally happened it was actually a relief. It had been fun but like all good things it had to come to an end. One noticeable change within the club environment, which had a bearing on my change of attitude, was that cocaine appeared to be overtaking ecstasy as the drug of choice. As anyone who's ever taken cocaine will tell you, it can turn people into, not just bastards, but boring bastards, especially when mixed with alcohol. From a club owner's point of view this was obviously preferable as they were never going to become rich selling a few hundred bottles of water a night. Euphoria, dancing and hugs were being replaced by posturing piss-heads spouting bullshit, basically. It was definitely time to move on.

The best thing to come out of Spectrum and Land of Oz was the effect they were having on the industry and culture as a whole. They, in addition to projects that the likes of Danny Rampling and Nicky Holloway had started post Ibiza, had spawned a plethora of impersonators, whether they be clubs, raves or parties. It was happening absolutely everywhere and to coin a very well-used phrase, nothing would ever be the same again. It's hard to get my head around it sometimes. I mean, if you think about what's happened in the thirty-five years since the four of us got on that plane to Ibiza. It's mind-blowing.

The most noticeable thing for me when we knocked Land of Oz on the head was an almost indescribable sense of freedom. God, it felt good. Ever since we got Spectrum off the ground I'd received offers to go and DJ all over the place, and although I managed to do a bit here and there I always felt restricted. Suddenly, I was able to accept these opportunities wholesale and didn't have to worry about a thing. But it wasn't just DJ'ing that was floating my boat at the time. Remixing and producing had been high on the agenda for a while, and by the time we finished Oz I had offers coming out of my ears.

One of the few jobs I'd been able to accept during my time at Heaven had been a remix of a Balearic staple called 'Jibaro' which had originally been recorded by a Colombian duo called Elkin & Nelson. I must have heard the song a thousand times in Ibiza, so when it came to entering the studio I was awash with ideas.

With regards to operating a studio, nothing had really changed for me since 'Girls Ain't Nothing But Trouble', in that I was still a bit of a novice, so in order to make it happen I was going to need help. Enter Mr Rob Davis – producer, songwriter and, unbeknownst to me at the time, the former lead guitarist with a band who'd had no fewer than eleven Top 10 singles including three number ones!

He's probably almost as well known these days as being a songwriter as he either wrote or co-wrote some of the biggest hits of the noughties, including 'Toca's Miracle' by Fragma, which was a massive hit all over Europe, 'Groovejet (If This Ain't Love)' by Spiller, which you'll know, 'I Can't Get You Out Of My Head' by Kylie, which he wrote with Cathy Dennis and which sold about 4 million copies, and another smash hit by Kylie called 'Come Into My World'.

Back then, however, Rob was primarily known as being the guitarist out of Mud. That's right, 'Tiger Feet' and the Christmas one that sounds a bit like an Elvis song. You got it. Although we got on like a house on fire pretty much immediately, I had no idea who Rob was, and because he's quite a modest young man he wasn't about to tell me. He was there to help me remix a track and so we got on with it. It wasn't until a couple of years later that the penny finally dropped. I was watching *Top of the Pops 2* I think it was, and they must have been playing 'Tiger Feet' or something. All of a sudden there's Rob on my screen wearing a massive pair of flared trousers, hair that should have had its own postcode and a ridiculous pair of earrings. Earrings were Rob's trademark during his Mud days, apparently. Anyway, once I stopped laughing I called him up on the phone and asked if there was anything he'd been keeping from me. 'You've found out then,' he said. I was actually really impressed. Glam rock had been my thing as a kid, and although I hadn't recognised him I was aware of what he'd achieved.

The name we used for the 'Jibaro' project was Electra, and when it was finally released in 1988 we formed a band (not featuring any actual musicians) to promote it. I think I played guitar on the video, although not the song, and despite sporting a mullet that would have put Patrick Swayze in his pomp to shame, the song barely troubled the charts. It did well at Spectrum though and became one of the most popular songs I played there. And at Land of Oz.

My relationship with Rob took me from being just an ideas man in the studio to an actual knob-twiddler. He was my mentor, basically, and taught me how to engineer and program, which would enable me to produce, not just other people, but myself. Through Rob, I met a studio engineer called Steve Osborne who'd trained at the legendary Trident Studios in Soho where, among dozens of other legendary records, David Bowie had recorded *The Rise and Fall of Ziggy Stardust and the Spiders from Mars*. For some reason we just hit it off, and sometime after that an offer came in that was right up our street. In fact, you could say we were mad for it. Ring any bells?

When Spectrum's reputation had started stretching beyond the M25, a contingent of Mancunians had started frequenting the club at least once a month. We already had a relationship with the guys at the Haçienda like Mike and Graeme, and this was an extension of that. A coachload of them used to come down and, as well as being massive characters, they'd all embraced the acid house ethos. They were out for a good time and nothing was going to stop them. Some of that contingent were members of an indie rock band called the Happy Mondays, and over time I got to know them pretty well. They'd had an album out, had another on the way and were causing a real stir.

By the time that second album appeared, which was called *Bummed* (lovely title), we'd all become good mates and whenever we went up there they treated us like honorary Mancs. One song on that album, 'Wrote For Luck', was crying out to be remixed and nobody realised this more than their manager, Nathan McGough. He ended up calling up Pete Tong who worked for the band's publisher and asked if he could recommend anyone. 'Why not try Paul Oakenfold?' he said. 'He did a great job of "Jibaro".' As Spectrum regulars, Nathan and the Mondays had been listening to 'Jibaro' for ages, and the moment Pete mentioned my name something clicked. Within a week Steve Osborne and I were in a studio, and the upshot of our efforts became the genesis of what's known as alternative or indie dance. Either or.

The rhythm and the structure of the original arrangement were wrong for clubs, and so what Steve and I did was to take a loop by N.W.A., put that underneath, and then add a top-line hook. There was obviously a bit more to it than that but you get my drift. Anyway, it worked like a dream, and the only people who became bigger fans of the remix than the band themselves were the public. In fact, the head of the legendary Factory Records who the band were signed to, Tony Wilson, credits that remix as the record that broke the band. Who am I to argue? Legend has it that the Happy Mondays first heard the remix while on their way to tour America in support of The Pixies and went completely off their nuts. But in a good way. Incidentally, some of the video for the remix was filmed at Spectrum in Manchester with acid house in full flow. How very appropriate.

That track really put us on the map as far as remixing was concerned and after that the offers came in thick and fast. 'Close To Me' by The Cure was one of the next ones we did, later followed by 'Waterfall' by The Stone Roses. We did loads of them. It's a big responsibility remixing somebody else's music. For a start, you're not doing it for fun. The whole point of remixing a track is to widen the music's appeal by introducing it to a new audience and so it takes a lot of thought. There's also a chance that whoever you're working for won't like the result, which can be awkward. Fortunately, that's only happened to me on a couple of occasions and I must have remixed hundreds of tracks over the years. When it does happen you just gather up the feedback and have another go.

What I find most disappointing is when I have to turn people down. This only happens when I don't think I can do anything interesting enough with the material, which isn't to say it isn't any good. It just isn't something that lends itself, in my opinion, to interpretation. You just have to be honest and over the years I've had to turn down some massive names – including David Bowie,

Peter Gabriel and Paul McCartney. The Paul McCartney case was awful, in the sense that I would have loved to have worked with him. Wouldn't anybody? He'd asked me to DJ at one of his daughter's birthdays and afterwards we had a chat in his studio. What an experience that was. He handed me a bass guitar and said, 'That's the one I used on "Hey Jude".' I was like, 'Really?' He then played me the material that he wanted me to remix which was on his new album. It was good stuff, but unfortunately it just wouldn't have worked on a dance floor and so reluctantly I had to decline. I didn't want to be associated with something that didn't work and I'm sure Paul would be the same. He was very understanding. I was gutted though.

One of the things I have going for me when it comes to remixing is a wide taste in music. I don't always like everything I listen to but nothing's off limits, which is the approach I always have when entering the studio. The endgame is obviously to take it to the dance floor, but the more ideas and material you have at your disposal the more chance you have of making it work. As I said, nothing should ever be off limits.

The Stone Roses remix led to me being invited to open for them at a gig they were doing at a place called Spike Island which is near Widnes. Frankie Bones, Dave Haslam and MC Tunes were also going to be on the bill and it sounded like fun. The only issue I had, although I didn't let on to anyone, was the size of the crowd. There were going to be close to 30,000 people there and the most I'd ever played to was about 1,500. Actually, that's not the only thing that worried me. I don't know if it was the drugs, but instead of putting me on the stage where I thought I'd be, they put me in the bloody mixing tower! I remember when they told me. 'Sorry, mate, but you're being sent to the tower!' 'Really?' The ladder leading up to it can't have been more than about 30 centimetres wide and as well as getting myself up there I had a box of about two hundred records. It was ridiculous. Good fun though.

For a variety of different reasons I don't remember a great deal about the gig itself (ahem), but it's gone down in history as being one of the most famous ever staged in the UK and, in 2020, I took part in a live stream event to celebrate the gig's thirtieth anniversary. It was put together by the founders of Gio-Goi, Chris and Anthony Donnelly, and had a line-up featuring Clint Boon from Inspiral Carpets, Rob Tissera – from Blackburn raves, Kissdafunk and Fantazia – K-Klass, Jay Wearden and the Happy Mondays' current tour DJ, Vince Vega. It was weird doing a gig online (it's a slightly different atmosphere!) but we raised a lot of money for charity. It was fun.

Probably my most high-profile remix from those early days came after an approach from Virgin Records. There was a sound coming out of Bristol at the time that was attracting a lot of attention. It was slower and more black and urban than indie dance and its main protagonists were Smith & Mighty, Tricky and a newish band called Massive Attack. It was Massive Attack who Virgin wanted me to work with and they asked me to remix four tracks: 'Hymn of the Big Wheel', 'Be Thankful For What You've Got', 'Safe From Harm' and the incredible 'Unfinished Sympathy'. I was really into what these guys were doing, so to be asked to remix four of their tracks was a big thrill. Fortunately all four were well received by the band, the label and the public, but the one that made the biggest impact was 'Unfinished Sympathy'. Do you know, that's over thirty years old now! It's frightening.

It was through my work with Massive Attack that I was asked by Virgin Records if I'd be interested in writing and producing a single of my own. 'Why not?' I thought. It was something I hadn't done before and it seemed like a natural progression. First of all I had to get a team together. Steve Osborne was a shoo-in as we were partners in the studio, and to help us with the writing duties we drafted in Rob Davis. The name for the project was Movement 98, as in 98 beats a minute, and our debut single, 'Joy and Heartbreak', was released in 1990. Based on the melody of Erik Satie's 'Les Trois Gymnopédies', it was a mid-paced lovers' rock tune featuring vocals by Carroll Thompson. It didn't make us millionaires but it reached a fairly respectable number twenty-seven in the charts and I was happy with that. We all were.

CHAPTER 12

Call the Cops!

Exactly six months after 'Joy and Heartbreak' was released, my maiden effort as a producer hit the shelves. Steve Osborne produced it with me and the record in question is the Happy Mondays' third album, *Pills 'n' Thrills and Bellyaches*. We'd obviously stayed in touch with the band after 'Wrote For Luck' and towards the end of 1989 we got a call asking if we'd be interested in producing their next album. Steve and I had been credited by the band as the people who'd put them on the dance floor and they wanted more.

The first track we produced for them, which was done some months before the rest of the album, was 'Step On', an old John Kongos track that was originally called 'He's Gonna Step On You Again', and which had already been covered quite a few times. Although a team effort, the magic ingredient on that track is the vocal provided by Rowetta. I think it was their manager, Nathan, who suggested we bring her in. We were all agreed that the track was missing something and had been wracking our brains trying to figure out what. I forget who, but somebody suggested putting on a female vocal which is when Rowetta's name came up. She'd been singing backing vocals for Simply Red and, so legend had it, was a big fan of the Mondays. It's her track really.

'Step On' was released as a single on 6 March 1990 and got to number five in the charts and shifted, in the UK alone, over half a million copies. Get in there! Steve and I were over the bloody moon. Not only had we enjoyed the experience but it had been a big success.

When it came to producing the album, the first thing we had to do was choose a location. Tony Wilson at Factory Records had given us a budget of £100,000 which was a lot of money. We could go anywhere, really. At the time of us agreeing the deal with Factory Records, the band were on tour in the States, and as they were finishing the tour in LA it was suggested that we record it there. I was game. Three months in California, all expenses paid? Yes bloody please. The next question was which studio we should use. The only one I'd really heard of over there was Capitol Studios which is where the likes of Frank Sinatra and The Beach Boys used to record. It's LA's version of Abbey Road, and when I suggested it to the band they thought it was a great idea. 'Groovy, man,' they said. 'Get it fucking booked!'

One thing I hadn't really considered while all this was going on was the enormity of what we were about to under-take. Not from a career point of view, although that was defi-nitely quite nerve-wracking. After all, we'd set the benchmark high with 'Step On' and Factory would be expecting more of the same. What I'm referring to is the small matter of spending three months in LA with six musicians from Hulme who, as well as being incredibly unpredictable were, shall we say, often quite high-spirited. Spending a week with them in a studio in the UK had been bad enough. They were very much a law unto themselves, and it was only when we were on the plane to LA that I began to consider what we might have let ourselves in for. I needn't have worried. Apart from reversing down a freeway, taking enough drugs to keep an entire festival going for a long weekend, starting various fights, hanging out with porn stars and their manager going missing, it was a relatively quiet affair. Oh yes, and Bez also ended up spurning the advances of an actress he'd never heard of called Julia Roberts. I shit you not.

By the time Steve and I arrived in LA they'd just about finished the tour. In fact, they had two gigs left, one in LA and one in San Francisco. This is where Steve and I got our first taste of what might lie ahead and it almost made us turn around and go home. The day after the LA gig, at which I DJ'ed, we were all due to fly to San Francisco. Then, after returning, we were due to enter the studio. Before we left for the airport somebody in the band got wind that Soul II Soul were going to be playing that night in LA and they fancied going. Subsequently, instead of meeting us in the lobby at their apartment block as arranged, they phoned down and said that they were cancelling tonight's gig.

The show had been sold out for weeks apparently, and within ten minutes the promoter was on the phone doing his nut, quickly followed by Tony Wilson from Factory who was back over in Manchester. Nathan, their manager, had to field the calls initially and when that all came to nothing they asked to speak to Shaun. Tony Wilson spent half an hour trying to persuade him and the band to go but they wouldn't budge. He was literally screaming at them. After that the promoter had a go. 'Look, you have to get on that plane,' he said. 'It's sold out!' 'I'm sorry, mate but we can't,' said Shaun. 'Why not?' asked the promoter. 'Aw, it's tragic, man. Our keyboard player, Knobhead, has an abscess on his brain.' 'Really?' said the promoter. 'God's honest truth, man. It's the size of a fucking football! He's been to see the dentist about it and he's told him he can't fly …' 'Look,' shouted the promoter, 'My partner's had AIDS for the last seven years and he still gets out of bed every morning and goes to work.' 'Ah well, if your partner's got AIDS,' said Shaun, 'we're definitely not coming!' With that, Shaun put down the receiver and later that day we all went to see Soul II Soul. Good gig.

Instead of putting them up in a hotel, which would probably have resulted in a diplomatic incident, the band had been secreted at a place called the Oakwood Apartments which are in a place called Woodland Hills. I'm not sure if it's the same these days, but back in the 1980s and '90s the Oakwood Apartments were used a lot by porn stars, and according to Shaun there were several in residence when they were there. Mick Hucknall from Simply Red was also staying there at the time, as was Christopher Quinten, the actor who played Brian Tilsley in *Coronation Street*. A load of drugged-up Mancunians, a soap star and a load of porn stars? Sounds like an evening at the Haçienda.

Despite what happened with the gig in San Francisco, or should I say what didn't happen, when it came to recording the album the band were well up for it and the ideas, which appeared to have been influenced by rap and hip hop mainly, came in thick and fast. Before working with them I'd always been a fan of indie but I never knew why. Then, when I worked with the Mondays, I realised that indie music leans a lot closer to dance music than rock. That's why I love it. You can move to indie.

Recording the band was a unique experience. For a start, and I don't mean this disrespectfully, they're not virtuosos when it comes to their instruments and some of the time they needed to be coached. For instance, Steve Osborne is very musical and would play the bass guitarist a line and he would have to copy it. A lot of other bands would have objected to that but the Mondays didn't. What they lacked in musical ability they more than made up for with enthusiasm, ideas and personality, which created a perfect vibe. Also, because the Mondays aren't what you'd call a traditional band – they're more of an entity, really – we decided to record them individually, which became key to making it work. Had we tried to record them as a band, which is traditionally the way it's done, it would have been a disaster and for a variety of reasons. One day we'd concentrate on, for instance, Mark the guitarist, and while we were all working on riffs and stuff, the rest of the band would be out playing tennis or getting wasted and arrested.

That line earlier about them driving the wrong way down a freeway and Bez turning down the advances of Julia Roberts are both true by the way. The Julia Roberts one, which has become almost apocryphal, happened on one of our first nights out. We were in a club and Julia Roberts walked up and started chatting to Bez. He really wasn't interested but out of politeness he asked her what she did for a living. 'I'm an actress,' she said. 'Well I've never heard of you,' said Bez. 'What have you been in?' While she started listing all the films she'd been in such as *Pretty Woman*, Bez lost interest and started talking to her minder. In the end she did the sensible thing and just gave up.

The other story also involves Bez, but to be fair most of the stories from that period do. Nathan, their manager, told me early doors that he was really into his cars, but there was one thing missing which was an ability to drive one. It quickly became apparent that Bez didn't just like cars, he liked anything with an engine, and if the opportunity ever arose he'd take whatever it was for a spin, regardless of who it belonged to or who was in it. He was a liability, plain and simple. After a few days of being in LA he'd had a rental car taken off him after running into some Americans who'd annoyed him. Obviously not at speed – at least I don't think so – but after confiscating the car he'd been forbidden to even look at another car as long as he was there. Not taking any notice of the ban, Bez found a vehicle with some keys in it, went for a spin, took a wrong turn and ended up driving the wrong way down a freeway. As you do. Or as Bez certainly does.

While we're on the subject of Bez, although he didn't sing or play an instrument he was as much a part of the band as anyone else and was integral to the vibe. I know I keep going on about 'the vibe' but that was what the Mondays were, and a lot of that came from Bez. He was the peacemaker, so when they were all coked up and on the verge of killing each other, he'd defuse the situation, make us all laugh and get everyone back on track.

Working with Shaun was fascinating. Revelatory, even. To this day I've never seen anyone improvise lyrics like that before. He's a big talent. Steve and I also encouraged him to tell us stories about growing up in Manchester and out of the stories came slang terms such as 'Call the cops' and 'You're twisting my melon, man.' How many of those terms were original to Shaun I have no idea, but at least half of his vocabulary was slang. The studio used to inspire him though and after recording with me and Steve for a day, he'd go back to his apartment, sit at his desk and start writing down lyrics. As far as I know Shaun had never written down lyrics before (they were always in his head) and what changed, I think, was that Steve and I were able to show him how they'd fit within a song almost immediately, which would inspire him and spur him on. Shaun later said that Steve and I made everything sound right, which was nice. He's a clever guy is Shaun. A good guy too.

When *Pills 'n' Thrills and Bellyaches* came out in November 1990, it went straight to number one in the UK charts and had pre-sales of almost 200,000 copies. The *NME*, who until now wouldn't have touched anything with my thumbprint on with a barge pole, named it as their album of the year. Better still, Steve and I won the Best Producer gong at the Q Magazine Awards and we were also nominated for a Brit. As a first effort at producing that wasn't too bad, but what made it really special – better than any awards or chart positions – was that it's a bloody good album and just being associated with something like that makes it all worthwhile.

Unfortunately, as much as I enjoyed the experience of working with the Mondays, it didn't really end well as far as me, Steve and Factory were concerned, and ended with Steve and I being – there's no other way of putting it really – ripped off.

Over the years I've been ripped off quite a few times, sometimes for just a few quid, such as when I did the remix for Jazzy Jeff and the Fresh Prince which I still haven't been paid for, and others for a small fortune. Or at least enough to buy a very nice new car. I was about to say that it's the nature of the beast in our game, but the fact of the matter is that it's everywhere, and as long as there are greedy and unscrupulous bastards in the world, there'll always be other people getting ripped off.

These days I'm quite philosophical about these kinds of occurrences and with regards to Factory Records it was more about bad financial planning and some poor decision-making than trying to get one over on us. Me and Steve were due the final payment of our deal to produce *Pills 'n' Thrills and Bellyaches* – about £20,000 each – and when we chased them for it Factory couldn't pay. To cut a long and quite boring story short, despite the success of *Pills 'n' Thrills and Bellyaches*, Factory had paid out a lot of money to other bands who had either disappeared without trace or had failed to deliver an album, and they were up to their necks in it. In the end Roger Ames at London Records offered to buy Factory for £4 million which would have saved them. I'm not sure if we'd have been paid or not but the label would have survived, at least for a while.

Anyway, shortly after agreeing a fee, Roger found out that Factory Records didn't actually own any of their artists' back catalogues, which basically meant that they had no assets and nothing to sell. Bang went the deal, bang went Factory Records, and bang went any chance of us getting our cash. But we weren't the only ones who were owed money when Factory went to the wall. According to their manager at the time, Nathan McGough, the Mondays were owed even more than us, so God knows what the total was. It was a real mess.

Tony Wilson and I had a bit of an exchange of words after the label went under, but things soon died down. When I said I'd become philosophical about these situations, what I really meant was that there's no point getting worked up about these things and as hard as it might seem sometimes, you've just gotta move on. Had Factory done me over on purpose like my ex-manager did, then it might have been different, but they didn't. They were just crap with money and made some bad decisions, that's all. As I said earlier, I had an absolute blast with the Happy Mondays and the album that Steve and I produced for them is a great source of pride for me.

At some point I made the decision to always try and make something good happen from something bad, and back in 2016 and 2017 I got the opportunity to spin my experiences with Factory in the same direction. The Los Angeles Music Academy had invited me to come in and run some workshops for them, but as opposed to just teaching the students DJ'ing, as had been planned, I decided to try and offer something that could potentially help them avoid some of the issues that had befallen me in the past and prepare them for life in the music industry.

DJ'ing obviously formed a big part of the workshops, but in addition to that I invited a lawyer, an agent and a manager to take part. Whether you like it or not, these kinds of people are now an essential cog in the music industry wheel, and although there's no cast-iron guarantee that you won't get messed about or ripped off, I wanted the guest speakers to tell the students why they mattered and what to look out for. It was fun and hopefully they all learned something. In hindsight what I should have done after the professionals had been in was ask Bez to give them all a driving lesson.

CHAPTER 13

Even Better Than the Real Thing

From a studio point of view, as in remixing or producing, it was always going to be difficult to top *Pills 'n' Thrills*. Then, a couple of years later in 1992, we received an offer that resulted in that actually happening. Certainly from a global point of view, not to mention my ongoing career.

We had been approached about producing the Mondays' follow-up to *Pills 'n' Thrills* but for a variety of different reasons it didn't come off. Although I'm not averse to working with artists or bands on multiple occasions, I can sense when something's run its course, and the partnership between Oakenfold and Osborne and the Happy Mondays was a case in point. For one thing they didn't have any songs, or even any ideas for songs. 'We'll sort that out when we get into the studio,' said Nathan. 'Really?' I replied. We were obviously all keen to see if we could build on the success of *Pills 'n' Thrills*, but in the absence of any material, not to mention the knowledge of how unpredictable they could be, both collectively and individually, it was too much of a risk. We did go into a studio for a couple of days to work on one track, but the vibe had completely changed. Some of the band might have been dealing, I think, and the ones who weren't were surrounded by people who, shall we say, weren't necessarily interested in the betterment of the band's career.

What I was more interested in doing rather than another Happy Mondays record, once I'd found out that they didn't have any demos or songs, was a gangster record with Shaun Ryder. That whole Manchester swagger and gangster vibe fascinated me (it still does), and Shaun was at the centre of that. I think we might even have had a conversation or two about it at the time. I was completely serious. I was going to get a rapper like LL Cool J on there. It would have been incredible.

The next production job that Steve and I took on was with Deacon Blue, believe it or not, and both the experience and the result was the antithesis of what had happened with the Mondays. According to Deacon Blue's label, Sony, they wanted to sound a bit edgier and at first we were hesitant. After all, they weren't exactly from my world.

After a lot of negotiations they managed to talk us into it, and so we went into the studio. After just one track the band decided that they no longer wanted to sound edgy, and from then on it went tits up. They had a single out that was massive and I think that's what spooked them. Deacon Blue ended up going their separate ways after the album was released, and it probably spelt the beginning of the end for Steve and me too, especially as a production team. Because of the band's change in attitude I'd lost interest in the project early doors, whereas Steve had remained on board. It highlighted a few differences, I suppose, although we never actually fell out.

Despite the Deacon Blue job, the vast majority of offers we received directly after *Pills 'n' Thrills* were remixes. At one point we were doing three or four a week. It was crazy. One of the most popular of that post-Mondays period was 'Move Any Mountain' by The Shamen. That one became a huge hit all over Europe and led to our manager at the time, Brian Reza, suggesting that we give ourselves a name. 'Oakenfold and Osborne not catchy enough for you?' we said.

We eventually decided on Perfecto, as in the record label. The reason I started Perfecto was because there were no dance labels out there at the time, or at least ones that knew what they were doing. The idea was to nurture new talent, and that's an ethos that hasn't changed from that day to this. In fact, if I had to choose one aspect of what I do that makes me as excited now as it did back in the day, it would have to be that. Playing clubs the world over, creating mixes and remixing and producing artists all come a close second, but what separates them from my work with Perfecto and new talent is that my enthusiasm over the past thirty years or so has been unwavering and I don't think that will ever change.

Anyway, back to this offer I mentioned. The act in question was U2, who at the time were probably the biggest band on the planet. Despite this, by the early 1990s the only songs by them that I was aware of were 'With Or Without You' and 'Where The Streets Have No Name' which were played at Amnesia. That's about it though. I knew they were huge, I just didn't know why.

When the band first got in touch – it was actually Island's A&R man, Nick Angel, who first suggested having their material remixed – it was about reworking a song they'd done called 'Mysterious Ways', which we duly did. We didn't meet the band though, so although I'd listened to more of their music and was beginning to get the vibe, I still wasn't a fan. A few months later I was doing a gig in Dublin and I received a telephone call from Nick asking if I'd like to meet the band in their studio. Having been on my radar now for even longer, I was far more aware of how globally influential the band were and I don't mind admitting that prior to the meeting I was nervous.

U2 had been turned on to the dance scene, as a band at least, after working with François Kevorkian in New York back in 1982. It was the time of 'Sunday Bloody Sunday' and I think he did about three mixes for them. Although they obviously remained a rock band, they came away from that meeting realising that disco and dance music weren't necessarily the enemy, and they remained open to the possibility of experimenting again.

Bono always says that the band didn't really get rhythm until they went on tour with BB King, and so while everyone else was partying and doing drugs back in the UK as part of the second summer of love, they were in Memphis getting into rhythm. 'I guess it came together for us with *Achtung Baby*,' he said. I didn't find this out until later, but the deal was that if U2 didn't like what Steve and I produced, then Island Records would pay the bill, so despite their enthusiasm they were still hedging their bets.

The meeting in Dublin went really well and I came away with a new appreciation, not just for how much the band understood music, but how they understood dance music. In that respect, I didn't really see them as a rock and roll band. They were more like a band of musicians who happened to play rock and roll. This was later on, but The Edge said that dance music made them jealous. 'It's wonderful to be in a rock and roll band,' he said. 'But it's limiting in so many ways. There are so many more possibilities with dance music as a form. That and the rhythm.' He also said that in his opinion it's almost impossible for a rock and roll band to match the excitement of being in a club and listening to good dance music. Having now seen the likes of U2 perform live many times, I'm not sure about that, but I totally get where he's coming from. Being turned on by a genre of music that's perhaps alien to you is a big thrill, especially to a musician.

EVEN BETTER THAN THE REAL THING

Of all the remixes that Steve and I did for U2 – I think we did five or six originally – our remix of 'Even Better Than the Real Thing' is the one that made the difference, both with the band, the label and, most importantly, on the dance floor. Legend has it that after delivering the remix for 'Even Better Than the Real Thing' to Nick Angel at Island, he listened to it once, went to his boss Julian Palmer's officer, kicked open the door and said, 'You have got to hear this!' Apparently they put it on and literally laughed with pleasure. They thought it was awesome. Luckily so did the band, and when interviewed later on Adam Clayton said, 'When everyone heard it, we thought, this is really it!' Adam also said, quite astutely, that the song had some Happy Mondays running through it which might have had something to do with Steve and me understanding where to take it, which I think we did.

We made some bold moves on that remix though. I came up with the idea of adding some female backing vocals that are there throughout and the feedback I received to the suggestion initially wasn't enthusiastic. 'You can't have female backing vocals on a U2 track,' everyone said. I went ahead regardless and as well as being the first voices you hear on the remix, they're so far up in the mix that they almost overpower Bono's lead vocal. I wasn't doing this for a laugh though. My attitude was that we'd been employed by the band to take them on to the dance floor, so whatever worked.

The thing is, Bono is one of the few rock singers I've heard who has genuine soul and his vocals actually sit well on dance records. Even so, the chorus and the verse needed lifting in my opinion. The next move was even bolder. 'The drummer's got to go,' I said. 'What! You mean you're removing Larry Mullen Jr from a U2 track?' 'Even if we added fills,' I said, 'it still wouldn't work.' The next to go was Adam Clayton, and for exactly the same reason, so that was half the band, gone.

Both of them were as cool as fuck about this because at the end of the day they understood that what gets people on to a dance floor is the beat, the rhythm. They trusted us. I know it might sound obvious but coupled with some cooperation and enthusiasm, trust is essential when working with a remixer. It doesn't always happen though. A lot of bands and artists, as with Deacon Blue, begin to get cold feet when people start tinkering with what they've created and that's understandable. Frustrating, but understandable.

My association with U2 was as much about good timing as anything else. It hadn't been our intention, but the remix happened to fit comfortably, not only with the band's new identity, but their musical direction and ambitions. The kind of material they were writing at the time didn't really fit into one category or genre, and I suppose I was in the same boat. We were all floating a bit in that respect and their positivity and interest in dance music surprised me.

Until then I think U2 had generally been viewed as being quite a serious, non-compromising stadium act, but that isn't the vibe I got. In fact, nothing could be further from the truth. They were humble, magnanimous and open. I couldn't have asked for more.

The only changes the band and label asked us to make were to the guitars — The Edge wasn't happy with the guitars at the beginning of the mix — and to the vocals. I was sitting in my studio not long after we delivered the remix to the band when my assistant rang through. 'I've got The Edge on the phone,' she said. 'You've got what?' I honestly thought she said hedge at first. 'The Edge, from U2. He wants to talk to you about the guitars.' 'Oh, right!' I won't try and recall the full conversation but The Edge wasn't happy about the guitars at the beginning of the mix. I forget what he said exactly but it was something really technical.

'Does it work though?' I said. 'Well, yeah,' he replied. 'It sounds great.' 'Then let's run with it. You have to trust me on this. We need to leave it like it is.' That's always been my motto, regardless of whether something works technically or not. If it sounds right, don't touch it! Once again, The Edge could have turned around and demanded that I put whatever it was right, but he didn't.

My acid test, by the way, for seeing if a remix works or not, is listening to it in my car. It sounds a bit daft but people listen to a lot of music in their cars, and so if it sounds good in there, as if it was on the radio, then that means it works. It's never failed me yet.

When it came to the vocals the band felt that we'd taken too much out, and on reflection they were right. 'Put more of the lyric back in and we'll have a bigger hit,' they said, and we did. For some reason it felt like there was a lot more riding on this job. It was as if we all knew what the possibilities were if we got it right. I think that's why the band became so involved. Not in a day-to-day sense, but with their input.

Things became really interesting when it came to deciding what to do with the remix. The boys at Island Records had an idea which, as well as being in the spirit of the band having taken a chance by letting Steve and I loose on their material, would also rip up the rule book with regards to the charts. 'How about having two competing singles in the charts at the same time?' said the Island Records boys to Paul McGuinness, U2's manager. Paul assumed that what Island were suggesting was releasing mine and Steve's remix alongside another track from the album, but they weren't. 'The same track,' they said. 'It's never been done before. Let's see if "Even Better Than the Real Thing" is better than "Even Better Than the Real Thing".' Despite the initial enthusiasm, once everyone had calmed down a bit it was decided that the remix would be released a short while after the original. The 'Perfecto

Mix', as it was called, ended up charting higher than the original so it was indeed, although only with regards to chart performance, Even Better Than the Real Thing.

CHAPTER 14

Moving Up a Gear

One of the first things I had to remind myself after being asked by U2 if I'd like to go on the road with them for their Zoo TV tour was that not one of the four or five million people who'd be attending the tour would be going to see me. That's quite a sobering thought when you think about it, and before accepting a job like that you have to make sure your ego is in check. Fortunately, I'd already had a few experiences like this such as Spike Island with The Stone Roses and, in addition to learning to accept the fact that I'm not the main attraction, or even an attraction, I'd learned to appreciate the benefits, apart from just the money.

The difference between this and the Spike Island gig, which had a lot of other DJs on the bill, was that I'd really have to think about what to play. I think U2 liked the idea of having somebody in support who could alter what they were playing in response to the audience which, as well as giving the public what they wanted, would put them in a better mood for when the band came on. If you think about what usually happens – a support band or bands will take to the stage prior to the main band and tapes will be played in between – it made perfect sense for all concerned. The crowd would be happy as they'd be getting what they wanted,

I would be happy with the response (hopefully), and so would U2, who would then perform to a nicely warmed-up audience.

Despite bands having had DJs performing for them as warm-up acts for quite a while, one of the first ones I'm aware of where they were hired to 'set the mood', if you like, was when the DJ Gary Crowley opened for Wham! on their first ever tour back in the early 1980s. Not only did he open the show but he went on in between the support acts. He was the host, if you like, and the concept worked a treat. Although on a much bigger scale, that's what I would be doing with U2.

The only thing that really worried me as far as the tour was concerned was how I'd be received. There was going to be no magic formula, so if I went down well somewhere one night it could be shit the next. You can never guarantee how well you're going to go down, but playing to your own audience obviously helps. What if the U2 crowd hated the concept of having a DJ there and I bombed every night? It was a big concern to tell the truth and for a week or so it kept me awake at night. In the end I decided to just own it. After all, unlike a support band I was free to play anything I wanted, and figured that as long as I did my home-work I'd be OK, or at least stand a chance of being OK. Whether I actually was would ultimately be up to the crowd.

Something else I did that would hopefully work in my favour was to have a rig built that complemented the scale of the events. Just plonking my gear on a table at the front of the stage wasn't going to work, so we had something built that, although tiny in comparison to U2's set, would at least kind of look the part.

When it came to the actual material, I went for a bit of a pincer movement. On one side I had all the remixes we'd done for rock acts such as U2, The Cure and The Stone Roses, together with the odd classic to drop in such as, for instance, 'Satisfaction', and on the other I had stuff that I knew for a fact was popular at that moment in time in whatever town or city we were in. In order to find out what that was, on landing there I'd go straight to the nearest record shop, ask the staff which two records were the most popular with the populace that week, and then buy a copy of each. I didn't always know what they were. It could have been Bill and Ben singing in Italian for all I knew. They were what the public liked and that's all that mattered. There were also some easy wins to be had. For instance, if we were on the east coast of America, I knew for a fact that Bruce Springsteen would go down well, which he did. It wasn't a science, as such, but a little bit of foresight and some effort went an awfully long way on that tour.

The way the evening used to pan out is that I'd go on first and play for an hour or so, then the support act would go on, whether that be Pearl Jam, Stereo MC's or Big Audio Dynamite (they changed them around a lot), then I'd go on again, and then U2 would go on. I think the band almost redefined the way that rock concerts were put on, or certainly stadium shows. Obviously you'd had dozens of bands and artists playing stadium shows before that, but the sheer size of the production, not to mention the line-up of which I was part, was all very new and ambitious. It kind of opened things up in a way and since then that world has become bigger and bigger. Everyone's in on it.

Away from the stage, being on tour with U2 was just crazy. Adam Clayton was going out with Naomi Campbell at the time, and every night a supermodel or three would turn up. One night it'd be Christy Turlington and the next Cindy Crawford or Kate Moss. It was hell! I remember I was asked to play Naomi's birthday party during the tour and at one point I had Claudia Schiffer, Kate Moss and Christy Turlington in the booth, all rifling through my record box saying, 'Can you play this please, Paul.' Then there were the aftershow parties, of course. They were never especially raucous affairs (it wasn't like the Happy Mondays) but you'd have the supermodels I just mentioned, Johnny Depp and Jack Nicholson, all at the same do. And me, of course, wondering how the hell I'd got there! The thing is, this would happen night after night after night. It was relentless. I'd had my fair share of success over the years, but this was in a totally different league. What's more, I loved it.

Whereas U2 and the support acts must have had about twenty or thirty people helping them out – roadies and assistants and what have you – I had just two. One was an old friend of mine who I'd known for donkey's years called Colin Hudd. As well as helping me with the music and with the gear, Colin, who is a very well-respected DJ in his own right, also filled in for me once or twice and acted as my tour manager. I also had another mate who I've known forever and who still works with me called Micky Jackson to help out, so between the three of us we had it covered. It doesn't matter how many people you're surrounded by in that sort of frantic environment, they'll all have something to do. And the chances are they'll have their own set of mates. Over the years I've had to get used to my own company, but just give me a record shop and I'm happy.

Although the band themselves and their management were all very kind and cooperative, some of the road crew weren't keen on having a DJ around as it wasn't very rock and roll. It was just a case of them giving me the cold shoulder here and there, but I didn't mind. Once they realised that just because I have turntables doesn't mean I can only play dance music, they came around and after a couple of shows they were fine.

As I just said, the band themselves couldn't have been nicer and as well as socialising with them – supermodels and film stars included – I also travelled with them. Nine times out of ten we'd go by private jet which was a big thrill. We'd have motorcades waiting for us at airports and police escorts everywhere. It was immense! I tried not to appear too excited and overwhelmed but sometimes I failed miserably. How long had I been a professional DJ? Two years? Yet here I was on a stadium tour supporting the biggest band on the planet and sharing a private jet with them.

As well as always getting on well with U2, I've learned more from them about various aspects of the music industry over the years than anyone else on earth, and because the majority of that happened quite early on in my career, it's paid dividends. For instance, I became what you might call a student of Bono during that first tour and used to watch him like a hawk backstage. The reason I started doing this was because I noticed early on how polite and kind he was. Not just to the roadies or the technicians, but to everyone he came into contact with, whether it be a wait-ress handing him a drink, a film star or a promoter. Everyone got exactly the same treatment and because he was the main man, that tended to filter down. Not everyone always followed suit, but if you behaved like an arsehole on that tour you stuck out like a sore thumb.

In addition to creating a good working environment and atmosphere, it also pulled everyone together and so as a working unit they were as tight as a duck's arse. All on the same page and all pulling together. I'm not saying Bono's behaviour was responsible for all of that, but it certainly set the tone.

What made it really special in my eyes was that you could tell he actually meant it. I'd always been brought up to be nice to people. Phrases like, 'If you haven't got anything nice to say, don't say anything at all,' were commonplace in our house. But to see it in that kind of environment, where the level of your importance so often goes in the opposite direction to the level of your behaviour, was a breath of fresh air, and I've always done my best to follow suit. He gets a bad press from an awful lot of people does Bono, but as well as being one hell of a musician and one of the best lyricists on the planet, in my opinion, he's a kind and very genuine human being.

I suppose it was about this time that the term 'superstar DJ' started being bandied about. I'm credited with being one of the first, if not the first, and what helped to lift me to that position, as well as touring with U2, was becoming the first DJ to play the main stage at Glastonbury, which actually happened about the same time as Spike Island. Not that I enjoyed it very much. When the offer came through I was like, 'Here we go. Glastonbury, man. This is gonna be massive!' Then when I got there, I realised very quickly that, instead of having developed an appreciation for dance music and its exponents and protagonists over the years, the people who ran it were basically just ticking a box. 'I'll tell you what, I know it's not our thing but that Oakenfold bloke's popular. Let's get him on.'

My suspicions were first raised when I realised that, instead of being onsite with all the other bands and musicians, I was based offsite and in a tent. I don't think they did it on purpose. They just didn't get or appreciate what I did for a living. To them I was probably a bit of a necessary evil, so when it came to actually accommodating me, on and offstage, they didn't give it much thought.

This was proved beyond all reasonable doubt when I found out that they'd scheduled me in between a couple of rock acts. Not exactly my natural habitat. To be fair, as the only DJ playing the main stage, there was only so much they could do, but still. Fortunately, the crowd seemed to be a bit more switched on than the organisers, and although it was a struggle I managed to win them round. The Cure were going to be headlining one of the nights so I kind of knew which way to go. It ended up being just like a gig at Future, basically, just with a much larger and less pilled-up audience. I remember dropping in a track by Bob Marley towards the end of my set and realising that, actually, this is going OK. Which kind of sums up my first Glastonbury experience really. It was OK.

After leaving the site I ended up going past the top field where all the travellers were and it was mayhem. Much more interesting than where I'd been. For a start, unlike the main site they had a couple of dance tents there and in one of them they had a sound system that was being powered by – get this – pedal power! Seriously, there were five people all on converted bikes pedalling as if their lives depended on it. Everyone took it in turns, including me. I had a ball up there. The following weekend I played another festival in Denmark called the Roskilde Festival. Once again The Cure were headlining, but the line-up was much more eclectic. My old mates and colleagues from The Orb were on the bill, as were the hip-hop legends, De La Soul.

What that initial appearance at Glastonbury should have been was a coming together of dance music and one of the world's most famous and iconic music festivals, and had they done it properly it could have been the start of something great. As it was it was just a bit of a damp squib. The next time I played there was 1999, and to be honest it wasn't much better. Other DJs have had similar experiences at Glastonbury over the years so it's not just me. The mentality there was always, 'All you do is play other people's music.' There was no understanding or appreciation for any aspect of what we did or do. I've had that a couple of times in my career and I came to the conclusion early on that it's their problem, not mine. It is a shame, though. I mean, why have Calvin

Harris, David Guetta or Martin Garrix never been asked to head-line Glastonbury? It's ridiculous. Instead they'll just get Coldplay or Paul McCartney back for the umpteenth time.

A few weeks ago I was asked to play a gig after the American F1 Grand Prix in Austin, Texas, and of course I was interested. I mean, these gigs are massive. 'Who would I be on with?' I asked. 'Billy Joel,' they said. 'Really?' I said. 'No, I think I'll leave it.' As much as I admire Billy Joel as a musician and a songwriter – and I do – that line-up wouldn't have worked in a thousand years. Once again, they must have thought, 'I'll tell you what, we've booked somebody for the older crowd, why don't we book someone for the clubbers too.' Do you know the average age of Billy Joel's core audience? I'm sorry, but the only way I could have warmed up his crowd was with a cup of cocoa and an electric blanket. I'd have bombed.

Another live damp squib that springs to mind is Net Aid, an anti-poverty gig organised by the United Nations that was obvi-ously inspired by Live Aid. Anyone remember it? Nope, I thought not. It took place at Wembley Stadium in October 1999 (with a simultaneous concert taking place at the Giants Stadium in New York), which in itself was a bit ridiculous. I mean, who puts on an outdoor gig in the UK in October? Nobody. The line-up was good though. We had George Michael, David Bowie, Bono, Eurythmics, The Corrs, Catatonia, Bush, Bryan Adams, Stereophonics, Robbie Williams, Sheryl Crow, Jimmy Page, Busta Rhymes, Counting Crows, Puff Daddy, The Black Crowes, Wyclef Jean, Jewel, Mary J. Blige, Cheb Mami, Sting, Slash and Lil' Kim. OK, it wasn't Live Aid exactly, but it wasn't far off.

Once again I was the only DJ playing, so in addition to not knowing where to put me, the audience were quite alien to me, and me to them. I didn't mind so much with that gig as the cause

Top: At Cream during the late 1990s. My residency there was a massive gamble for all concerned but it paid off big time.

Above: Same club, different year. Being invited back to celebrate Cream's 20th anniversary in 2012 was a huge honour.

Backstage and then onstage at Coachella in 2013. Coachella is one of my happy places and always has a great vibe – providing it isn't windy!

Base camp of Mount Everest, 2017. I must admit that my original idea of taking dance music out of the realms of a nightclub environment didn't include taking it to the world's highest mountain! As experiences go though, it's right up there.

Stonehenge, 2018. If somebody had suggested to me at the start of my career that one day I'd play a gig here. I'd have asked them what drugs they were on. I'm so glad it happened though. What an experience!

Top: Vegas baby! Las Vegas is all about excess and for some reason it's always brought out the best in me.

Above: Reminders of my days on the road.

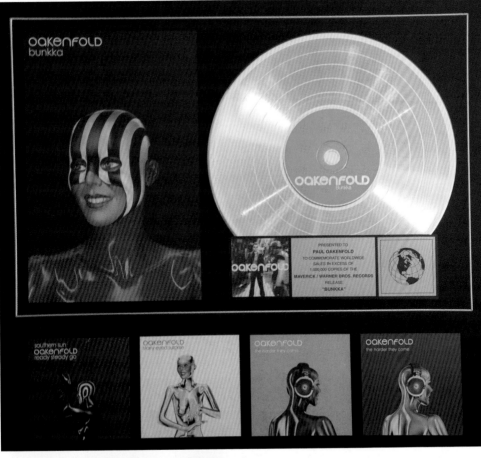

Top: *Bunkka*, 2002 – A source of pride. Becoming the first DJ to have a hit album as a solo artist was a big deal for me.

Left: My office at home. So many memories!

EIIR

The Master of the Household
has received Her Majesty's command to invite

Mr. Paul Oakenfold

to a Reception to be given at Buckingham Palace by
The Queen and The Duke of Edinburgh
on Monday, 13th October, 2003 at 6.00 p.m.
to mark the contribution of Pioneers to the life of the Nation

RSVP
The Master of the Household,
Buckingham Palace,
London SW1A 1AA.

Dress: Lounge Suit/Day Dress

Guests are asked to arrive between 5.15 and 5.50 p.m.

Top: My invitation from Her Majesty. Mum was gutted she couldn't come with me.

Above: As pleased as I was being recognised by the Queen, being recognised by the readers of magazines such as _Musik Magazine_ is far more gratifying.

With my beloved record collection that's still growing to this day. This my real happy place!

was all that mattered. I just went on and just did my best for half an hour.

I suppose I was a kind of prototype, in a way. As one of the first mainstream exponents of electronic dance music and that kind of DJ'ing, I was the go-to man when people who weren't familiar with the genre were forced to dip their toes in the water and book somebody. This meant that as well as receiving the majority of the big opportunities and invitations, I also bore the brunt of much of the prejudice. Which, given where we were in the genre's history, was always going to be inevitable. Luckily, I've got a very thick skin and knew for a fact that this new culture of ours was growing, and would continue to grow, exponentially. I was at the forefront of something special and as far as I was concerned the haters could do one.

Next year I'm going to be doing an arena tour around America with the Pet Shop Boys and New Order and in the same capacity as with U2, in that I'll go on first, then New Order, then me again, and then the Pet Shop Boys. Actually, I have a feeling that New Order and the Pet Shop Boys might flip who headlines night by night, but things for me will stay exactly the same. Saying yes to that gig was a complete no-brainer and the music I play will obviously be unashamedly 1980s. I'll play Eurythmics, Culture Club, Wham!, A-ha, the lot. I'll do one hour before, half an hour in the middle – BANG! There you go. These kinds of tours are great as they're a celebration as much as anything else and everyone's in a great mood. In fact, the only thing that could spoil it is if I went on and played Billy Joel all night!

The best thing about doing stadium tours with rock groups isn't the private jets and the money, or even the supermodels. It's the stadiums themselves. I'm gonna have to be careful not to go on here as I appreciate that not everybody reading this will be as mad about the beautiful game as I am, but that's definitely one of the things that made me want to say yes.

A good few years later I went on tour with Madonna and got to play the Maracanã in Rio. That was special. We played two nights at that place in front of a combined audience of about 200,000 people. To me though, it wasn't the size of the venue or the audience that I found impressive, it was what it meant to football. The one that ticked all the boxes though, and to this day makes me go a bit weak at the knees, is Wembley – *quelle surprise*. As an England fan who also happens to hail from London that was always going to be the case, and so far I've been lucky enough to play Wembley six times. At least I think it's six. I played there once with Madonna, four times with U2 and once at Net Aid.

The first time I played there was with U2 and before the set was erected and the boards went down over the hallowed turf, I tried to organise a football match with the crew. When I asked the groundsman at Wembley I was told in no uncertain terms that this would not be possible and from then on, in his eyes at least, I became a marked man. I get it though. From a groundsman's point of view the turf they look after will indeed be hallowed and they'll have to guard it with their lives. When the groundsman walked off, my assistant Micky, who was with me at the time, grabbed a ball and he and I had a kickabout. We knew we'd get told off for it but we thought, 'What the hell.' There were no goalposts, obviously, but we didn't care. At least we could say we'd played at Wembley. The groundsman must have gone for a break or something as fifteen minutes later Micky and I were still living the dream. It was a real bucket-list moment.

After that we decided to go and have a look at the dressing rooms, which is something I always try and do when I visit a stadium. This was the old Wembley though, and apart from a few benches, hooks and a communal shower, there was nothing much to see. Once again, this wasn't the point. We were in the home dressing room at Wembley Stadium where the legendary World Cup-winning England team of 1966 would have been both before and after beating Germany. Incidentally, when I played at the Millennium Stadium with Madonna a few years ago, Madonna had the home dressing room, the dancers and musicians had the away dressing room, and I had the ref's room! That was weird.

Anyway, just as we were standing there taking it all in and imagining Bobby Moore triumphantly carrying in the Jules Rimet Trophy into the dressing room from the tunnel with the rest of the team following on, this geezer came in who was obviously on the payroll there and started berating us. I tried to explain who I was and that I'd be playing there in a few days but he was having none of it. He even accused us of trying to steal things. 'But there's nothing to steal,' I said. 'Unless we want to try and walk out of here with a bench under our arms! Look, all we were trying to do is have a look around. You're more than welcome to escort us if you like.' Once again he wasn't interested and Micky and I were literally escorted from the stadium. I've been asked to leave a venue after a gig before, both ceremoniously and unceremoniously, when things have become a bit rowdy, but never before! It was a first.

CHAPTER 15

Mix Me Some Goa

In 1994, which was the year after I finished touring with U2, I came of age as a musician. This was thanks partly to my old friend, Danny Diamond, and partly to U2 themselves who had inspired me, as I had them with the remixes, to move further out of my comfort zone.

After leaving the UK, Danny had gone to LA where he'd ended up working for a trance label called Dragonfly Records. Through that, he'd come across a new sound from Goa called Goa Trance. 'It's going to be the next big thing, man,' he said. 'We have to go there!' Funnily enough, I had actually come across Goa Trance before then. Back in 1990 Steve Osborne and I had been asked to remix a song from a dance album by Michael Hutchence from INXS and his collaborator, the producer and songwriter, Ollie Olsen. The project was called Max Q and when Michael and Ollie first approached Steve and me we were well game.

Michael Hutchence was probably the first rock star I got to know, and believe me he epitomised the term. I remember being at a party in Sydney once, which is where we first met, and when he walked into the room everyone stopped what they were doing and just stared at him. He didn't say anything or even look in anyone's direction. He just stood there. We all looked at him though, most in admiration I should think, a lot in awe, and one or two with a hint of the green-eyed monster. He just oozed it. I'm pretty sure that the reason they asked Steve and me to remix the tune was because we'd remixed INXS's 'Suicide Blonde', although I could be wrong.

Anyway, Michael's mate Ollie was heavily into trance at the time and I remember him playing Steve and me something in the studio one day that he said had come from Goa. Apparently they were having wild parties in the outback at the time and this is what they played. These days that all makes perfect sense, but at the time, as I hadn't really got into trance yet, I don't think I took much notice. The whole Max Q thing should have been massive really and if you've never come across it, and I imagine that the majority of you reading this won't have, I urge you to have a listen. There's some good stuff on there.

Bearing in mind what had happened in Ibiza, I did experience one or two feelings of déjà vu when Danny started talking about Goa and it really got me going. 'Oh my God, here we go again!' I thought. I'm not sure if I mentioned it earlier, but when Danny and Trevor were over in Ibiza running bars and things, they used to ring me up regularly and go on and on about Amnesia and the Balearic Beat. As I said before, Danny can be very convincing when he wants to be and he made the whole Goa scene seem just as exciting as Ibiza. There was clearly an opportunity and I couldn't wait to get there.

The big difference between the two movements, apart from the music, was the drugs. Instead of taking ecstasy, which was obviously part of the whole Ibiza thing, people who were into Goa Trance (now called psychedelic or psy trance) were taking acid. At first that put me off slightly as I've only ever taken acid once and hated it. And I mean really hated it. Actually, I didn't take it willingly. I was spiked one time in a club and had to really fight to keep things together. After thinking it through, I realised that because I loved the music and the energy that Goa Trance created, I could concentrate on that alone. No temptations. No distractions. Just me, the music and the people. It was quite a prospect.

What acid did do, as well as making the parties last much longer, was turn the experience of the crowd into something far more intense. It's a much wider experience, if you like. Your senses are more alert when you're on acid and there's a lot more going on. It was only when I saw it first-hand though that I began to appreciate the correlation between the two. It might not have been my thing, but in order to truly understand and appreciate the music I had to have at least an idea of how the two married up.

When we arrived in Goa one of the first things I did was have a motorbike accident, as you do. I'd borrowed an old Enfield bike from somebody and while taking a rather sharp corner I went one way and the bike another. After that Danny suggested that we go on foot so I ditched the bike and we hit a couple of parties. The parties were all outside, either in the jungle or on a beach. 'This is cool,' I thought. What's more, they were all free, and the people were wearing all kinds of gear. There was no dress code; you just did your own thing. This kind of easy-going mentality only lasted until you tried taking a photograph, because as soon as you did that somebody would be on you. 'No cameras!' they immediately shouted. I've never got to the bottom of exactly why that was the case at these parties, but I suppose it might have something to do with the fact that everyone was taking acid, and you tend to do things a bit differently on acid.

Speaking of which.

As with the drugs, the reaction of the crowd at these events, at least the ones where everyone was on acid, was at odds with what I'd been used to in Ibiza and in London, and once again it unnerved me slightly, at least initially. Instead of everyone being as one and facing the DJ, which had been the reserve of almost every club in Europe for the last few years until cocaine had reared its ugly head, the crowds were in a world of their own – literally. You did get some groups who'd be as one and just going for it, but the majority of experiences were glaringly individual. I'll be honest with you, it took some getting used to. I was used to witnessing collective euphoria on a grand scale and this, although generally euphoric, was much more fragmented and a lot more spontaneous.

What I liked about the music, apart from the energy, was that it sounded like a natural successor to acid house, which is something that in my mind hadn't arrived yet. As well as millions of septums and personalities being eroded, cocaine had also eroded the togetherness that you felt when visiting a club and the music, although interesting at times, had pretty much followed suit. Old tracks speeded up. That sort of shit. There was no emotion or spontaneity any more. No glitz or extravagance. No creativity, even. Or very little. In fact, and this might sound a bit dramatic, the entire scene was beginning to lose its soul. Goa Trance and trance in general, which was still an emerging genre, was like a breath of fresh air.

Danny and I arrived back in the UK with exactly the same amount of enthusiasm as we had on arriving back from Ibiza what, seven years before? Blimey. We held parties in disused bank vaults and even in a former butcher's in Smithfield Market. Danny and three mates of ours called Andy and Dino Psaras and Mike McGuire went one step further by starting a regular night called A Concept in Music in a warehouse underneath Old Street roundabout.

My own interest in the music was heightened on our return after hearing Dino Psaras, who was a DJ, playing Goa Trance in a new London club on New Oxford Street called The End. He was playing stuff by a former techno artist called Martin Freeland and to cut a long story short I ended up signing Martin, who recorded as Man With No Name, to a specially created offshoot of Perfecto Records called Perfecto Fluoro. Martin had been plying his trade as an engineer for the producer Youth at Butterfly Studios in Brixton.

Youth had been one of the early champions of trance in the UK and Butterfly Studios was where it all happened. To me, the most talented young protagonist out there was Martin and when he played me a tune that he'd composed and produced called 'Teleport', which would go on to become the first and I think only trance tune to break into the UK Top 40, I knew I had to sign him. After that we signed artists such as The Infinity Project, Section X, California Sunshine, Virus and Johann Bley. It wasn't mainstream, at least not generally, but it was successful.

Unfortunately, I did receive some criticism for what I did in the Goa Trance world. At least at the very start. Some of its protagonists wanted to keep it as their little secret and didn't want the likes of me trying to popularise it and take it to a wider audience. Why, I have absolutely no idea, but that's how it was. Once Man With No Name hit the charts with 'Teleport', that was it. It was game over. Or game under way, whichever you prefer. The thing is, the underground was now networked, so nothing, or at least nothing worth listening to, could remain a secret for very long. Once word got out that was it, and what you had to hope for, and work towards if you could, was that whoever did the popularising did it justice.

When it came to popularising psy trance, which is how I'll now refer to it, this went stratospheric on 18 December 1994 when a mix that I'd produced for Pete Tong's Essential Mix on Radio 1 went to air. The show's producer, Eddie Gordon, had approached me some months earlier about producing a mix for the show and as trance and psy trance were at the forefront of much of what I was doing at the time – producing, spinning and releasing – I bit his hand off. To me, it was a perfect opportunity to showcase the genre – a genre that I was trying to champion via the artists I'd signed and by my own work – so I went straight into the studio.

Because the potential audience for the mix was going to be in the millions, I decided to make it as eclectic as possible. Just because it's called 'The Goa Mix' doesn't mean it's all psy trance. Heck, no. Sure, it's trance, but the word Goa is there because that's what initially inspired it. Funnily enough, in summarising what he thought I'd achieved with the mix, the boffin who wrote my biography, Richard Norris, actually summed up perfectly what I'd had in mind before writing it. He said that 'I'd created an immersive sonic journey full of peaks and troughs, tension and release, a perfect headphone trip that manipulates its source material with edits, segments and cinematic interludes.' Even with a dictionary and some English lessons, I quite literally could not have put it better myself, and the fact that he thought I'd achieved that makes me grin from ear to ear.

The cinematic interludes he mentioned come from *Blade Runner* mainly, and a few bits from the soundtrack to Francis Ford Coppola's *Dracula*. To this day it's one of the hardest mixes I've ever done and that's mainly down to the arrangement. The different keys were definitely a problem, but I was using a lot of music that didn't have a beat to it, such as the film scores. Usually that's what you're mixing – beats – but this was all about keys and the spoken word. I was mixing ambiance, basically. The majority of this was completely new to me so in many ways it was like starting from scratch. I can honestly say that I have never worked as hard on anything in my entire life.

The research alone to find music that might complement my original ideas took me about three months and it was another three or four to compose the mix and put it together. At one point I almost gave up. I thought, 'Fuck this for a game of soldiers. I'll just do a DJ mix.' What kept me going was the opportunity. Radio 1 giving me a two-hour slot with no boundaries was a big deal and it was my chance to take psy trance and trance to the next level. The ones who wanted to keep it underground could piss off. The music was all cutting edge and I'd been waiting for an excuse to mix film music with the kind of trance I liked for ages.

The only thing that matched the excitement of completing the project, which went into overdrive towards the end, was the anxiety of how it might be received by the public, which went exactly the same way. By now I'd already established my own style of trance which was quite melodic. As far as I knew, nobody on earth had ever created anything like this before, and because it was so new and extreme I had a feeling that the public and press alike were either going to love it or hate it. Which was it to be, a magnum opus or Frankenstein's monster?

The reaction of Radio 1, in fact, was going to be just as important as the public or the press, if not more so. If they'd turned around and said, 'What the fuck have you created, Paul?' then it wouldn't even have been played. All that work down the drain. I'm not sure what that would have done to me, and had I considered the possibility shortly before submitting it to Eddie Gordon (fortunately it didn't come into my head), I might have had a heart attack.

I'm trying to remember what reaction I was actually hoping for. I obviously wanted it to be positive, but as I said earlier I wanted to take the listener on a voyage full of highs and lows. I didn't want them to just say, 'Yeah, that was good.' I wanted it to jump-start people's imaginations in some way and make them think – and feel – outside the box, with or without drugs. In fact, because I wasn't into acid they never even figured. I have to be careful not to sound too self-indulgent and pretentious, but I'd been in situations like that myself such as at Paradise Garage, Amnesia and in Goa. Seminal moments that, even if they don't change you as a person, you remember for the rest of your life.

Fortunately, the reaction from the public, the industry and the press was as extreme as the composition itself, in that everyone seemed to love it. One thing we didn't do immediately though was release it, and rather ironically it ended up being bootlegged heavily by Cream who would soon become my employers.

I'm often asked if I'd ever attempt anything as ambitious as the Goa Mix again, and until about five or ten years ago I'd have said, 'Never say never.' In fact, my own personal favourite when it comes to my Essential Mixes isn't the Goa Mix at all, it's the Havana Mix that I did in 1999. Since then people's attention spans have rapidly started to shrink, so the thought of me producing a two-hour mix for Radio 1, while still attractive creatively, just wouldn't generate the interest and it would have the phrase 'diminished returns' written all over it. Things like Essential Mix were a thing of their time, and while we obviously salute their influence, life and everything in it has moved on. I've said it before and I'll say it again, if I don't think that there's at least a fighting chance that I can improve on something, I will not touch it. It doesn't always work out the way you want it to, but apart from making music, what gets me out of bed in the morning is the proposition of breaking new ground. Always has been, always will be.

Speaking of which.

CHAPTER 16

Double Cream

In 1996 I came up with an idea for the nightclub scene that, although not exactly new, was pretty damn radical for the scene at the time, and should it actually work it would change the way things are done. Not just for the clubs, but for DJs and the crowd.

For years now, like every other DJ in the UK, I'd been playing here, there and everywhere, and with shiny new venues and upcoming DJs appearing almost by the minute, the thought of playing the same venue more than a couple of times a year was becoming a rarity.

One of the first people to actually take up a residency in a major club in the UK was yours truly. In fact, just a few weeks ago I spent an incredible night at the O2 in London helping them celebrate their thirtieth anniversary. Any ideas?

Ministry of Sound, which is based on Gaunt Street in Elephant & Castle, opened its doors for the first time in September 1991 and I was its first resident DJ. Yeah, I know. Good eh? Like me, a co-creator of the club, Justin Berkmann, had been a disciple of Larry Levan and had been as taken by the music, atmosphere and ethos at Paradise Garage as I had. Subsequently, when it came to him and his business partners, James Palumbo and Humphrey Waterhouse, trying to create an English version of the club, he contacted me. The secret to Paradise Garage's success, by the way, was simple. In addition to an inclusive door policy they had the best DJs playing the best music through the best sound system. That really was it. Being an aspiring DJ and sharing exactly the same vision as a prospective employer is an almost electrifying prospect, and when Justin first called me I don't think I slept for a couple of days. I was so excited.

The residency, which was every Friday, ended up lasting only six months and unfortunately that initial expectation and excitement soon evaporated. The idea behind a residency from a club owner's point of view is pretty similar to a football manager looking to buy a player. You want somebody who, as well as being at the height of their powers, is going to complement your team and your vision. From a DJ's point of view it's the same, in that once you've signed you'll do your best to deliver until something goes wrong or until you get itchy feet.

To cut a long story short, the boys at Ministry tried to bite off a bit more than they could chew in those early days which left them unable to pay the DJs what they were worth. As a gesture of goodwill I said that they could pay me down the line, and when that didn't happen I decided to go. I don't think it was intentional, which is why we never fell out and eventually carried on working together. They just got carried away with everything. Thirty years later and Ministry of Sound is still one of the most famous and iconic nightclubs on the planet, and because they look after the club and the brand so well I can't see that changing.

As well as having dipped my toe in the residency arena I'd also seen first-hand how a genuinely successful long-term residency can work having studied the likes of Levan, Alfredo and Frankie Knuckles, to name but a few. The thing is, when the idea to have another go at securing a residency in the UK first came into my head, the UK dance club scene was in a pretty good place, so I was half expecting everyone to come back and say, 'Look, mate, if it isn't broken, why mend it?' Even so, I decided to run my idea past the big four, which were Gatecrasher, Ministry, Renaissance and Cream.

Rather surprisingly, all four of them replied in the affirmative, but the ones who shouted the loudest were James Barton and Darren Hughes from Cream. According to them they'd been talking about exactly the same thing for quite a while, so my approach seemed like karma. I'd also guested at Cream many times previously and had always had a blast there. James and Darren were good guys and I'd long since been a lover of Liverpool and its people.

The next step was to see if a deal would be done. I knew this could get complicated so I kept well away. I had a vision for what I wanted to happen if I had a residency, and if that was going to come to pass I had to make sure that my relationship with James and Darren remained as healthy and uncomplicated as possible. Me getting involved in contracts, etc. would just muddy the waters.

David Levy, my agent at the time, began the negotiations as soon as we found out that Cream were game. As well as being highly respected, David had a reputation for getting his clients the best possible deal, so I knew I was in good hands. As it turned out, what actually occurred during these negotiations became the stuff of legend and as well as giving me a reputation for being a bit of a diva, which I completely and utterly refute and in a moment will explain why, they also paved the way to ensuring that DJs were treated a lot more like music artists than just club acts. The difference was David's approach. He had a lot of big artists on his books at the time and instead of going into the negotiations like he would have if he were representing a DJ, he put his artist head on instead.

All I can say is, vive la difference!

Because this deal was the first of its kind in the UK, a lot of chat began to occur within the industry and with that came a lot of rumours. Phoney rumours. First of all there was the money. According to some sources I was going to be on £50,000 a week, which in today's money would be at least double that. This was just ludicrous. Of course I was going to be paid handsomely, but fifty grand? I wish. After that came the rider. If you think Ozzy Osbourne's blue M&Ms story is amusing – which I still don't know whether it's true or not – wait till you hear this. Apparently, in addition to several cases of Krug champagne, enough assistants to fill a football stadium and several lobsters, I'd demanded a selection of class A drugs to be delivered to me on a silver tray every week. There was loads of other stuff and 99 per cent of it was bollocks.

Lastly came the length of the contract, which although spurious on the face of it became the thing that reinvented the wheel, so to speak. Under normal circumstances, if you even had a contract to play a gig, it would be no more than a page or two long whereas the contract that David had drawn up for the residency was over twenty. Although standard practice for a rock band or an artist, this was unheard of for a DJ and it obviously got everyone thinking.

The only thing in the contract that on the face of it might have appeared a bit starry (but was actually quite necessary) was the arrangement to get me to the club every week. If Chelsea were playing away from home it would just be a simple case of me getting myself to Liverpool Lime Street at a decent time and then making my way either to the club or to the Adelphi Hotel, which was my base. If they were playing at home, however, things would be different. In that event, because time would be against me, a car would pick me up from Stamford Bridge and drive me to the club and if that couldn't be arranged then it would have to be a flight. The clause that made it sound starry was that if no commercial flights were available then Cream would have to hire one. Given the way that DJs were normally treated at the time it was incredibly forward, but at the end of the day if you don't ask you don't get. Cream were desperate to hire me, I was desperate to play there and watch Chelsea. Needs must when you've got a lot going on.

One of the reasons why DJs hadn't been offered residencies in the UK yet was that the club owners didn't always trust them to turn up. To be fair, a lot of DJs did have a reputation for being unreliable, so the disparity between how DJs and musical artists were treated, while perhaps disproportionate, wasn't completely without reason. What separated me from them was the experience of working with people such as U2. Consummate professionals, basically, who are obviously very highly paid but who always deliver. Before we agreed the contract I let James and Darren know that that was basically what they'd be getting and they believed every word.

What surprised me slightly about all this was the reaction from the industry press. Instead of saying, 'Good for you, mate,' they were outraged that a club had agreed to such demands and seemed to think that, as a mere DJ, I had ideas well above my station. There was still a certain amount of disdain shown towards DJs that to this very day still hasn't been eradicated, and probably never will. Could I give a toss though? Could I heck. Contractually I was now safe and sound but professionally – and creatively – I was in seventh heaven. In my eyes Cream were the most forward-thinking club in Europe at the time and the fact that we were going into partnership together, which to all intents and purposes is what was happening, felt amazing.

I alluded earlier on to the suggestion that a club hiring a DJ for a residency is like a football team signing a new player, so when the deal was eventually agreed and Cream and I were looking for ways to celebrate the partnership, there was one idea in particular that stood out. 'Why don't we do a press call down at Stamford Bridge?' somebody suggested. 'You could even sign the contract on the pitch.' Twenty years before, the Sex Pistols had signed their contract with A&M Records outside Buckingham Palace, and although I'm not a fan of the band I knew it had happened. Me, at Stamford Bridge? What a brilliant idea. I could obviously appreciate the publicity value of such a stunt, but for me personally, as a Chelsea fan? Well, it'd be amazing.

After discussing the idea with Chelsea and getting the go-ahead, me, David Levy, James and Darren headed down to Stamford Bridge with the contracts. Just before the photo shoot, James had the bright idea of going to the club shop and buying a Chelsea shirt with Oakenfold printed on the back. Except he didn't get one with Oakenfold printed on the back at all, he got one with OAKFOLD printed on it. Unfortunately we didn't realise this until the shoot started. 'Get the shirt out then,' said Darren. 'Here we go,' said James, proudly handing it to me so I could hold it aloft. 'Hang on a second,' said one of the journalists. 'They've spelt your name wrong!' 'Eh? You're joking, aren't you?' After running back to the shop it turned out that the only replacement they had available was a size XXXL which was the size of a bloody beach towel. No matter. We had to work with what we'd got so after finding the missing E and N we had my correct name printed on the back and were ready to go. With a beach towel.

One of the other factors that made me so keen to go with Cream was the crowd. I speak as a Londoner myself, but down there people are spoiled for choice when it comes to entertaining yourself whereas up north it's different. Cream was like a Mecca in the city of Liverpool and the interest, attention and passion it was shown by the faithful created an atmosphere that is difficult to describe. When I started my residency I became a part of that vibe and it was special. I love having links with the North West. It's a home from home.

For the first year of my residency at Cream I played in a room called the Annexe, which to this day is one of the most intense environments I've ever played. As well as having a very low ceiling, health and safety was non-existent and the amount of people you'd have in there made it feel dangerous. I used to have a very loyal following who, if you'd left it at that, would have filled up the room nicely, but during the night people would mooch in from other rooms. That's when it started to go crazy and I don't mind admitting that after a while it became a distraction.

I used to spend most of the week choosing the set. Not all day every day, but you know what I mean. Although I only played there once a week, Cream was never far from my thoughts and every Monday morning after having recovered on the Sunday I'd sit down with Darren, who I became very close to, analyse the set just gone and see where I could take it next time. In my eyes, I don't think I've ever played a perfect set in my life and I don't think I'd ever want to. I've come close once or twice, but achieving perfection is like being at number one, in that from there the only way is down. Some people might disagree as far as the sets are concerned, but from my own point of view I always like to remain within touching distance.

I don't know whose idea it was but in an attempt to build on the amazing response we received after the launch of the partnership, or should I say the signing, we started leaking stories to *Muzik* magazine. True stories, that is. A sort of running commentary about what was happening in the world of Cream and Oakenfold. This idea quickly gathered pace and before we knew it a kind of soap opera had been created featuring a cast of about a dozen people, and as the word began to spread, people started buying *Muzik* magazine just to catch up. That's the joy of being involved in a genre that's still quite young. It was a proverbial blank canvas in many ways, but with the benefit of knowing what's worked in the past for other genres and what hasn't. We had such a lot of fun.

After a year in the Annexe, Darren and James decided that I should move into a bigger space. For all its issues I loved playing the Annexe and so at first I wasn't keen. It might sound pretentious but in order to do or change anything in my life I need a motivation – or a challenge even – and other than potentially playing to more people I couldn't find one. 'I'll tell you what then,' said James. 'Here's your motivation. You design the room with us. How's that?' He didn't have to say another word. I was in.

After a lot of hard work the new room, which was called the Courtyard, was ready. It's funny but because I'd been so involved in the preparation, when it came to actually playing there for the first time I became quite nervous. Whereas you might have had four or five hundred people in the Annexe, you could get around two thousand in the courtyard. It was different strokes.

Incidentally, one of the things that fascinated me most at Cream, and there were many of them, was how people used to stand in exactly the same place week after week. You'll obviously only notice something like this if you're doing a residency, and when I began to cotton on it opened up a whole new realm to the proceedings. A feeling of community, basically. All of a sudden I was able to build up a rapport with my audience on the dance floor, and when I went down to speak to them at the end of the night, which I always did, it was like picking up a conversation that had already started. I'd never experienced anything like that before in my life, and to me it's one of the main attractions about doing a residency. The relationships.

The Cream PR machine went into overdrive about my move to the Courtyard and come the first night there was a genuine buzz of excitement. Unlike the Annexe, the DJ booth in the Courtyard was quite high up, so instead of the crowd being able to see me arrive and get ready to take over from my support DJ Paul Bleasdale, which used to get everyone going, I was able to sneak in unannounced. This gave me something I hadn't had before which was the element of surprise and an opportunity to make an entrance. What's more, I intended to use it.

When Paul finished his set the lights went down, and after putting on a simple rhythm track I turned the volume down by roughly 50 per cent. This changed the dynamic completely, and because everyone had an idea what was happening, all eyes turned to the DJ booth. I was still out of sight at this point and as I very slowly increased the volume of the rhythm track, the energy of the crowd followed suit. I'm not sure how long I held out – two minutes maybe – but when the crowd were literally fit to burst I put an absolutely banging track called 'Flaming June' by the electronica musician BT on the turntable, stood up, raised an arm to the crowd and let the room go bang. And it did go bang! The level of intensity was off the scale, like the Annexe times ten. For the first time ever I could hear the crowd in a nightclub roar and chant like they would at a football match. It was insane. Better still, they were chanting my name, or at least my nickname, which is Oakey. It might sound slightly arrogant but at that moment everyone in the DJ booth, which was Darren, James, David Levy and myself, was thinking exactly the same thing. This has to be the best nightclub in the fucking world.

From then on things went from being very good indeed to absolutely fucking incredible. The thing is, I can't put my finger on what changed really, apart from the location. I was putting the same amount of effort into preparing the sets as I normally did and everything seemed the same. Except, that is, the response from the crowd. As well as chanting my name, all these banners started to appear in the room. I'd be standing there in the booth completely locked into the music and there'd be two thousand people dancing and chanting my name while surrounded by a load of banners with Oakey, Oakey, Oakey written on them. They also started coming from much further afield and never a week went by without Darren or James coming in and telling me that they'd just been speaking to a bunch of people from Ireland or Scotland or somewhere. 'What you've all created is a church,' one of the club regulars once said to me. 'Every Saturday night a congregation religiously turn up to worship the music.' 'But that would make me the vicar, wouldn't it?' I replied. Anyway, I wasn't sure about that. Churches are usually very cold places and Cream was just a sweatbox.

It was during this golden period at Cream that the term superstar DJ was first coined. *Mixmag* interviewed David Levy one day and after asking him about the DJ culture we were creating, he said, 'Well, there's models and supermodels, and there's DJs and super DJs.' The following issue they printed David's statement which gave birth to the superstar DJ, or at least the term. He always says he wishes he'd never said it.

The only downside to what was happening at Cream was the amount of attention I was receiving, not just inside the club but outside too. It started off with people bringing presents to the club. Teddy bears and things like that. Then they started appearing at the hotel, together with the people who'd bought them! I didn't want to be rude or anything so I accepted them, but I found it a bit weird. One girl used to give me plants and clothes she'd made for me. Every week she'd bring them to the club and at first I was OK with it. She was a really nice girl and seemed normal. Then, as time went on, she got a bit strange and started following me to the hotel. It all came to a head one night when she tried to climb into the DJ booth. Luckily the security guards got hold of her before she could make it in there and then threw her out. I did ask them to go easy on her but they ended up banning the girl for life. After that she started turning up at other gigs and things. It really wasn't healthy.

The biggest problem the club had, which again started shortly after I moved into the Courtyard, was with gangsters and dealers. They were in danger of taking over the club at one point and the only option open to James and Darren was to work closely with the police. This meant that on a Saturday evening, in addition to having a police helicopter flying overhead, you'd have armed police officers outside the club for most of the night. Somebody once said that they thought it added to the theatre of what was going on and I'd have to agree with them. I liked the edge that it brought to the proceedings. It was raw and very real. It reminded me a bit of what went on at Spectrum. I used to meet a lot of villains there and their presence used to add a sense of danger. The criminal presence at Cream, however, was on a much bigger scale which is why they had to work with the police.

I suppose much of the above could come under the banner of being careful of what you wish for. Everything comes at a price, and turning Cream into a super club and me into a super DJ (David Levy's words, not mine) — given that we had nothing really to compare it to — was always going to create problems. Surmountable ones, fortunately, but problems all the same. At the risk of sounding even more clichéd, it was a character-building exercise and I for one learned a lot. Not just about stalkers and police helicopters, but about myself and what I wanted out of life.

After the end of the second year of my contract James and Darren tried to talk me into extending it and moving into the main room. This time there was no motivation to be had at all, other than playing to more people for more money and it was time to call it a day. For a start I didn't like the main room at Cream and I felt that quitting while I was ahead would be a sensible move. I also hadn't been able to travel much during the last two years and that was really starting to bug me.

I'm not one for regrets but in hindsight, instead of quitting Cream altogether, what I perhaps should have done was take a few months off, jump on a few planes and then come back for one more year in the Courtyard. I was leaving the best room with the best sound system and the best crowd in the country, if not the world. Everyone who's played there knows how good it was. But regardless of whether I was right or not, what I can say without fear of contradiction is that what we all achieved at Cream was very special indeed and we can all be very proud of ourselves. I certainly am.

Whereas the Goa Mix is undoubtedly the piece of music that people most want to talk about when they meet me, my residency at Cream seems to have had more of an effect on more people than anything else I've done in a club. Also, the enthusiasm with which they talk about it is touching, but it isn't surprising. I was there, remember, and saw the looks on their faces week after week after week. You never forget that.

CHAPTER 17

Cracking America

There's an old saying in the music industry that if you make it in America you'll make it around the world, and by the late 1990s I was ready to give it a go. That's not to say I didn't have a following elsewhere in the world other than the UK. I did. Being big in America though carries with it gravitas that, whichever country or territory it is you're visiting, carries you in on a massive cloud. It's like another level of fame.

The tour I'd done with U2, which had gone all over America, was kind of irrelevant in this situation as the people I'd played to hadn't been my audience, nor were they ever likely to be. In fact, apart from the odd gig, the only time I'd ever gone over there for more than a week or so was for the Factory/Haçienda tour which I did with Mike Pickering. Since then the time had never been right, although I'd been keeping a close eye on things. Carl Cox, Digweed and Sasha were over there on a fairly regular basis, but so far no DJ had tried to crack America once and for all. That was my plan. The question was, when?

The two things that gave me the confidence and the impetus to try and crack America was a certain amount of success I was now having there and a piece of advice I received from U2. The success had been bubbling away for some time. My albums were selling well (I'd sold well over a million over there up to then) and I was getting quite a few offers to play. Not thousands, but enough to make me think that there might be something in it. Also, every time I spoke to a promoter about going over there they used the same words. 'There's a buzz about you over here, Paul,' they said, or words to that effect. The likes of Cream and Ministry were already stuff of legend in the States and as a former resident of both I was part of it.

The advice I received from U2 happened on the tour and was imparted to me after the idea about cracking America had first come into my head. U2 were the biggest band there by a country mile at the time, so with dreams of conquering the country fresh in my mind it seemed like a good idea to ask the boys what the secret was. As expected, there was no magic ingredient for cracking America other than perseverance and hard work, but on a scale that would be foreign to the majority of bands and artists.

In the late 1980s when everyone else was in Europe getting off their heads during the second summer of love, which I was obviously involved in, U2 were touring the length and breadth of America and had been doing so on a similar level for years. 'At first they hated us,' said the boys, 'which was really hard. But Instead of being put off and staying away, we went back for an even longer tour. Things got better so we went back again, and then again. We were relentless.'

It's only when you get to know America that you actually realise the enormity of what they mean. If you tour the UK, for instance, even extensively, you'll be looking at twenty or thirty gigs tops, and it's the same for every other major European country. In America you could go on tour for six months and still not have covered everywhere. That's why, if I wanted to have a go at conquering it, I knew for a fact that I would have to commit to the country, and to the project, fully. It was all or it was nothing. There was no other way.

Once I'd made up my mind to do it, I quit every project I was involved in in the UK. I quit my residency at Home, which I'd taken up a few months after leaving Cream. I quit the lot. The only thing I didn't quit, which to be fair was a going concern as opposed to a project, was Perfecto Records. We'd been doing good business in America for a while, and before I went over there I checked to see how we were performing in each state. Although it wasn't an exact science it helped me gauge the kind of attention that each state might require. One thing I was sure of, however, was that I would leave no stone, or in this case no state, unturned. Even if it looked like I'd be on a hiding to nothing, you've gotta start somewhere and you never know where it might lead.

The first venue I played on the first tour was the infamous Viper Room in LA. Traditionally a rock and roll joint, I'd been told by the promoter that this would be a kind of industry event. Any gig that has the word 'industry' attached to it generally means that it's gonna be an invited crowd as opposed to your own crowd, so I was managing my expectations.

As I drove on to Sunset Boulevard, which is where the club was based, I suddenly saw a huge line of people that, as I continued driving, appeared to start at the club itself and must have been about two hundred yards long. 'Jesus Christ!' I said to myself. 'This ain't no industry do!' Apparently the promoter almost lost control of his car when he turned on to Sunset and ended up getting a $300 ticket! What a start to the adventure, and what a night.

One of the strangest and most daunting places I remember playing on that first tour was Birmingham, Alabama which was right inside the Bible Belt. The venue was basically just a bar with some sawdust on the floor and about fifty locals. I have no idea whether they even knew who I was, but it ended up being an amazing gig. They'd probably never seen anybody playing electronic dance music before and I'd certainly never played in a bar with sawdust on the floor.

Regardless of how much of an anomaly I was in these places, you could always guarantee that a dance audience would exist, so providing the promoter did their job, we at least stood a chance of getting a half decent crowd. These kinds of unknown quantities coming up trumps was easily the most pleasurable part of it all as it was basically confirmation that it was working, or at least going in the right direction. I even DJ'ed in Alaska during that first tour. I wanted to go to Anchorage for some reason but the only local promoter said he couldn't afford to pay me. 'Just pay for my airfare and a hotel,' I said, and he agreed. We ended up getting over 250 people. Which for Anchorage, which was definitely not a hotbed for nightlife, was unheard of. Wherever I went, my attitude was always, 'You might not think you want me here, but you soon will, and I'm going to keep on coming back till you love me!'

Until now, the mistake that the majority of British DJs had made was to play the east and west coasts to death and then bugger off home, thinking that they'd cracked America. They used to do twenty or thirty shows over there max, with the majority taking place in either California or New York and New Jersey. They completely ignored the rest of the country which is mad when you think about it. It's like going to the UK, playing London and Edinburgh and forgoing Glasgow, Manchester, Birmingham and everywhere else, but on a much, much grander scale. I won't pretend that it wasn't daunting at times, because it was, but what helped to keep my head up, in addition to U2's words of advice which I used to repeat to myself ad nauseam, was that it was a completely new experience for almost everyone concerned.

I was trying to popularise electronic dance music in America and they loved it.

The only slight oversight when I started the tour, which became glaringly obvious even after the first show, was that I didn't have anything to sell or promote. People were coming up to me after the shows asking for stuff, as were the promoters, but I had nothing for them. This led me to sign a deal very quickly with a newish dance label called Thrive Records who were distributed by WEA. Founded by a man called Ricardo Vinas, who ended up A&Ring *Bunkka* for me in the States a few years later, they've worked with some big names over the years such as Sasha, John Digweed, Danny Tenaglia, Sander Kleinenberg and Deep Dish. I got on with Ricardo like a house on fire and managed to persuade him that we should release a compilation album featuring ten tracks sharpish. This, although established practice in the UK, was a fairly new concept in the States as EDM was still underground. The crossover was in progress but the whole point of me being there was to help it over the line, and when the album was released we shifted over 200,000 copies in no time at all. That may not sound like a lot to some people, but for what was ostensibly still an underground genre it was massive, and the album, not to mention my relationship with Ricardo, became a very important building block.

For every ten Birmingham Alabamas or Anchorage Alaskas we'd have something more akin to the Viper Room, as in certain parts of the country the crossover had already taken place. The first example of this post the Viper Room was when me and my support DJ, Dave Ralph, turned up in the tour bus that we'd hired – which used to belong to country-and-western legend Willie Nelson – at the Burning Man Festival in the Black Rock Desert, Nevada.

Although I'd played festivals and outdoor gigs many times before, I hadn't played anything like this. As well as taking place in a desert, which was a new one, it must have been at least 40 degrees out there, which is about 104 in American money, and when the wind got up, which it frequently did, a virtual sandstorm would take place. It was fucking madness! Seriously, it's hard to put into words what Burning Man is like if you haven't been there.

One of the first things I remember seeing on arriving there was a London double-decker bus, in the middle of the bloody desert, with about fifty naked Americans running around it laughing their heads off. The only thing that would have made it weirder was if they'd all been singing Cliff Richard songs!

After that I saw a car that had been customised to make it look like a shark racing across the sand at about 100mph followed by a float with about twenty people on it that was decked out in black-and-white leopard skin. I don't think I'd ever been as far removed from reality before in my life, and as an experience it was just extraordinary. Like a modern-day version of Woodstock but with different music, different drugs and more public transport. It wasn't just dance music that had crossed over there, everything had! I remember going down like an absolute storm when I played, but I have a funny feeling that everyone did. I've been back to Burning Man several times since and each time I see something, or should I say some things, that either make me howl or terrify me. Sometimes both.

It was during this tour that I was contacted by the *Guinness Book of World Records* who informed me that I would be entering next year's book as the world's most successful DJ. I genuinely thought it was a joke when they rang me up. I mean, how on earth do you measure these sorts of things, and how on earth do you react? I tried to be as polite as possible but it all seemed like a bit of a laugh really. It was only later on that I realised that it actually might mean something. Mum and Dad thought it was amazing! With dance music and clubbing obviously not being their thing, it was something they could relate to so in that respect it did me a favour.

My promoter for that tour, Gerry Gerrard, claims that the gig when everything fell into place with regards to a DJ performing in the same natural environment as a major rock band for the first time was in a converted theatre called the Mayan in LA. He brought in a load of visuals for the show and as he stood there at the side of the stage he saw the audience facing me, exactly as they would a rock band. The point being that at the end of the day the audience doesn't give a shit how you make the music, so long as you do make it, and as long as they have visuals of some kind to pull them in they'll be happy. We also had a lot of Hollywood celebrities in that night such as Demi Moore and Charlie Sheen, so it could just as well have been a Guns N' Roses gig. This was confirmation, in Gerry's mind at least, that dance music had now crossed over into the mainstream, and it wouldn't take me long to follow suit.

I carried on touring the USA on and off for the next year or so, and in 2001, after having taken a well-earned break, I got a call from Moby one day asking me if I'd like to take part in a tour he was planning. What, another one? Or at least my manager got a call from his. He was planning a festival tour called Area: One, and wanted me on board.

After sending us the details the only thing that concerned me was that the tour would be taking place in amphitheatres, which in my mind would be like playing a football match under water. You can't play dance music to people in seats? The following day Gerry Gerrard called Moby's people back and suggested a compromise. 'Look,' he said. 'He'll do it as long as he can do his thing in a tent and not an amphitheatre. What's more, he wants his own line-up.' As I was basically demanding a separate stage for the tour, I was fully expecting Moby and his people to turn around and tell us to bugger off, but they didn't. They said yes. 'Really?' I remember saying to Gerry Gerrard. 'Wow, man. We've got some work to do here!'

Moby's people ended up hiring a tent that held about 2,500 people, which for me hit the nail on the head. Not just because the audience would be standing up, but because in order to get in they'd have to queue up in a line outside. This might sound a bit daft but that kind of thing wasn't common in Middle America and I wanted to recreate the full nightclub experience.

Joining me on the bill, but not necessarily in the tent, would be the likes of OutKast, Nelly Furtado, New Order and The Orb, so it was a real mix. These kind of uber eclectic line-ups had been the staple of many a European festival for donkey's years, but not in the States, which is what made it such a daring move. Moby was convinced, however, that the mood was finally shifting in the States and people's tastes were becoming broader. He was right.

Joining me in the dance tent as my support DJ would be none other than Carl Cox, who was one of the few European DJs other than me who'd been making a genuine effort to make inroads there. He did get a little bit of a rude awakening though, or a 'reality check', as he called it, when it came to the set-up. For a few years I'd been building myself a customised DJ booth that I could obviously take on tour with me, but would be mine and mine alone. This, like so many other things, had started with U2 and had been honed during my residencies at Cream and Home.

To Carl and others it might have seemed quite pretentious or outlandish, but it's where I was professionally. When Carl turned up for the first soundcheck on the Area: One Tour he assumed that he'd be using my booth, but was pointed by my tour manager in the direction of his decks which were on a table on the other side of the stage. He had no visuals. Nothing. At first he probably felt badly done to but I think it taught Carl that our status as DJs was now changing within the pantheon of popular music. In fact, I know it did because a few years later when I saw him performing in Miami he had the biggest fucking DJ booth I'd ever seen in my life, and enough lights and visuals to keep Madonna happy! It didn't take him long to catch on and catch up.

The only nightmare I had on Moby's tour was when my touring assistant forgot to bring my records to a gig. We were playing at a place called Jones Beach in Long Island and as nightmares go it doesn't get much bigger for a DJ. *Rolling Stone* magazine had come to do a feature on me at the gig, and when my touring assistant told me that he didn't have my records, my stomach literally hit the floor. 'You're fucking kidding me,' I said. 'But our hotel's three hours away?' I was due on in about an hour. It was a disaster.

The organisers looked into getting it helicoptered in but it was all too late. Boy, did I get a talking to. The only person who offered to help me that night was a DJ I knew vaguely called Liquid Todd who offered to go on in my place. With no other options available I accepted his offer and he ended up getting dog's abuse. He was booed and had things thrown at him, the lot. It was awful. To be fair, it didn't seem to bother him that much and he just carried on spinning. Now I've got to know Liquid, who is a massive character, I can understand why he carried on. Things like that don't faze him. What a kind and brave thing to do though.

Although it happened slightly before the Area: One tour, the event that kind of rubber-stamped the fact that I might have cracked America was playing the main stage at the legendary

Coachella, which is basically America's answer to Glastonbury (but with a more forward-thinking approach to dance music). Plenty of DJs had played the festival before but never on the main stage, so in that respect it was Glastonbury all over again. Where the two festivals differed, which became clear when I saw the line-up, was that they had almost as many DJs on the bill as bands and solo artists. Fat Boy Slim, The Chemical Brothers, Squarepusher, Aphex Twin. They had some big old names on there. What made it extra special for me was that instead of being stuck somewhere in the middle, I was on right before the headline act, Jane's Addiction. That sent out a big message and I'd finally arrived on that big cloud I mentioned earlier.

The experience of playing Coachella for the first time is something I'll never forget, but unfortunately for all the wrong reasons. Don't get me wrong, the gig itself was fine from a spectators' point of view, and to this very day I get people coming up to me and saying how much they enjoyed it. I'm not sure whether these people were under the influence of something strong during the gig, but the fact that they never mention what happened onstage during that gig makes me think that perhaps they were. Anyway, allow me to explain.

Back then I was still playing vinyl and behind my set-up onstage was a large black curtain. Behind that some roadies were setting up for Jane's Addiction who were on directly after me. My entourage, incidentally, consisted of a friend of mine called Swedish Egil who, as well as being a DJ, is my producer on SiriusXM Radio and also has his own show. That was it. Just him and me. We were very self-contained.

The moment I took to the stage at Coachella and started playing, the road crew who were setting up Jane's Addiction began testing all the microphones. 'One, two. One, two. One, two.' I obviously had monitors next to me but they were being drowned out. Egil went behind to ask them to stop but they refused. In fact, I have a feeling that they might have used some rather colourful language. The organisers might have been pro-dance music, but there was still a 'them and us' situation and especially when it came to the rock crowd.

As soon as the mics were done they started checking the drums, which was obviously even worse. The crowd wouldn't have been able to hear anything, but up onstage it was flaming bedlam. 'Please, Egil,' I pleaded, 'Just tell them to fucking stop.' The look on his face when I asked him was a picture. 'What?' he must have been thinking. 'You're going to send me back there – AGAIN?' Unfortunately I had no choice, so while Egil went back into battle, I set about trying to hear myself think.

After having thought about it for a minute, I'm fairly sure that it must have been done on purpose as normally you'd test the instruments and mics closer to the time. And certainly not when the support act's on! What a bunch of tossers.

After about twenty minutes they finally buggered off which just left me, Egil and about 50,000 people who, despite everything, appeared to be having a bloody good time. About five minutes later I felt something touch my back and when I looked round I realised that the curtain, which must have been a couple of inches thick and weighed an absolute ton, was starting to ripple. Because I'd been lost in what I was doing, I hadn't realised that the wind had started to pick up and now everything was beginning to move. And I mean, everything! The first thing I did was ask Egil, who was still recovering having been verbally abused by half a dozen sweaty road crew, to try and stop the curtain from whacking me on the back and pushing me forward, which is what was starting to happen. While he was doing that I tried to stop the needles from jumping on the records which was damn near impossible. It gets worse though. At some point a gust of wind got right underneath the curtain and lifted it over my record box, which then pulled it about 10 yards behind us into the land of Jane's Addiction. Egil, who was still busy trying to stop the curtain from hitting me, couldn't do a thing to help as had he moved, the chances are the curtain would have taken me and my console out.

Until now I'd managed to prevent the needles from moving around too much on the records, and although I'd obviously noticed the odd discrepancy here and there, the crowd fortunately hadn't. Literally a second or two after the curtain had kidnapped my record box, the needle on a record I'd just started playing jumped from the beginning of the track to about a minute before the end. I had nothing lined up on the adjacent turntable and my record box was about 10 yards away behind an iron curtain. 'Fucking hell!' I cried. Even if I could get hold of a record, how the hell was I going to be able to mix it before the end? By this time Egil had changed tack and was lying on the floor behind me trying to make the curtain rigid. This, although preventing the curtain from hitting me, was also preventing me from being able to get to my record box. It was all fucking happening.

Although the majority seemed oblivious, there were definitely some people towards the front of the stage who could see what was going on and in the end they started trying to tell the security staff what was happening. It didn't make any difference. They, like the road crew, couldn't have given two hoots about our predicament and probably thought it was funny.

Right at the last minute I asked Egil to go underneath the curtain and grab the box, and while he did that I braced myself for a battering. Although he was only under there a second or so it felt like a minute. Fortunately, I only got hit a couple of times by the curtain and managed to remain upright, and after passing me the box, Egil assumed his position on the floor as my windcheater-in-chief. He did a bloody good job too. In fact, if it hadn't been for him the gig would have been over in minutes.

I think I did about an hour at Coachella, and when I went to take a bow at the end of the gig, because of what had happened, which had left me quite disorientated, and the fact that it was still windy, I almost fell off the bloody stage. The people who'd seen what was happening and had tried to help were especially generous with their applause and I made sure I gave them a special wave. God knows what Egil and I must have looked like when we walked offstage. We were both all over the place and looked like we'd been involved in a fight as opposed to a gig. I suppose we had really. A fight against the elements. We were bruised and a bit battered, but we managed to get through it in one piece.

I think I've played Coachella four times since then, on various different stages, and the last time was in 2013. Would I ever play there again? It's hard to say really and I'd obviously have to be asked first. Coachella's changed though. Back then you had a real mixture of artists whereas these days it's primarily about new and emerging talent. Although I'm all over that concept, I'm ever so slightly past that stage in my career. I remember having a conversation with my agent about this not long ago, and even if I was invited back there I'm not sure I'd accept. There's no reason at all why you shouldn't have old talent and new talent on the same bill together, but I've been there so many times. Old or new, give somebody else a chance. Also, it might be a little bit hypocritical of me bearing in mind what I said about Glastonbury inviting the same people back. I'll definitely go back as a punter one day. Hell, yeah. But as an artist? I don't know. Let's see what happens. These days I'm far more interested in taking dance music out of the realms of a nightclub or a festival environment and to new and incredible places. I'll come on to that in a bit, but suffice to say that the idea of an old and more established DJ championing dance music in new locations is a lot more attractive than an old and more established DJ playing in the same old places and, potentially, in the place of new talent.

The thing that's stayed with me the most about that two- or three-year period in America, and is one of the reasons why I love it as much as I do, is the sheer variety of audiences, locations and experiences that I was lucky enough to encounter. One day I'd be playing a gig to the faithful in somewhere like New York, LA or Miami alongside, for instance, the aforementioned Chemical Brothers or Carl Cox, and the next I'd be trying to spread the word in a dusty old backdrop somewhere. Had it been just one or the other, and especially over such a long period, then it wouldn't have worked and it certainly wouldn't have been as much fun. Ultimately though, it was always the potential that kept me going, and even after having supposedly broken America, I was still like a dog with a bone. In fact, I still am to a certain extent. Had I done it the other way around and scored a massive radio hit, which would have prevented me from having to tour that extensively, I'd only ever have seen the major towns and cities. As it was, I ended up seeing more of America in three years than most Americans would in a lifetime. What's more, I wouldn't have it any other way. Radio hits? Who needs 'em?

CHAPTER 18

It's Just Not Cricket

It was estimated some time ago that I must have played to over 20 million people since I started performing, which is roughly the same size as the current population of Sri Lanka. Some of the gigs have obviously been more memorable than others, but the one that sits alone in terms of the experience it provided, and what it did for me professionally, was a gig I did on Clapham Common in August 2001. Instigated by Channel 4 in order to celebrate the fact that they'd won the rights to show the Ashes from the BBC, it is to this day the biggest solo gig I've ever done.

It actually started out as a support slot for the cricket. Channel 4 had decided to erect some big screens on Clapham Common in order to show the final Test of the series and the idea was that once that was done I would come on and we'd all have a jolly old time. Come the end of the fourth Test, Australia had already won the series which rendered the whole cricket thing a bit of a damp squib. In reaction to this Channel 4 decided to change how the event was promoted and it went from being a cricket match with a DJ at the end to a DJ with a cricket match at the beginning, if that makes sense. All of a sudden the billboards, which were situated all over London, had my name on them instead of Darren Gough's, so I'd been elevated to the main event and was no longer playing second fiddle.

Despite it being a free event they weren't expecting hordes of people, and as well as a couple of food stands there were just a few toilets and a handful of police officers. They were expecting a couple of thousand people max, I think, and with the sun beating down it looked like we were on for a good day. A civilised game of cricket that means nothing followed by some banging tunes courtesy of yours truly. Who could ask for more?

I have no idea what happened with the cricket as it isn't my thing, but by the time I arrived for my shift there must have been at least 50,000 people there, which later swelled to at an estimated 70,000. By this time I'd played to lots of big crowds with U2 and whoever, but none where they'd come to see me. The police, however, were extraordinarily nervous about the crowd, and had they been able to disperse them I'm sure they would've. As it was, all they could do was pray that nothing went wrong, and fortunately it didn't. I do realise that we were probably quite lucky in that respect as anything could have happened as there were next to no police there. I remember one of the officers kept on running into the DJ booth. 'Have you seen the amount of people?' he said. 'They just keep coming!' Because of all the lights I only got a glimpse of the burgeoning crowd on a few occasions, but when I did it took my breath away. What made me laugh though was the screen that was stuck in the middle. With just a couple of thousand people expected the screen they'd ordered was quite small, which stuck in the middle of 70,000 made it look like a portable television.

The immediate aftermath of the gig, at least for me, was amazing. The atmosphere had been incredible and although the police had been very nervous it had obviously been a big success. 'We should do this every year,' I said to my manager. 'You're not serious,' he said. 'Why not?' I replied. 'We could feature all the artists who are signed to Perfecto and I'd headline.' The general feeling seemed to be that we'd got away with something and should leave it at that, but I wasn't having any of it. Next time we'd have everything in place, especially the right amount of police. In my opinion it was no coincidence that there hadn't been any violence or bad feeling and I wanted to go again.

After arranging a meeting with Channel 4, I laid out my grand plan which was to hold the event on the same day every year going forward. I thought it went well but unfortunately they were having none of it. Like everyone else (except me) they felt like we'd dodged a bullet so it didn't even get to first base. To me that just wasn't logical as with everything in place surely there'd be less chance of it going wrong.

For a couple of weeks I was full of regret of what might have been (I even had a name for it which would have been Oakenfest), but as time went on that went and I was left with memories of what had actually taken place. Beautiful memories. Had we gone again these would have been diluted over the years, but as it stands they're as strong now as they were twenty years ago. Yep, that was definitely one of my better days.

Speaking of Channel 4, when people talk to me about the *Big Brother* theme, the question on their lips is usually whether or not I get a royalty every time the theme's played. What generally happens with TV themes these days is called a buyout, so instead of paying you money every time it's played on TV you get a flat fee at the start. If the show only lasts a few weeks then it doesn't matter, but if it goes on for years it can grate a bit. That's just the way it is though and unless you're a Paul McCartney you just have to toe the line. Back in the 1970s and '80s, an American called Mike Post was the go-to guy when it came to catchy theme tunes, and because these shows were shown all the time all over the world, he made a fortune. Good for him. Just get this list though – *Magnum PI, NYPD Blue, Law and Order, The A-Team, The Rockford Files, Quantum Leap, Hill Street Blues*. That's some CV, don't you think? The guy's a genius.

I have no idea when it happened exactly, but because of the amount of money the producers were having to pay to guys like Mike, eventually they decided to call time on it which is when buyouts came along. When the producers of *Big Brother*, Endemol, first approached me about writing the theme tune for it, I was hesitant. Because the idea for the show was so original – a bunch of strangers thrown together in a house for several weeks with a load of cameras and only each other for entertainment – I had a funny feeling it was going to be huge, especially in the UK. After all, we're a very inquisitive nation, are we not? If it did do well I had a hunch that I could end up feeling ripped off and I didn't want that to happen. The money wasn't huge, so to all intents and purposes it was the same as writing a piece of library music. Had that been the norm in my world then fine, but it wasn't. If something I wrote or produced did well, I was used to being remunerated.

I was living over in Amsterdam at the time which is where Endemol are based, and when I tried to negotiate away from having a buyout they said that I could take it or leave it. 'We've got some other people in mind,' they said. 'If you say no we'll just move on.' At least I knew where I stood. After several conversations with my manager at the time, I decided that, even if it did do well, it would be a nice little string to my bow so I eventually agreed. Me and Andy Gray ended up writing the tune together based on a riff I came up with and we released it under the name of Elementfour. If you're writing for TV you obviously want to go for something as memorable as possible, and this seemed to fit the bill. During the initial discussions with Endemol I suggested that whatever we came up with should have club and chart potential, and they were all over the idea. When we played it to them they loved Elementfour, and when we released it as a single it became a massive hit, not just here but all over Europe. The only radio station in the whole of Britain that wouldn't play the tune was Radio 1 as the show was on Channel 4. Petty or what? It still reached number four in the charts though, which wasn't too shabby. Had it been played by Radio 1 it would definitely have got to number one but that's just the way it is. We followed it up with an album featuring some classic dance tracks that had appeared in the first series, and once again it did very well indeed.

CHAPTER 19

He Shoots, He Scores

From a personal point of view, I'd kind of fallen in love with America, and after having committed to it professionally, at least for the last few years, in 2002 I started entertaining the idea of me possibly committing to it personally too.

For all my claims about the UK being more accepting of dance music and dance culture generally than America, by the early 2000s a movement was under way that was in danger of eroding that. Dance music appeared to have peaked in the UK but as opposed to allowing it to regenerate like you would any other genre, because it was relatively new some people sensed a kill – especially the press – and decided to put the boot in. In layman's terms, the problem that dance culture had was that it had grown very big very quickly and, like anything in that situation, it can't keep growing forever. Claims that it had got too big for its boots and had morphed into nothing more than a money-making machine were commonplace. Even Ministry of Sound's own magazine started putting the boot in by questioning the existence of dance culture. It's bad enough being attacked by the wider press, but when your own press start attacking you, you know there's something wrong. There was a very negative vibe in the UK at that time. Not just with dance culture but generally.

Obviously, the worst didn't happen when it came to the predicted demise of dance culture, thank God, but instead of trying to fight both that and the cloud of negativity that seemed to be sitting above the nation, I decided to use it all as a catalyst, not just to up sticks and leave the UK, but to quit one industry which I was at the top of in favour of another in which I barely even registered.

Back in the mid-1990s I'd written and produced a couple of tracks for a British film called *Shopping* starring Jude Law and Sadie Frost, and a couple of years later a track for the godawful remake of *Get Carter* starring Sylvester Stallone. As you know, I'd been harbouring ambitions about writing film music ever since I was a teenager, and when the offers finally arose I was ecstatic. Had I not been remixing and producing other acts, touring with U2 and on the verge of attempting to conquer America, etc., then I would definitely have pursued it there and then. It was just bad timing. Six or seven years on I was in a very different position, as was the genre I'd been championing all these years. It was better in the States, but less so in the UK.

The thing that made me pack my bags and buy a plane ticket of the one-way variety was a telephone call from the film producer, Joel Silver. He was about to produce a film starring John Travolta and Halle Berry called *Swordfish* and wanted to know if I'd be interested in providing the music. Not just a couple of tracks, but the entire score. At this moment in time I can't think of a comparison from my work as a DJ with regards to what it did to me emotionally. It was stratospheric. Me, scoring a Hollywood movie?

When I walked into Joel's office for our first face-to-face meeting, my excitement went into overdrive as although I'd obviously heard of Joel Silver, I wasn't that familiar with his CV. The posters on the wall educated me very quickly and I was left in no doubt about the man's credentials. *Brewster's Millions*, *The Matrix*,

HE SHOOTS, HE SCORES

48 Hrs., Commando, Jumping Jack Flash, Lethal Weapon, Die Hard, Predator. It just went on and on and the more posters I saw the more enthusiastic – and nervous – I became.

I had a good long chat with Joel and although he didn't go into any details, during the conversation he happened to mention the budget. 'We're talking about a $100-million movie here,' he said, or something to that effect. And this was over twenty years ago when $100 million was a lot of money! I tried to appear nonchalant but I think I failed miserably. A hundred million bucks. That's almost as much as I earned at Cream every week.

I later found out that one of the reasons Joel asked me to score the movie was because during their research for the film, which is all about coding, they'd spent some time with some people in Silicon Valley and had found out that coders generally like working to dance music. Let's face it, if you're sitting there looking at a screen for ten hours a day you won't want to listen to Adele. It'd do your head in. I'm not sure whether my name was mentioned during those conversations but at some point somebody must have thought of me, and thank God they did.

I left Joel Silver's office on cloud nine. Seriously, I was fucking buzzing. Right then, I thought, 'I'm going to immerse myself in this. Give it everything I've got.' At the time I genuinely believed that this would be my future. I really did.

At the time of our meeting the film was in production, and after dotting the i's and crossing the t's with Joel and his people, I was invited on to the set. They were shooting a scene in Frank Sinatra's old house which is about 40 miles outside LA, and when I arrived there with Micky, my assistant, I was completely blown away. After showing us around, Joel allowed us to sit in the producer's and director's chairs during a break in filming. 'What do you think?' said Joel. 'Are you impressed?' For one of the first times in my life I was genuinely speechless and had I been able to vocalise the words that were in my head, I'd have said something along the lines of, 'Well of course I'm fucking impressed, you dollop. I'm on a Hollywood film set!' I remember looking at Micky who was in Joel's chair and he looked back at me as if to say, 'Don't look at me, mate. I'm as speechless as you are.' About ten minutes later Joel came walking up with what looked like not one, but two Halle Berrys. 'This is Paul,' he said to the Halles. He's going to be scoring the film. It turned out to be Halle Berry and her double, but I could barely tell the difference.

Because I'd already written a couple of tracks for movies, I was already vaguely familiar with the process of writing a film score, which is basically – and I mean very basically – to enhance various cues you're given. If it's a love situation you go in that direction and if it's action you go in another. I could be wrong but I have a feeling that Joel and his people thought that I was a little bit further down the line with regards to writing film music, but I wasn't going to say anything. If I had I might have lost the job. I had faith in my abilities and had I had serious doubts about whether I could deliver I'd have turned the job down. Or would I? I'm not sure to be honest. I'm as brave as I am daft sometimes.

One thing I did do was confide in one of Joel's assistants, a lovely lady called Melina. Not because of a lack of confidence in my abilities, but because I was a new boy in town and was actually slightly nervous. I've always been a firm believer in the notion that you should always treat people as you'd have them treat you, and because I was always very polite to Melina and her colleagues, which perhaps they weren't used to, she went out of her way to help. Once again it was about building the right network of people and as important as the bigwigs such as Joel Silver undoubtedly are, he wasn't going to help me in this situation. In fact, he might have seen it as a weakness and fired me. I was once told by my dad that if you ever work in an office you should always get to know the boss and the receptionist. It was the same principle here. He knew what he was talking about.

In the time-honoured tradition of being a serial remixer and seeing potential in other people's work, instead of scoring the entire movie from scratch like I'd originally planned, I decided to amalgamate some existing tracks too. This happens all the time, of course, but instead of using the originals, or even existing remixes, I reworked them all especially for the film. I used 'Unafraid' by Jan Johnston, 'New Born' by Muse, 'The Word' by Dope Smugglaz, 'Kneel Before Your God' by Lemon Jelly, 'On Your Mind' by Patient Saints, 'Lapdance' by N*E*R*D and 'Planet Rock' by Afrika Bambaataa and the Soul Sonic Force which became a hit in the UK.

For certain parts of the film we thought that orchestral music might be more appropriate so Joel drafted in a lovely man called Christopher Young. This was arguably the most intimidating part of the whole experience as I went from basically working alone with an engineer to working with him and – count 'em – a seventy-five-piece orchestra. To say it was overwhelming would almost be an understatement, but I did my best to hide it. Everything had gone swimmingly so far and Joel and the director, Dominic Sena, seemed happy with what I'd been producing, not to mention the ideas I'd been coming up with. Was I finally about to be found out? I think they call it imposter syndrome these days and when I first walked into the room where the orchestra was situated I had it big time.

I've worked with orchestras many times since then, but probably my most nerve-wracking experience happened in 2007 when I was invited by the composer Felix Brenner to join him onstage at the Boston Symphony Hall to perform a composition of his alongside the world famous Boston Pops Orchestra. It was the

Boston Pops who actually commissioned Felix to write the piece and the idea was that while the orchestra, which was a ninety-six-piece orchestra this time, played Felix's composition, I would mix digital instrumentation and samples of the original music over the orchestra using turntables, CD players, effects and electronic keyboards. A drummer was brought in to add further texture so it was basically a live remix. I've been in situations before where an orchestra has been accompanying the music I'm playing, such as the gig I told you about at the O2 very recently, but never the other way around. When an orchestra is following you, only they can mess up and because there are usually multiple players of each instrument nobody really notices. When you're following them there really is no place to hide, and despite the fact that we rehearsed it long and hard when it came to the performances – I had to do it twice in front of almost three thousand people a time – it was bloody petrifying. Fortunately it went down a storm, but it could have been very different.

The only way I could get over having to work with so many people on the *Swordfish* soundtrack was to keep on reminding myself that I was there for a reason and Christopher, who I ended up getting on very well with, never once tried to patronise me. We were in a similar boat really as he was an orchestral composer having to complement what was ostensibly an electronic score that I'd started. The trick to our relationship was communication. Communication and a mutual respect. And tequila.

Like Joel, Christopher, who's about five years older than me, had worked on some big films in his time and I was more than happy to defer to his experience. What made it easier was that he was keen on taking as many of my ideas on board as possible, so it actually turned into a genuine collaboration. It did take some getting used to though. At first there was a barrier because, despite us both being musicians, we spoke very different languages, and for the first few days nothing was getting through. On either side. When I spoke he'd sit looking at me open-mouthed and vice versa. It was funny, but it was alarming too as without being able to communicate it wasn't going to work. Slowly but surely things started to get through, and from then on it became a blizzard of ideas.

Bearing in mind I was interested in forging a career in the film music industry at the time, this was obviously an opportunity to take a lot of very important stuff on board, and after that initial trepidation and the language barrier I grabbed it. There are some people you just click with creatively and Christopher was one of them.

On the flip side to this, about two years later I was asked to work with the Wachowskis on their film, *The Matrix Reloaded*. A film music co-ordinator called Jason Bentley got me the job and although it was just a couple of cues, it was a huge opportunity. I met the Wachowski brothers at their offices and they told me exactly what they wanted, and so off I went. After delivering something that I believed met their brief, they immediately got in touch to say that it was all wrong. 'OK,' I said. 'Tell me what I need to do to put it right and I'll do it.' I forget how many times I went back to them but each time I did I got the same reaction. 'It's all wrong, Paul.' Luckily I'm not precious about things like this and I appreciated the fact that it was their vision I was trying to bring to life. Subsequently, I ended up having to work a full twenty-four-hour shift before they were happy and I almost lost the plot!

What that initial experience with *Swordfish* taught me, in addition to the fact that, if not the whole of my long-term future, film music would play at least a part in it, was that I should really start thinking about finding myself somewhere to live and settle down instead of living out of a suitcase in a hotel. After having lived in LA for a few months I knew that I'd made the right decision. I enjoyed the vibe, not to mention the weather, and now had a couple of friends out there. It was all good. Because the life of a DJ is so transient, unless you have a residency, of course, it doesn't really matter where you live, but with industries such as the movies it's obviously different, and especially when you're trying to make your mark. Look at actors and actresses. They all migrate to Hollywood when they're trying to make it big. You have to be where it's at.

At the time I'd been living on Connaught Square which is close to Marble Arch and I was actually really happy there. I had a lovely house in a lovely area and had a lovely life. It was perfect. As soon as I realised that *Swordfish* might not be just a one-off gig, that all went out of the window and the only thing I could think about was being close to the action. I was over there for three months to write *Swordfish* and almost every day that passed I received a telephone call asking if I'd be interested in a job of some kind. Most of them were just cues, so one or two tracks, but some of the films were massive. Tim Burton's remake of *Planet of the Apes* was one of the early ones. The composer of the film, Danny Elfman, is a genuine Hollywood A-lister as far as score is concerned, and working with him was amazing. After that there was *The Bourne Identity* starring Matt Damon, then *Collateral* with Tom Cruise. I also did some tracks for the *Blade II* soundtrack just after *Swordfish*. Seriously, it was a mad old time.

Twenty years on and I'm still living in LA, although I'm about to move to Austin. I must have worked on at least twenty film scores in that time – a mixture of cues and complete scores – and I've got to a point where, although not what you'd call an established film composer, I've had enough experience and have enough contacts to not have to be on the doorstep. What excites me about Austin is that it's new and fresh and, despite it being full of talent and promise, doesn't have a reputation of being a big music town. In a way it's like dance music was when me and the other DJs started taking it mainstream. There are no boundaries and no preconceived ideas. Just a load of talent, an amazing vibe, some incredible venues and a whole lotta promise. Whether it becomes a musical Mecca or not isn't the point. What's made me want to move there is the prospect of being at the start of something that, whichever way it goes, I fully believe in.

Apart from writing and producing the soundtrack to a film, which had been an ambition of mine for donkey's years, the primary ambition I had at this point in my life that would fit nicely within the parameters of breaking new ground was putting out a song-based album of my own material, from pop and big-beat to trance. And, under my own name. I'd released lots of different albums under pseudonyms such as IRS and Grace, but nothing under Paul Oakenfold, or just Oakenfold, as it would transpire.

Although it had been an ambition of mine to eventually release some songs under my own name, it had always been quite a quiet one and the reason for that is because I had reservations about potentially becoming a pop star. That's actually underplaying it somewhat. I was shit scared! Suddenly being thrust into the lime-light and doing talk shows was the stuff of nightmares as far as I was concerned. Even as a DJ, ever since breaking America that had become quite a regular thing and it made me feel uncomfortable. The thing is, if you won't promote a single then the record label won't get behind it, and if the record label don't get behind it, it won't become a hit. Why then, you'll be asking yourselves, would Paul Oakenfold want to produce an album full of potential chart songs under his own name?

It was actually Steve Osborne who persuaded me to do it as in his eyes, after all the remixing and production work, it was a natural progression. Also, the whole superstar DJ thing was still in full flow and despite my reservations about becoming a pop star I was overcome by the opportunity. Not just of making a potentially successful record, but by being ahead of the game by becoming the first ever DJ to release an album of mainstream songs under their own name. Another consideration, which was part of Steve's argument, was that over the last ten years or so he and I – either separately or together – had made hits for literally dozens of bands and artists. 'Why not make some of your own?' he said. Easier said than done, of course, but it was worth a try.

Actually, I almost forgot what is perhaps the biggest consideration of all. You see, when I started working on *Bunkka* in the year 2000, I still hadn't realised my dream of composing a soundtrack for a film, and one of the reasons it hadn't happened was because nobody recognised me as a composer. In the last few months alone I'd been in the Top 10 twice with songs I'd co-written – 'Bullet in the Gun' and the *Big Brother* theme – yet because they'd appeared as pseudonyms nobody knew.

Despite making the decision to go ahead, I decided to keep quiet about it and didn't go public about the project until the album was complete almost two years later. I'm not sure why that was really. I was changing management at the time though, and that had been weighing heavily on my mind for a long while. It just never seemed like the right time.

When it came to finding a label for the record, the favourites initially were London-Sire. That is until Madonna's label Maverick made an approach. I'd recently remixed a hit for Madonna called 'American Life' and she and I had become friends.

The first time I met Madonna I was on my knees rifling through a box of records. Her manager and mine shared an office at the time and I'd popped in for a visit. I just looked up and there she was. Funnily enough, the first time I met U2 I was on my knees rifling through a bunch of records. This will probably surprise some people but in my experience the bigger the artist or the star the less attitude they have. I know there'll always be exceptions but perhaps I've just been lucky. As well as being very polite, Madonna is also extremely charismatic and I won't pretend that the above didn't have a bearing when it came to choosing between London-Sire and Maverick.

The next thing I needed to do after choosing a label was to get myself out of London. All the management shit had been getting to me and if I was going to produce something decent I needed to escape. I ended up setting up camp at Peter Gabriel's studio near Bath which is called Real World. There are several studios at Real World including The Big Room, The Wood Room and The Red Room, but none of those seemed right. They were all massive and I needed something more intimate. In the end the staff there suggested a room that Peter Gabriel used to use but wasn't advertised called the *Bunkka*. It was perfect. Not just as a studio, but as a name for the project. I loved it.

The biggest problem I had once I started writing the album was choosing the style of music, or should I say styles of music. In the end I opted for a kind of soundtrack to my life, so something incorporating pop, which had influenced me heavily as a child and as a teenager, hip hop, indie and dance, of course. Every element of who I was musically, apart from perhaps film music, had to feature in that record, and did. This in itself made it a nightmare to A&R as there was no continuity. Love her or hate her, if you listen to Madonna you know it's Madonna. End of story. Therefore, when she puts out an album you don't need to worry about finding an audience, and providing the material's up to scratch, they'll love it. A&R is obviously more complex than that, but you get my drift. What I was creating was another potential Frankenstein's monster, and this time without a captive audience.

Because of my experience I ended up doing some of the A&R myself, which is when I realised how important things like continuity are. You can imagine sitting down with the head of a big radio station. 'What sort of music is it then? If it's Oakenfold I suppose it's trance.' 'Nope. There's a bit of everything really. It's eclectic.' 'Not interested.' One thing I've learned over the years is that you cannot be all things to all people all at the same time. It's impossible. To be fair, that isn't what I was trying to be. The problem I had, however, was that at no point during the writing and recording process did I sit down and think about whether a 'soundtrack to my life' was going to be a good idea.

What we did get right was the artwork for the album which we did with a man called Anton Corbijn. If you don't know the name, as well as being a world-class photographer and movie director he's also responsible for some of the most iconic music videos ever made. He's one of those people whose name and work results in words such as visionary being used and I was a big fan. I'd got to know Anton on the U2 tour and when it came to *Bunkka*'s artwork he was the first person I called. Fortunately, he was keen to get involved and after having a very long chat and sending him the material, we jumped on a plane to Marrakech for a photo shoot. The artwork he produced alone ended up winning all kinds of awards and in my mind it still looks iconic. The marketing campaign too, which was based on Anton's artwork, was absolutely on the nail, so providing the material was up to scratch, regardless of it being eclectic, *Bunkka* still had a chance of doing well.

Ah yes. The material. The first track I worked on for *Bunkka* was 'Ready Steady Go', a trance effort featuring Asher D from So Solid Crew on vocals. Although it wasn't part of a soundtrack, 'Ready Steady Go' had been written with TV and film in mind, so to all intents and purposes it was a musical trailer for a movie that hadn't been made. That's the best way of describing it. I was absolutely obsessed with soundtracks at the time, so although the material doesn't always allude to that, that was the basis for much of the album. Rather ironically, not to mention happily, 'Ready Steady Go' has gone on to be used in several soundtracks including *The Bourne Identity*, *Collateral* and *Stormbreaker*, not to mention a shedload of TV ads. In fact, I do believe that, globally, 'Ready Steady Go' is still my most successful record to date. Not from a sales point of view but the whole caboodle – films, charts and TV, etc.

That is the way forward though – singles that cross over. People just aren't interested in bodies of work like albums any more. We're back to the attention span thing again. Look at Calvin Harris. He's made four or five studio albums since he started out which have done OK, but he's either produced, written or collaborated on an absolute ton of successful singles. It's like The Beatles in reverse really. They started off as a singles band, which is what the public wanted at the time, and graduated to an albums band. Basically, the whole thing has gone full circle and we're back to 1962.

Because of the different genres featured on *Bunkka*, and because I can't sing for toffee, I ended up having a lot of guests on the album, anyone from Tricky, Nelly Furtado and Perry Farrell to Ice Cube, Tiff Lacey and the Icelandic singer, Emilíana Torrini. I even had the legendary author and journalist Hunter S. Thompson on the album. Now there hangs a tale. Actually, let me tell you about that one first. I might need a drink afterwards.

I must confess that although I was up for keeping things as eclectic as possible on *Bunkka*, I hadn't really envisaged collaborating with a journalist and author. Least of all one who had a reputation for being constantly angry and who could destroy people at the drop of a hat using either the written or spoken word. The reason I thought of Hunter was because a lot of people I knew at the time seemed to be reading his 1971 novel, *Fear and Loathing in Las Vegas*. A film adaptation of the book starring Johnny Depp had been released a year or two previously, so that had obviously rekindled people's interest. As well as reading the book, which took me an age but I enjoyed, I started researching Mr Thompson and the more I read the more fascinated I became. He was the man behind something called gonzo journalism which is a style of journalism that features the author as its protagonist, simultaneously experiencing and reporting on a story from a first-person point of view. He also had a reputation for speaking his mind and being a bit of a hellraiser, and although I had no actual ideas as to how we might collaborate, I asked my A&R man for the album, Ricardo, to see if he could make contact.

It took a while but Ricardo managed to get Hunter's number and after ringing him up he explained who he was and why he was calling. 'FUCK YOU!' shouted Hunter, and then put down the receiver. When Ricardo reported back to me I apologised for having put him through that and then thought about what to do. By now I'd spent so much time thinking about Hunter S. Thompson and researching him that I just couldn't let it go, so instead of leaving it I decided to write him a letter. I don't know the exact story but apparently Hunter's assistant at the time, Anita, who ended up becoming his wife, intercepted the letter and so before he could read it and then send me a tirade of expletives or just put it in the bin, Anita explained who I was and, as importantly, that what I was suggesting might be something worth doing. A few days later I received a letter from Hunter saying that, and I quote, 'You are the soundtrack to youth and one of the most sincere artists of your generation.' I don't know if it was the letter itself, Anita's intervention or a mixture of both that changed his mind and made him bestow upon me such a massive compliment, but I didn't care. We were on!

The first thing I did was ring Hunter up for a chat which gave me a chance to tell him more about the album and the kind of material we'd created so far. This led to another call and then another until Hunter finally suggested that we should meet in LA. 'Meet me at my hotel,' he said. 'At midnight.' It was a funny old time to hold a meeting but I didn't mind, and after buying him a bottle of absinthe on the way to the hotel by way of a present, after having read an interview with Johnny Depp in which he said that Hunter liked it, I went to his hotel, found his room and knocked on the door. When Hunter answered it was clear that he'd had a few and he greeted me like a long-lost brother. 'Come and meet some of my friends,' he said ushering me in. These 'friends' of his happened to be Keanu Reeves and Sam Shepard and it took all my legendary poise and restraint not to stand there open-mouthed and say something like, 'Fuck me! Hello, boys. How are ya?'

About half an hour later Sam and Keanu did one, which left Hunter S. Thompson, me, a DAT machine and a bottle of absinthe. I left the DAT machine running throughout the entire conversation. We talked about politics, football, the Hells Angels, who he'd once spent a year riding with in order to research a book about them, and of course, drugs. As he was talking I tried to make him move around the room more as when he did he became a lot more animated. Then, just as he was giving me a brilliant story about a politician he'd met, there was a knock at the door and in walked Sean Penn. Then, a minute or two later Harry Dean Stanton shuffled in. Apparently Jack Nicholson had been in there shortly before I arrived. He knew everyone! I wish to hell I hadn't brought the absinthe though. I'd never had any before and within half an hour I'd lost the power of speech and sight. I was a wreck! Hunter, who was already three sheets to the wind when I arrived, had most of the bottle to himself and he was absolutely fine.

After finally getting down to business and discussing our collaboration we settled on an idea based around the American dream and ended up calling it 'Nixon's Spirit'. Hunter wanted to talk about being young and having dreams, and the way that society tells you that as you get older there are certain things you can and can't do. I went back the following night to complete the conversation and once again he had half of Hollywood either on the phone or coming through the door. 'Hang on a minute,' he said at one point. 'I've got Johnny Depp on the phone. Yes, Johnny. Whaddaya want? I'm busy.' I think everyone was terrified of him to a certain extent, but everyone was also fascinated. He was a genuine one-off.

Although the sessions with Hunter went well and I got what I wanted, including an appalling hangover and a couple of autographs, when it came to his remuneration things didn't go quite as smoothly. A lawyer in London was dealing with that side of things and when she sent Hunter the contract (she'd been instructed to write the most anodyne contract possible as we knew he could be volatile) she received a reply that would have made the devil himself blush. I have it framed on my office wall and as a piece of expressive literature it is first class. It's a series of highly graphic and extremely fearsome insults basically and ends with a description of exactly where and how he's going to stuff the lawyer's head once he's ripped it off and then what he intends doing with the corpse. It's a depraved masterpiece, but what makes it even more special is that it was cc'd to Johnny Depp, Sean Penn, David Letterman, Don Johnson, Nick Nolte and about ten other people I've never heard of.

The poor lawyer was in tears when she received it and after sending her a big bunch of flowers and an apology, I instructed her to pay Hunter what he wanted. I should have seen it coming really. We'd gone from him telling me to fuck off to us having a really good and productive time together, so it was time for another insult. This one, though, was just epic.

I'm pretty sure that our collaboration was one of the last things Hunter did as in February 2005 he ended up taking his own life. Despite what happened at the end I was really upset. He was obviously a very complicated human being, but if you cut through all the booze and drugs and the vitriol he could be very kind and very sweet. Not to mention a master of the written and spoken word, of course. It was a real shame.

What's almost as interesting as the tracks that ended up on *Bunkka* are the ones that didn't quite make it. For a start there was a collaboration with Billy Corgan from Smashing Pumpkins that unfortunately didn't quite make the grade. I'm not quite sure what went wrong but neither of us were really happy with the result so we just left it. That does happen sometimes and as mouth-watering as a collaboration might seem sometimes, if it doesn't work you have to move on.

There was one omission from the album that to this day gives me a knot in my stomach. I'd decided to write an operatic track for *Bunkka* – I know, it was a bit left field – and hired the services of an operatic soprano called Summer Watson. The track, which was about nine minutes long, contained some samples from the second movement of the third symphony of a then living Polish composer called Henryk Górecki who, for the symphony's libretto, had used religious texts. When it came to seeking clearance from Górecki, he claimed that because we'd only taken bits of the symphony, the words could be taken out of context, even though they were in Polish. We tried to seek a compromise but he just wasn't having it, and so in the end, very reluctantly, I had to walk away.

The biggest chart hit from *Bunkka* was 'Starry Eyed Surprise', a catchy little pop tune that I wrote and performed with Shifty

Shellshock from the American rap rock band, Crazy Town. The idea for the song came from the soundtrack to the movie *Midnight Cowboy*, which was scored by a hero of mine, John Barry. It's a well-known fact that I am a James Bond fanatic (there's even a Bond chapter later on) and it's still my opinion that the late Mr Barry is responsible for some of the most iconic film scores ever written. The man was a genius, end of. Anyway, I was sitting watching *Midnight Cowboy* one night when suddenly I heard a guitar loop on the title track, 'Everybody's Talkin'', which was written by a man called Fred Neil and sung by Harry Nilsson. A good song is like a good painting, in that you notice something new every time you listen. I must have heard that song at least a hundred times yet had never noticed the loop. Within a minute I was sitting on my sofa playing this loop on my guitar. I had no idea what I was going to do with it at the time, but I was hooked.

The first idea that came to me when I started working on it was to turn it into a rap record and ran it past first LL Cool J and then Jurassic 5. Neither were particularly interested so I put it to bed for a while. A few weeks later I was doing a show in Seattle and came across a band called Crazy Town. Apparently they'd just had a big hit with a tune called 'Butterfly' but to be honest I'd never heard of them. They were on the same bill as me though so I went out to watch them. The singer, a white rapper called Shifty Shellshock who was also the group's lyricist, reminded me a bit of Shaun Ryder (sounds mad but there were similarities) and after the gig I asked him if he'd be interested in adding a lyric to the tune I'd now come up with based on the guitar loop. I gave him a brief, which was basically partying and getting wasted, and left him to it. When he came back with his effort I was shocked at first. It was basically an out-and-out pop lyric and all I could think about initially was what the dance music industry would do to me, not to mention my core fans. Discounting film music, just about everything I'd released before now had fitted somewhere within the genre of electronic dance music.

One of the first people I played it to was Marc Marot who'd looked after U2 at Island Records. 'It'll be a smash,' he said. 'I guarantee it.' 'Really?' I replied. 'But it's pop.' 'So what?' said Marc. 'It's hot.' I suppose I felt slightly embarrassed. I shouldn't have, but I did. I was part of the dance music establishment and was about to sell out. At least that's how some people would see it. It wasn't a case of me being disloyal to the genre exactly. More a case of whether the genre, and its audience, would remain loyal to me. In my mind, I'd simply found something that I think worked and wanted to try it out. It was all part of my obsession with breaking new ground, I suppose, so was I about to be hoisted by my own petard? We'd have to see.

Despite the majority of people believing I had a hit on my hands, I was hesitant about including the tune on *Bunkka*. In fact, I was adamant we wouldn't. This was a kind of compromise, in my mind. Letting the dance industry and my core audience know that instead of selling out and becoming a pop star it was just a one-off. A moment of madness, if you like. Unfortunately, when it came to being adamant, the people at Maverick put me to shame and the conversation as to whether it would be included on the album didn't last more than about two or three minutes. They had me over a barrel and it was fair enough. After all, what record company in their right mind would agree to exclude the most commercially promising song from an album?

Within just a few weeks, Maverick's decision to include 'Starry Eyed Surprise' on the album was justified, at least commercially. After playing it to Capital Radio they decided to use it for their TV advert a full three months before it was released. This meant that when the song did finally appear it went straight in at number six in the UK and received more radio play than any of us could ever have wished for.

It ended up going Top 10 in no fewer than twenty-three countries and went some way to ensuring that *Bunkka*, which had been released two months before, went on to sell well over a million copies. In order to try and combat the possibility of me turning into a pop star, which was brought well and truly home to me in America one day when I was asked to appear on the annual Kiss FM Jingle Ball alongside Destiny's Child and Justin Timberlake, I decided to turn the whole thing into a concept as opposed to a solo record, and after dropping my Christian name and just using Oakenfold I assembled a band around me for live performances and promo appearances. I had a guitarist, a drummer, Shifty Shellshock on vocals, another vocalist called Spitfire, and I was on keyboards.

When it came to playing songs with other vocalists we just had videos of them on a screen behind us as it would have been too expensive to take everyone on tour. I'm not sure if it prevented the world and his wife from completely disbelieving that I was morphing into a pop star but it certainly made me feel better. All in all, and despite the lack of direction, I was happy with *Bunkka*. I've made two more artist albums since then – *A Lively Mind* and *Trance Mission* – and have another coming out in 2022, but I think that might be it as far as studio albums are concerned. As I've already said, people just aren't interested in this kind of stuff any more. They want it short and they want it sharp, and who am I to argue? Give the public what they want, that's what I say.

CHAPTER 20

Madonna

When Madonna and Maverick signed me, the only other dance act they had on their books at the time was The Prodigy which made us kind of special. I don't mean that in an arrogant way but because we presented a different set of opportunities to the label we received a different kind of attention. This went to a different level when I started remixing more and more of Madonna's material which eventually lead to me co-writing and producing a couple of tracks with her. These were basically bonus material for a new *Greatest Hits* LP she was releasing and one of them became the single 'Celebration' which went to number one all over the world.

Anyway, in 2006 I received a telephone call from Madonna's manager, Guy Oseary, asking me if I'd like to go on tour with her. Given the amount of material of hers I'd remixed and the fact that her audience would be, if not a dance audience necessarily, at least dance-orientated, I ripped his hand off. The last time I'd done a tour on this scale was with U2, but with an audience who'd be more on my side, so to speak, I was keen to see what the difference would be. I wouldn't be disappointed.

You might not believe this but my rider for this tour was bigger than Madonna's, the dancers and the musicians put together.

For a start she doesn't drink and neither did the dancers or musicians. Apart from a bit of food, that's all there was to it. I, on the other hand, had about twenty bottles of beer and a few bottles of wine on my rider. On any other tour, and certainly in a nightclub, that would have seemed pathetic, but on this tour it made me seem like the Rolling Stones in their heyday.

The main difference between this and the U2 tour, apart from being the only drinker and the fact that I was a bit older and more worldly wise, was the atmosphere. Although joyous at times, the mood at a U2 concert is a roller coaster and over the course of an evening they'll evoke every emotion. That's the nature of their material and the audience are obviously prepared for that. With a Madonna gig, there's only one thing on people's minds and that's to have a good time. No ups and downs and no politics. Just anticipation, passion and freedom. It's the kind of audience I'm used to really and I fed off that big time.

By far the most difficult audience I've ever had to cope with, as in we were absolutely poles apart, was the one I encountered when I opened for Lenny Kravitz. The audience was primarily straight and white and I died an absolute death. It felt similar to the main stage crowd at Glastonbury that I'd encountered years before, but with none of that spirit you get at a festival. And it wasn't through want of trying. I moved it around all over the place but it didn't make any difference. They just stood there like robots. Literally. The problem you have with someone like Lenny Kravitz is that his audience, unlike Madonna's or even U2's, aren't easy to define and despite doing my research I found them hard to pin down. Even if I had managed to identify them, I'm not sure it would have made any difference. It was one of those situations when it felt like they'd made up their minds beforehand that they weren't going to have a good time, at least with me on the stage. We're back to the old adage that nobody's there to see the support act so I shouldn't really grumble. You live and learn.

The thing that U2 and Madonna have in common is their approach to what they do and once again, if it hadn't been for what I learned from U2 I'm not sure I'd have lasted very long with Madonna. This really came to light when she invited me to write and produce with her. As well as being an amazing performer her professionalism was the thing I'd noticed most when we were on tour, so when it came to entering the studio I made sure I was on point. When she arrived at 9am I'd been there since 7.30am prepping, so when she walked through the door and said, 'I'm ready,' I said, 'OK, so am I.' It was one of the few situations, certainly in a studio environment, when I've felt nervous. Partly because it was Madonna, but mainly because I had no idea how she liked to work. Complete honesty is a prerequisite in that environment and there were going to be times when I'd have to tell her that I didn't like what she'd sung or that she'd sung something wrong. It was a daunting prospect. It shouldn't have been, but it was. Because my approach was as professional as hers, and because I explained everything when I did pull her up, she was fine. Forthright, but fine.

In 2013 I produced a song for Cher called 'Woman's World' and that was a completely different experience. She has her own vocal producer so you get what they deliver, end of. This makes it easier in a way but the lack of input can be frustrating.

I ended up doing three world tours with Madonna and if you take into account the songs we wrote together and the remixes – not to mention the fact that I signed to her label, of course – I've probably collaborated more with her than any other artist or band. The thing I admire most about Madonna is her ability to move with the times and tap into the current zeitgeist. Not everybody can do that, believe me, which is why so many people get left behind. Madonna's ruthless in that department, although I think that most of us would agree that she's now reached a similar stage in her career as, for instance, the Rolling Stones, U2, Queen and Paul McCartney, whose fame and relevance, although significant, is primarily down to what they've done, as opposed to what they're doing now. Like it or not, nobody's interested in them making new music any more, no matter how good it might be. In fact, if you went to see the Rolling Stones in concert and you heard Mick Jagger say the words, 'Here's a song from our new album,' I guarantee that the audience would let out a collective groan. She may or may not like it, but that's exactly where Madonna is now. Give them the hits and enjoy the experience. That's what I say.

CHAPTER 21

Viva Las Vegas

To paraphrase the creator of the modern dictionary, Dr Johnson, which I'm sure you've been expecting me to do since the very beginning of my book, when a man is tired of Ibiza he is tired of life. Well, in addition to not being tired of the place – far from it, in fact – in 2007 I had an idea based on what I'd been doing in Ibiza that would once again ruffle a few feathers and raise more than a few eyebrows within the EDM establishment. Basically, I wanted to take Ibiza to America.

To be fair, things had been levelling off in Ibiza for a while and although it was still popular and a lot of fun it seemed to have lost its way a bit. Instead of waiting for something to happen I decided to have a go at recreating the island's glory days else-where, and because I was living in the States that seemed like the natural choice. The question was, where? LA was my first thought as that was my home but the restrictions with things like opening hours and fire marshals made it a non-starter. 'OK then,' I thought. 'What about New York?' Again, this didn't get past first base as the flight time alone, which is over five hours, would have made it impossible for me, not to mention the time difference. Sure, I could have relocated, but I was happy in LA and felt like I'd already done New York. The only other obvious option was Miami and although it's a shorter flight it was still too far. This created a quandary as LA, New York and Miami were still the only cities in America where EDM was established in all its forms. If I was going to go ahead I'd have to find somewhere new and basically rewrite the rule book. Given what I already knew about America I saw this as an opportunity and the more I thought about it the more convinced I became that America was ready for a fourth hub.

For about two days I sat there with a map of America in front of me trying to figure out which town or city might buy into the full Ibiza experience but there was nowhere obvious. The country seemed to have accepted the fact that it had three hubs for EDM and that was that. Still not disheartened, I decided to take an exploratory trip to Las Vegas which, as well as being the enter-tainment capital of the world, was much closer to home. Even so, the EDM scene there, although not exactly underground, was still very much in its infancy and trying to turn it into a hub would be a monumental task.

Throughout the 1990s there'd been parties held at various locations throughout Las Vegas but it was only in 1996 that the scene started going mainstream. The catalyst was something called the Desert Move Party which was the first of its kind to attract sponsors and receive radio station support. You could also purchase tickets through the likes of Ticketmaster, which had never happened before, and some of the acts they had on in those early days included Josh Wink and Derrick May. The parties used to take place in the desert outside the town and everyone would be taken there by bus. It was like a shorter, less bohemian, and far more commercial version of Burning Man, I suppose, and would attract every key player from the local scene.

Sometime after that a nightclub called Utopia opened which, by 2007, which is when I arrived and started exploring, was still the only place of its kind on the strip. Build-up and tear-down events such as Desert Move continued appearing, but that was the closest Utopia came to having any kind of competition and the closest Las Vegas came to having an EDM scene worth talking about and one that actually might attract partygoers from elsewhere.

The opportunity then was obvious. Or was it? Perhaps things hadn't happened for a reason. After all, the actual population of Las Vegas is zilch and any kind of major club scene would, just like Ibiza, have to rely on a high turnover of visitors. At first that put me off the idea slightly as I wasn't sure if the traditional Las Vegas audience would be up for it, which would basically mean we'd be trying to attract a brand new market. Half of me had a kind of 'build it and they will come' sort of attitude and the other half was saying 'run to the hills'. What made me lean towards the former was the fact that I knew literally hundreds, if not thousands of like-minded people who visited Las Vegas on a regular basis so although I didn't have the exact figures I knew that times were changing.

After deciding to look more closely at the idea I began thinking about a suitable venue, and the only one that sprang to mind was Palms Casino Resort which is just off the strip. The reason I thought of Palms was because a popular MTV reality show called *The Real World* had been filmed there and everything about the place seemed to be geared towards catering for younger people. It was also run by younger people and they even had a recording studio there. It seemed perfect.

After approaching the people in charge they gave me a guided tour and I was well impressed. The nightclub held about five thousand people, which was well big enough, and it felt perfect. My idea, by the way, if you haven't already guessed, was to become the first major DJ ever to have a residency in Las Vegas. Not only that, I wanted it to be my production so instead of just turning up and playing once a week I'd have a hand in every aspect.

What I think was changing in Las Vegas, in terms of entertainment, was that instead of the place being overrun with crooners, magicians or the Céline Dions of this world, you were starting to get some pop acts playing there. This wasn't a clear indication that an EDM revolution was on the cards but for the first time ever it was a definite possibility. What also made it a possibility was the ethos of the town, not to mention its licensing laws. There are no rules in Vegas and if we wanted to remain open until 4am or beyond we knew that it wouldn't be a problem.

After finally deciding to go for it I set about building a team around me and then started thinking about a concept. As I just said, there are no rules in Las Vegas (or at least ones that people take any notice of) and the show would have to reflect that. We couldn't just chuck up a few big screens and some lasers. It had to be a production, and in the Las Vegas sense of the word.

For a few years now the Perfecto brand had been going from strength to strength. The label was doing really well and we'd been using the name for all the spin-offs such as tours. With that in mind we decided to call the concept Planet Perfecto which is the name we'd adopted for the project behind 'Bullet in the Gun', which was actually me, Ian Masterson and Jake Williams. With the name of the night all sorted, which was eventually elongated to 'Paul Oakenfold Presents Planet Perfecto at Rain', which was the name of the club, we started thinking about the production. I got my inspiration from three sources: the Burning Man Festival, The Australian Pink Floyd Show, which I'd seen a few times and was a fan of, and Cirque du Soleil. We had a fire show, screens the size of double-decker buses, trapeze artists, men on stilts who swept the crowd with lasers, a seven-foot-tall drag queen with a motorised grinder on his chest, arms and crotch that sent sparks flying everywhere. We even had some ninjas who would crawl along the walls and then hang from a net that was suspended above the dance floor.

As I said at the very start of the chapter, the EDM establishment were not at all impressed when they found out what I was up to, nor did they think it would work. As far as they were concerned, you only went to Las Vegas at the end of your career and they said that having somebody like me going there would potentially damage, not just my own image, but the image of the genre. 'Au contraire,' I thought when I first heard the rumours. For a start, people do not just go to Las Vegas when their careers are washed up. In fact, a lot of artists and acts actually make their careers there. Also, the whole point behind Las Vegas, as well as having a bloody good time, is to keep on reinventing things and make them bigger and better than they were before. Why on earth couldn't dance music be part of that?

The magazines in particular had a right go at me. 'His career's over,' they all said. 'He's finished.' It all seemed to mirror the kind of ungracious and hurtful comments you sometimes get in the British tabloid press and I don't mind admitting that for a short time it really pissed me off. It felt like I'd become an enemy of the establishment and it felt like they were willing me to fail. By now I had a bit of a track record for trying new things, and breaking new ground, and although not everybody liked what I did, there was no denying that the EDM industry had benefited from my endeavours. So why weren't they backing me? Were they jealous because they hadn't thought of it? All I was trying to do was put dance music on the map in Las Vegas, which just happened to be one of the biggest tourist destinations on earth. Also, unlike Ibiza, which gets a lot of repeat business, the majority of people seeing me would be doing so as a one-off, so in shopping terms we'd be talking to, and making, a lot of new customers. Anyway, I wasn't doing this for them. I was doing it for me, for the people who would hopefully come and see us, for Las Vegas, and for dance music.

All that the above did was make me even more determined to make it work and by the time the opening night was upon us we'd left no stone unturned. The team had done an amazing job and the buzz that they'd created was massive. We were ready. The venue was ready. All we needed now were the punters. Even I was surprised by the amount of press we received after opening and I was left in no doubt whatsoever that the town of Las Vegas was ready and willing to become America's new EDM hub. The move had been a good one.

One of my favourite reviews after the opening night came from the *Las Vegas Weekly* who said, 'We're not in Vegas any more, Toto. Hell, we're not even on this planet. Rain nightclub slipped the surly bonds of Earth around 11.30pm – aided in part by a sexy onscreen flight attendant – to touch the face of a god of progressive trance music, Paul Oakenfold.'

The review went on for about five paragraphs and almost every line was a compliment.

Another review I saw, but can't remember where, complimented me on the fact that, instead of playing nothing but well-known crowd-pleasers which, given how commercial things were was probably what people had been expecting, I played a lot of non-commercial tracks and promos, so despite all the visuals and special effects, the music was still paramount. A testament to this being the case, and having the desired effect, is that I received just as many questions about the music I played from the crowd in Las Vegas as I did at Cream or anywhere else.

That residency ended up lasting the best part of three years and according to the *Las Vegas Entertainment Guide* I'm something like number eight on the all-time list of the most popular artists who've appeared on or around the strip. It really was all-encompassing though. It takes everything from you.

About halfway through my tenure there, British Airways began flying daily to Las Vegas from Heathrow, and in order to promote the venture they got me and the Mayor of Vegas to help them out. I took a couple of flights, I remember, and shook a hell of a lot of hands. I also started doing Perfecto Pool Parties after that, which people have copied and are massive to this day, and then later on Perfecto Day Parties, which are also on the menu.

There then followed a tidal wave of new EDM clubs that since then have consolidated the town's position, not just as an American hub of electronic dance music, but a global hub. You had XS at the Encore at Wynn which opened about seven months after me, then Marquee at The Cosmopolitan of Las Vegas, Surrender at the Encore at Wynn, Hakkasan at the MGM Grand, LIGHT at Mandalay Bay, Zouk at Resorts World, OMNIA at Caesars Palace, JEWEL at ARIA. The list goes on and on and these days they're everywhere. In fact, between me opening in 2008 and 2015 alone, the electronic dance clubs were estimated to have contributed almost $2 billion to the Vegas economy. In addition, an EDM festival that you'll no doubt have heard of dating back to the late 1990s called Electric Daisy Carnival Las Vegas, which had hitherto been attracting modest crowds of around 50,000, suddenly began drawing in crowds of up to half a million people, giving it the title of North America's largest music festival. I'm not saying that all of that's down to me, but I certainly started it. What's more, I don't mind taking a bit of credit for it either. It was certainly a big finger up to all the industry doubters and haters, some of whom have since acknowledged the fact that, looking at the bigger picture, it might not have been a bad idea after all.

After two and a half years I was both frustrated and exhausted which is when I started making plans to quit. Most people who live in Las Vegas live in the suburbs and hardly anybody lives on the strip. Partly because it's obviously not a residential area but also because you'd never get any sleep!

Since about six months before opening I'd been spending three or four nights a week there and because what I did was quite public I rarely got a minute to myself. Then, when all the British Airways and Perfecto Pool Party stuff started happening I was spending even more time there with even less time to myself. I suppose I became wrapped up in what always happens in Las Vegas which, as I've already said, is to continually try and make everything bigger and better. That kind of hard-core commercialism isn't where I'm at and towards the end of the final year I wasn't enjoying it. You can have too much of a good thing, and I'd had a bucketful.

Everybody assumes that I must have taken a long break after Vegas but not at all. I'm OK with hard graft and providing I'm working somewhere or on something that interests me, or am putting in the hard yards required at the very beginning of a project, I'm happy. What I found frustrating and exhausting about Vegas, apart from the fact that creativity has to eventually give way to commerciality and having no time for myself or other projects, was the fact that, because it's so commercial and transient, it really has no soul. I don't mean that disrespectfully but it was almost like living on a movie set for three years, in that lots of famous and very important people would turn up day after day and lots of very important things would happen. Then, at the end of each day, they'd all leave and it would just be me. I needed my friends and family back, and I also needed to give my passport a hammering.

Since officially finishing my residency in 2011 I've been back to Vegas dozens of times. In fact, just six months after leaving I went back to do a big Halloween show at a club called Butterfly in the Chateau Las Vegas. By then the whole EDM vibe had really taken hold and the night was an absolute blast. The last time I played a major gig there was in 2019, again at Butterfly. I was also offered a new residency there about this time and after thinking about it for about five seconds I said, 'No thanks.' Covid happened soon after that so even if I'd said yes it wouldn't have happened. Not that I ever would. A residency in Las Vegas these days would be the death of me. Then again, what a way to go!

CHAPTER 22

Sound Trek

I forget when it was exactly but one day in the dim and distant past I came up with the interesting and yet potentially challenging idea of playing DJ sets in iconic places and settings around the world. It's something that over the years has taken up more and more of my time and my initial motivation was to raise the profile of dance music. After all, I've always believed that, despite having started a few in my time and having played in literally thousands, dance music should be played far and wide not just in clubs. Also, Paul Oakenfold live on Mount Everest or at Stonehenge has a much better ring to it than live in a nightclub.

The first idea I came up with, which took place in 2003, was to play a set on the Great Wall of China. I had to start with something big and, in the absence of any impending attempted moon landings that I could hitch a ride on, it seemed to fit the bill. Also, I'd already been to the Great Wall of China with Danny many years previously and however small, a link still existed. I wanted to go back.

Knowing what I know now, if we'd had that initial discussion again and somebody had suggested the Great Wall of China I'd have had them arrested. Honestly I would. For a start, the amount of permits we had to apply for was off the scale. This was understandable I suppose as we weren't attempting to hire a venue. We were attempting to hire a UNESCO World Heritage Site and one of the most famous landmarks on the planet. The Chinese government, it's fair to say, are as protective of their Great Wall as I am of my record collection and start to finish it took us well over a year to arrange. That's for one gig.

In order to make it more feasible, both logistically and financially, I coincided the event with a tour of Asia. Just like my visit to America at the end of the 1990s, I decided to go all out and play markets that no other major DJ had ever played before. Then, literally a week or two before we were due to fly to Asia from Australia and begin the tour I got a call from my manager. It was all about something called SARS which apparently was going to kill millions and he'd been advised to advise me to come home. 'Absolutely no chance,' I said to him. 'I'm having a great time. Leave me alone!' About a week later he called me again and reiterated the advice. 'We really do think you should all come home,' he said. 'Look,' I replied. 'We've got over a thousand face masks in our luggage and they're coming with us to China.'

I wasn't being gung-ho about it and when it comes to things like that I'm normally very careful. My assistant Micky and I had been watching the news, however, and had come to the conclusion that, providing we were careful, we should be OK. In fact, we probably had more chance of falling off the Great Wall than we did of catching SARS at the time.

With SARS taking up the majority of the headlines at the time, we wondered whether there'd be any space left for us, but we needn't have worried. In addition to eventually granting us permission to play the gig and film it using six cameras, they allowed members of the international press to be present. That in itself instigated a mini-tidal wave of publicity that would have cost us thousands to buy. As well as becoming the first ever DJ to play a set on the Great Wall of China, we were also raising money for charity and the two seemed to strike a chord.

The section of the wall where I'd be playing was about a two-hour drive outside Shanghai, and as we set off from the hotel the heavens began to open. Fortunately, the people of Shanghai are as used to rain as we Brits are so nobody seemed to care. The organisers, on the other hand, were not so happy. 'This is a bad sign. It's the spirits. The spirits don't want us to be here. They don't want you to be here,' they said pointing at me. 'So you want me to go home then?' I asked them. Suddenly, the suspicion lifted and we made our way from the vehicle cavalcade containing all the gear to the wall itself. The only issue we had just prior to the gig was that four of the six cameras we were using suddenly stopped working. Perhaps the spirits were pissed off after all? Or at least a bit camera shy.

Despite it being able to hold a lot more (I shudder to think how many people you could get on the Great Wall of China) the Chinese government had only allowed us to sell five hundred tickets, although the promoters ended up selling at least three times that amount. This meant that when it came to the gig itself we had people trying to get in from all angles. Apart from Mongolia, that is. It was just mad.

Despite everything – the venue, the rain, the broken cameras, the interlopers (with tickets!), and the spirits, of course – the gig went off without a hitch and I was surprised by how well it went. We later released the mix on Perfecto under the name of Perfecto Presents – Paul Oakenfold, Great Wall and it ended up selling really well.

Bizarrely enough, the majority of issues we faced with that gig, which included the preparation beforehand, actually took place sometime afterwards. I was doing something called the Thirst Tour which took me all over Asia and South America, and when it came to entering China again I was told that it wasn't happening. We'd played a gig in Hong Kong the night before and were due to play two high-profile gigs in China.

According to my manager at the time, the Chinese government were under the impression that because we were attempting to enter the country again having already played the Great Wall, we must have been part of some kind of weird subversive organisation and were ultimately a security risk. We had ten people and 15 tonnes of gear. They ended up getting me in on a tourist visa at first but the Chinese watched us like a hawk and refused to let me play. It was those bloody spirits again. I'm sure of it. After much toing and froing (not to mention one or two brown envelopes being passed around) the Chinese government relented and so the final show went ahead, which was better than nothing. Despite what we encountered I've been back to China many times since then and would go again in a heartbeat. Visually, it's a stunning place and although there's a lot that separates us, the people there love to dance and love their dance music.

It was a whole eight years before I dared to try something like that again. Partly because I just didn't have time but also because I now knew that attempting to perform live in places that are natural venues brings with it a plethora of challenges and I had to be ready for both physically and mentally.

When the time came we eventually chose a place in Argentina called Ushuaia which is the southernmost city in the world and the last inhabited place before Antarctica. 'That'll do,' I thought. There were enough people living in Ushuaia to make the gig work, at least potentially, and because of its geographical significance it should generate some publicity.

We ended up spending about a week down there and once again we tied it in with a tour. The Planet Perfecto Tour of South

America, to be exact. Saying that, the detour we had to take in order to play Ushuaia was probably about 1,000 miles, so it may as well have been a stand-alone gig. What a place though. Although it's classed as a city the population is tiny and we had to take the final leg of our journey by helicopter.

Instead of playing it safe and booking a club or a venue in Ushuaia, which would have made sense, some idiot suggested that we do a gig in the rainforest instead. An even bigger idiot called Paul Oakenfold said, 'What a good idea,' and so we set about seeing if it might be possible. You might have thought I'd have had enough of grandiose gestures like this but apparently not. Fortunately, the local government in Ushuaia were a lot easier to deal with than the Chinese government and were a lot less precious about their rainforest. Sure, there were plenty of hoops to jump through, but they made it easy for us.

I spent the first couple of days there choosing and then running through my set, and when that was all sorted the team and I decamped from the hotel in Ushuaia to the site where the gig was taking place. One of the locals offered to take us fishing when we arrived there and in a moment of pure madness my assistant Micky Jackson and I said yes. I love the great outdoors but sitting on a boat holding a fishing rod for several hours isn't my idea of fun. That trip quickly descended into chaos when, while trying to cast out, I ended up hooking Micky – literally. The wind must have taken hold of the line and the hook ended up in Micky's back. He had a coat on as thick as a duvet but Micky's always maintained that it broke his skin. There's actually a video diary on YouTube of this gig and I'm standing on the boat pissing myself laughing. Unlike Micky.

Because it was part of the Planet Perfecto Tour which was sponsored by Samsung, we managed to get plenty of PR for the gig and ended up attracting a couple of thousand people. It was winter over there so the temperatures were close to freezing but nobody cared. Although it wasn't as high profile as the gig on the Great Wall it was far less problematic and left me wanting to do more. The question was, where.

Because of work constraints, over the next three years or so I only had time to dream about where in the world I could play. It was quite fun really. In spare moments I'd think of places that would scare and excite me in equal measure and then go to bed planning the sets. The idea that kept on coming back to me time and time again was playing a gig on Mount Everest, or at least on the highest point possible which would be base camp. I'd already played at the southernmost point. Why not the highest?

As well as ticking all of the original boxes this also ticked a new box that I'd dreamt up which was to challenge myself physically. Taking dance music out of the realms of a nightclub was a challenge in itself, but apart from filling in forms, trying to get permission from various governments and overcoming numerous logistical obstacles, where was the challenge for me? I was also getting on a bit now so I thought why not kill two birds with one stone? If I'm going to do something for the betterment of dance music, why not my health? I also had a desire to push myself creatively, but until I got over there I wasn't sure how.

Another difference to the previous events was to make this more professional, so instead of throwing it in as part of an existing tour and doing a quick video diary to accompany it, I decided to make it a stand-alone project with an accompanying film. I'd also thought of a name which would be 'Soundtrek'. Not bad, eh?

Such an outrageous and outlandish idea was always going to require an outrageous and outlandish personality to help make it happen and I knew just who to call. For the past few years my old mate and partner Danny had been working as a promoter in Kathmandu (I know, he gets around) and I knew for a fact that he'd at least be able to put me in touch with somebody. A few days later Danny called me back and suggested I meet a DJ and producer who was local to Kathmandu called Ranzen. 'If anyone can help you, he can,' said Danny.

Believe it or not, Kathmandu has a thriving underground electronic music scene and when I arrived there to meet Ranzen for the first time and talk about the project I was well impressed. I even ended up DJ'ing with him at a club there and it was banging. It ain't all monks and mountains, believe me.

Ranzen put us in touch with all the right people and while my team started making the arrangements, Ranzen and I discussed how we could both make it work creatively. The original motivation, as always, had been to promote dance music and raise some money but this was becoming bigger than that. It was a coming together of cultures and in order to make it authentic I not only wanted to play alongside somebody who belonged in Nepal, but I wanted to learn what music meant to the people.

I won't bore you with the planning details as it would take weeks, but suffice to say that arranging to play a gig on Mount Everest is no easier than arranging to play a gig on the Great Wall of China. In fact, if anything it's more difficult as you can't exactly drive a truck up there with all your gear in it. Also, as dangerous as China can be sometimes we were going to be up against some of the most dangerous terrain on the planet, not to mention the weather and the altitude.

I think it took us about a year and a half to plan the gig which was half a year longer than the Great Wall. This included six months for my own training regime which started the moment we got the green light. Everest base camp is over 5,300 metres above sea level and the list of things that can go wrong at that kind of altitude is staggering. I ended up hiring the services of a very famous mountaineer called Kenton Cool, both to help me prepare and to act as our guide to base camp. At the time Kenton had no fewer than twelve Everest summits under his belt, and as well as living up to his name and being as cool as fuck he had the respect of the local people, which was so important. He also oozes confidence. The man's a legend.

With Kenton on the practical side, Ranzen on the creative side and a brilliant team of people back home sorting out the details I had all the bases covered. I thought, 'I'm coming for you, Everest.' It was going to be a doddle. Yeah, sure!

Incidentally, something that Ranzen specialises in is recording everyday sounds and then using them in his music, and before we set off to base camp he came up with the idea of recording the trek and then amalgamating some of the sounds into a piece of music that the two of us would write along the way. I couldn't think of anything that would encapsulate both the project and our burgeoning friendship better. It was perfect.

The journey from Kathmandu to base camp took almost two weeks and I could feel as we went along that the six months training had been essential. This first became apparent when we stopped off in a place called Khumjung which is in full view of Everest. The school there has a football pitch outside it and we ended up playing a match against some of the local kids. Naturally, you'd expect a bunch of Nepalese teenagers to run rings around some old farts like us, and they did. What we had not bargained for, however, was the change in altitude. Instead of being fairly useless we were worse than useless and the final score was Soundtrek United 1, Khumjung Rovers 4. Or was it 5? I can't remember. It certainly gave us a wake-up call though, that's for sure.

By far the most emotional moment on the entire trip, at least for me, happened on day eight when we stopped off at a climber's memorial (sometimes called a stupa) that's situated on a place called Dughla Pass which is in the Solukhumbu District. It had originally been built by Sherpas in 1996 in memory of a famous mountaineer called Scott Fischer and since then a rock had been added to the memorial for every mountaineer or Sherpa who had lost their lives, not just on Everest but on every Himalayan mountain. The significance of the memorial obviously means a lot to Kenton and as he told us about it he began to shed a few tears. He didn't go into any detail but you could tell that at least some of the rocks on that memorial had been placed there for people who he must have known personally. The fact that we were all very tired did nothing to quell the emotions that had clearly suffused the group, and after Kenton had finished speaking we all went off in separate directions, in some cases to have a bit of a cry, I should think, and in some cases to try not to. You know what us blokes are like.

As the trek drew to a close, thoughts about the gig itself began to invade my consciousness but because of the lack of sleep, and probably the altitude, the worries I had were somewhat inflated. How and where would we set up the equipment? Would the equipment work? Would we have an audience? What about the weather? That was obviously the big one as if it didn't play ball we'd be screwed. Eighteen months in the making, a two-week journey just to get there and it could all very easily come to nothing. Also, unlike the other two gigs no stage could be erected beforehand, so even if the weather was OK and the equipment worked it would just be a case of finding a suitable spot and then giving it a go.

Throughout that trip there were hundreds of examples of just how far me and my team were outside of our comfort zone.

That's excluding Kenton, of course, who was as happy as a pig in you know what. One of the only times we struggled collectively was when we spent our first night in a tent. For the majority of the trip we'd stayed in villages and although they weren't always comfortable at least we had a bed. Some of us had obviously slept in a tent before and some of us hadn't, but because of where we were – and because, at the end of the day, we were actually just a bunch of cosseted townies – we were all as useless as each other.

The morning after our first night in a tent was like the night before the last day on earth. Except for Kenton. As well as freezing our arses off and not being able to sleep, nobody had dared go for a pee because there were yaks walking around. Oh yes, and it was also very dark which none of us liked very much.

Before we set off on the final day of the trek, which happened to be the day after our first night in a tent, Kenton made a speech to the group. It was a proper, 'Once more unto the breach, dear friends!' affair and had we been in a bar in Kathmandu after having had eight hours' sleep each we'd have screamed in the affirmative. As it was we were all shagged out and grumpy so when Kenton called out the climax to his speech which was, 'One in, all in,' which we were all supposed to repeat there followed an incoherent collective murmur.

Although I was knackered, when I finally reached base camp later that day the sense of achievement I felt did the size of the task justice. It was massive. Everything I'd achieved over the past however many years, apart from having children, had been about music. Sure, that might have been part of the endgame, but no matter how well it went it wouldn't have anything on this. In fact, I would urge anybody my age – you know, a well-maintained forty-something – to do something like this. Not necessarily trekking to Everest base camp, but you know what I mean. Taking yourself well outside your comfort zone and pushing some boundaries. It's gotta be done.

The biggest problem I encountered once we were up there was getting to sleep. For the first night or two I was in a tent again with no mat and it just wasn't happening. Because of what it requires of you – physically and mentally – sleep is absolutely essential and if you don't get what you need you'll be in trouble. People were getting airlifted off left, right and centre so the dangers are ever-present. Luckily, they have these mini camps up there that cost a dollar a night where, as well as having heaters inside, they have little wooden benches where you can put your sleeping bag. It might not sound like much but compared to a tent on the mountain floor it was luxury and after a couple of nights in there I was fine.

When it came to choosing the set for the gig I had to take into account the fact that people wouldn't be able to dance or jump around as much as they would in a club. In addition to the altitude, which suppresses you, you're often fighting the elements up there. Whether it be sun, rain, wind or snow, it's almost always on the extreme side up there.

Some of the Sherpas, who it has to be said would make astonishing stage crew if they ever decided to switch jobs, had managed to erect a stage for us at base camp using rocks with Everest in the background. As backdrops go it was pretty damn amazing and it definitely put a spring in our steps.

I'm not sure how much truth there was in this but somebody had suggested during the trek that the music might cause an avalanche and once we'd set the gear up on the stage it became one of the main topics of conversation. I'm 90 per cent sure that it was bollocks but there was enough ambiguity floating around to make us all a bit nervous and when it came to doing the soundcheck we erred on the side of caution.

Unlike the Great Wall, where 1,500 tickets were sold for a gig where only 500 were allowed in, we had no restrictions whatsoever and we certainly didn't try and sell tickets. First of all, it's a big old space and had there been 100,000 people with a penchant for dance music trekking Mount Everest at the time there'd have been plenty of room. How on earth would you police it though? 'Sorry, sir, your name's not on the list so you're not coming in.' 'Want a bet?' You'd need about a million bouncers.

Fortunately for us, the Nepalese government, who I'm pleased to say had backed the project 100 per cent, put the word around so by the time we arrived at base camp everyone who was trekking Everest at the time, and there were literally hundreds of them, knew about the gig.

Including the Sherpas there were probably twenty or thirty people in our group and by the time our fellow trekkers arrived that number must have swelled to about two hundred. We had people from all over the world there and some of them were even fans of mine. Yes, I do still have some fans. The gig was a celebration really of everything we'd been trying to achieve and everything we'd encountered on the way – music, friendship, adventure, different cultures, camaraderie, compassion. The euphoria that created, with a bit of help from the music, of course, not to mention a few bottles of tequila that I'd managed to squeeze in the luggage, was off the scale, and to this very day I don't think I've ever experienced anything quite like it. It was a feeling of unbridled togetherness and I'll never forget it. Just as I'll never forget having to sleep in a tent on a load of rocks!

CHAPTER 23

Do Stonehenge

My latest adventure took place in 2018 but instead of me having to make a two-week trek up Mount Everest to a height of 5,300 metres, I simply flew into Heathrow, got on the M3, came off at Junction 8 and then took the A303, turned on to the A360 until I hit the A344, at which point I then ventured right for about 500 yards and there I was. Stonehenge – which I'm reliably informed is a paltry 100 metres above sea level. Pathetic.

This particular event was the brainchild of a friend and business partner of mine called Alon Shulman who, as well as being the man behind a company called Universe who promoted the gigantic Tribal Gathering festivals of the 1990s is also a special adviser to English Heritage.

When Alon first suggested this I thought it was a great idea. After the exertions of Everest I was looking for a challenge that could potentially be as high profile, if not higher, but with far less planning and preparation. There can't be many places on earth that are as historically significant and as celebrated as Mount Everest but as soon as he suggested Stonehenge I knew that we'd found one. My first question to Alon was if he was sure it hadn't been done before and he assured me it hadn't. In fact, the closest anyone had ever come to playing a DJ set at Stonehenge was in the 1970s when they'd held a series of free festivals with the band Hawkwind. The chances are somebody will have played records between the bands during these events but because they took place in fields adjacent to the stones it didn't count. What Alon wanted to do, as did I, was to play a set right in front of them.

The reason he suggested it was because English Heritage were having the majority of their government funding removed and were desperately in need of support. Not just cash, but promotional support too as apparently visitor numbers were also suffering. One of the reasons they thought this might be a good idea was because of awareness. People from the ages of eighteen to fifty, for example, which is about my target demographic, either wouldn't even be aware of places like Stonehenge or would have no idea of their historic significance, and by allowing someone like me to play in front of the stones it would at least get people inter-ested. And let's face it, they're pretty damn impressive. In fact, if I was eighteen years old and I saw a DJ playing a set in front of something as iconic looking as Stonehenge I'd get straight on my phone and start Googling it, which is basically what everyone does these days. OK, so not everybody's going to rush down there, but you never know where it might lead.

Although the negotiations didn't take nearly as long as the other events, this was the first time ever that English Heritage had officially permitted a live performance to take place at the monument and the compromise was that instead of selling tickets to the event as had originally been requested I could only play in front of a small and specially invited audience. 'How many people?' we asked. 'Ooh, about fifty?' they said. Wow, that was small! They were nervous though, which was fair enough.

After thinking it through we came to the conclusion that the amount of people in attendance didn't really matter. For a start, the event was going to be live-streamed so anyone could watch it and with a live audience there'd always be a chance of something going wrong, especially as we'd be playing until dawn. 'Maximise the audience,' they said, 'and minimise the risk.' Job done.

Among the people we invited were the actor and director Andy Serkis, and some old and aforementioned friends of mine including Danny Rampling, Carl Cox, Terry Farley, Nancy Noise and Mark Moore. Having people like that there simply underlined the fact that this was an unashamed celebration of electronic music and club culture. A club culture that was now celebrating its thirtieth anniversary.

The set for this gig gave me more headaches than you'd have in an Irish pub on Boxing Day and my notes look like the scribblings of a madman. I shudder to think the amount of times I'd had to time my set to coincide with a sunset, primarily on Ibiza, of course. Sunsets are obviously dramatic things and the questions I usually ask myself are, how do I build up to it and how can I touch people emotionally? The sunset at Stonehenge posed a different set of questions, partly because the majority of people watching would be doing so from the comfort of their own homes and would probably be alone, and also because of the setting. Just the name Stonehenge can evoke all kinds of emotions and it's easily one of the most dramatic and thought-provoking places I've ever been to. Do I try and shock people, I thought, or do I try and make them think? Choosing the right music to complement a place like Stonehenge is hard enough, but choosing, and correctly timing, a piece of music that will complement a sunset? Having never seen one there I had to just trust my judgement. It was a big moment.

Because of noise pollution we had to keep the live sound right down but the people watching at home would be able to have it as loud as they liked. It was strange though as the speakers by the DJ booth had to be turned down so low that they were sometimes drowned out by the sound of traffic. Because of this, the event to passers-by must have looked both spectacular and a bit baffling, not least because it had all been kept secret in case any fun seekers tried to descend. Anyone driving past would have seen Stonehenge in silence lit up in red and blue with about fifty people dancing around wearing headphones. I'm surprised the police weren't called.

As night fell and the gig began, Carl Cox joined me behind the decks and we ended up sharing the DJ'ing duties. If you watch the coverage of that on YouTube you'll see that, despite the reduced volume and small crowd, Carl and I are having an absolute whale of a time. I mean, come on. You've got two old mates who've known each other forever standing on a stage flanked by one of the most famous landmarks on the planet (which just happens to be covered in lights and projections of flames while spotlights blitz the sky) doing something that they both love in front of more friends who love it just as much. Life doesn't get much better than that, believe me. Grandiose gesture number three had been completed.

Grandiose gesture number four happened in September 2019 and made more headlines than any of them. This was actually an invitation from a man called Jeremy Corbell but it merits an entry simply because of where it took place, which was just outside Area 51 in the Nevada Desert. If you're not aware of it, Area 51 is a highly classified United States Air Force facility situated about 150 miles north of Las Vegas and in addition to conspiracy theorists believing that the US military are hiding crashed flying saucers and alien bodies there, the guards are authorised to shoot trespassers. As one of the most secretive and mysterious places on earth it seemed like a good idea and as soon as they went public with the gig I began to appreciate the power of its reputation. Every music magazine in America wanted to know about it and *Mixmag* even asked me to report live from the location throughout the day. OK, so there was no charity angle to this one but it was something nobody had ever done before and would help spread the word. Jeremy Corbell was launching a new documentary he'd made called *Bob Lazar: Area 51 & Flying Saucers*, which later became a big hit on Netflix and before I took to the stage he showed a screening of it.

The main difference between this and every other event I'd done so far was the crowd. Because it was free it was open to all comers and a lot of those happened to be UFO hunters. I don't know if you've ever encountered a UFO hunter before but they take their extraterrestrials very seriously indeed, and the ones who weren't dressed up as aliens were carrying either home-made ones or an inflatable one. It was strange to say the least but they certainly knew how to have a good time.

A slightly more worthy mention in this category, which again was an invitation and also took place in a desert in 2019, was when I was asked to perform at the opening ceremony of the Special Olympics in Abu Dhabi. The Special Olympics is the world's largest sports event for children and adults with intellectual and physical disabilities and has been going for over fifty years. As somebody who has dyslexia, as do both of my children, this obviously rings a big bell with me and I was honoured to take part. I've always been about overcoming obstacles and I'd argue that, instead of hindering me, my dyslexia has actually pushed me to do things I'd never have done. Anything that celebrates the fact that people with disabilities can achieve great things deserves to be celebrated, end of story.

Instead of just appearing as part of a line-up I was the official DJ, no less, which meant I had to plan, not just a set, but an entire evening. Avril Lavigne, Luis Fonsi, CeeLo Green and a host of other artists opened the show with the official World Games anthem, 'Right Where I'm Supposed To Be', which had been written, produced and arranged by Greg Wells, who produced the soundtrack for *The Greatest Showman*, Ryan Tedder from OneRepublic and the legendary Quincy Jones. My big moment was playing while the athletes and officials entered the stadium and it's a moment that will live with me for the rest of my life. You could almost touch the euphoria in that stadium. It was astonishing.

The focus these days with regards to my motivation for these events has shifted well and truly towards climate change and two of our next challenges will be dedicated to raising awareness. The first one, God willing, will be a DJ set in Antarctica which I can't wait for. It'll involve another trek, of course, but at least it'll be fairly flat. We did think about cadging a lift on one of the scientists' planes, but as well as charging about fifty grand a ticket, which is rather steep, where's the fun in that? I want huskies, man!

The next one after that, which we're already working on, will hopefully be in Machu Picchu in Peru. In addition to raising awareness about climate change we'll also be trying to build a music school there. It's all about using your contacts. I've played in Lima about five times and am very good friends with the main promoter there. As well as helping me set up the gig, I know for a fact that when it comes to building the school he'll be instrumental in making it happen. What's the point of me meeting all these important people and not utilising their influence once in a while? My hope is that somewhere along the way some other DJs will start doing the same thing because this isn't about me. It's about the community of electronic and dance music working collectively to achieve great things, if that doesn't sound too flowery. As popular music's newest and brightest genre we haven't been around for much of what's taken place for the greater good and it's up to us to let the world know A, who we are and B, what we're capable of. Any takers?

CHAPTER 24

Somebody Special

You may have noticed by now that I'm not really big on divulging much personal stuff. I never have been really. I much prefer talking about what I do for a living as opposed to what I do when I go home or in my downtime. I've had a lot of girlfriends over the years and have also been married but neither have ever come close to defining who I am. You already know that I love football and if you took that and music away there wouldn't be much left. Apart from family, that is.

I suppose this might sound a little bit clichéd but the reason I've never managed to make a personal relationship work long term is because I'm married to music. Actually, that's probably an uber cliché. It is true though. God knows I've tried over the years and in addition to music being the reason for these relationships going wrong, or at least at the heart of it, it's what I use in order to pick myself back up again. Does the thought of never having another serious or meaningful relationship with a woman again bother me? Absolutely not. Does the thought of having to cease my involvement with the music industry altogether bother me? Abso-bloody-lutely! It horrifies me.

I've got another cliché for you though and that's music is my life. It's that simple. Whether it's producing, remixing, promoting, composing, scoring, performing, managing, teaching, publishing or mentoring. I don't care. Over the years I've worn every single hat there is so just let me get on with it. I wish I'd realised this earlier as it would have prevented a lot of heartache, but the fact of the matter is that for as long as I'm called Paul Oakenfold, whoever I form a relationship with is always going to play second fiddle to music. With kids it's different as although I'm married to music – happily married, it has to be said – I'm still the father of my children. What's more, I love them dearly. It's not been easy though, and I'd hazard a guess that in a few years' time there'll be a conversation or two about why I wasn't there for them at certain times or at certain events. The thing is, if I'd traded in my life in music for a nine-to-five job or to work as a chef on becoming a father I'd have been a right miserable git, and who wants a miserable git as a father?

The reason I mention that is because one of many things I remember about my own dad, who I'm about to tell you about, was how happy he was and one of the reasons he was happy, apart from having fantastic children and a loving wife, was because he looked forward to going to work and enjoyed it. I'm like a well-travelled version of him basically. I love what I do and look forward to it every day. Actually, because of the hours you work as a chef I wouldn't have seen the kids much anyway. And I'd have been knackered all the time. There, I've convinced myself. In all seriousness though, I certainly wouldn't have been able to provide for them in the way I do, and believe me, that's a big part of my motivation. I mean, what parent doesn't get at least some satisfaction from being able to provide for their kids?

From my own point of view, missing things like seeing them walk for the first time or hearing them say their first words has been a source of regret over the years but that's just the way it is. Just a few weeks ago I was given the timetable for Roman's football matches (he plays for his school team) and because of my timetable I can only make one or two. A lot of people might say, 'Well can't you just change your plans?' but it's not as simple as that, more's the pity. Most of the things I do, whether it be scoring a movie or a video game or DJ'ing or mixing a track are booked months or even years in advance. They're also contracted which means if I try and change the goalposts I'll either cause a lot of people a lot of hassle or I'll get sued. Either way, it's not going to do my career any good so what's the use? Whether you like it or not, sometimes you have to make sacrifices and I've been doing that most of my adult life. I still have a good relationship with my kids which is the main thing and I'm hoping that as they get older we'll be able to make up for lost time.

The ultimate motivation for the above, as in the thing that enables me to be absent so often and make these sacrifices – in addition to providing for my kids, that is – is a desire to be the best in my field. Or should I say, the best in my fields. Ever since I started working in the music industry I've had a desire to be the best at whatever it is I do and despite my advancing years that desire burns as fiercely now as it ever has. Do I think I'm the best at what I do? Of course I do. Anyone who is the best thinks they're the best, and if they try and tell you otherwise they're lying.

The first six months of Covid I actually loved as it forced me to put a pause on life for a bit and take stock. I can't remember the last time I did that (if at all) and it did me the power of good both physically and mentally. It's unfortunate that I had to wait for a pandemic to sort myself out but you always have to look for the positives. By the time things started opening up again I was desperate to step back on to the treadmill of life again, but not to the same degree. I'm conscious of the fact that my time as a DJ is probably coming to an end – or at least a gigging DJ – and so instead of taking everything that was offered to me I decided to be more selective.

With regards to travel, my wanderlust burns as brightly as ever, except that instead of turning up at an airport and going straight to the nearest city and then to a hotel or a club or a venue like I would if I was playing somewhere, I can do what Danny and I used to do back in the day and explore. That's the thing, you see. Excluding America, which I've explored at length, I shudder to think how many countries I've visited over the years but have never gone off-road, if you get my drift. Also, because I usually have people on the ground in the places I'm visiting – promoters, assistants, managers, etc. – I'm rarely what you'd call left to my own devices and the only thing I ever have to think or worry about is the job in hand, whether it be a gig, a remix, a public appearance or a recording session. I'm always well looked after but although it's comfortable I'm not getting the whole experience. I'm not exploring! Travelling's good for the soul – or at least it's good for my soul – providing I'm doing it warts and all.

One of my biggest ambitions in life at the moment is to be able to give my two kids an experience at either Christmas or on their birthday other than the usual stuff like a phone or designer clothes or whatever. I want to be able to take my kids to China for a few weeks. I want to take them to Beijing, Shanghai and Chongqing. At the moment I can't do that as I'd have to take them out of school and apparently that's not the done thing. I almost managed to get my son Roman to come to China with me a couple of years ago but then Covid kicked in and messed it all up. I'll get my opportunity though.

Anyway, on to my dad. The reason I'm putting this chapter here is because it's about ten years since we lost him and the reason I want to talk about my dad, in addition to me still loving him with all my heart, is that he's always been a massive influence on me, even after his death. Not just personally, but professionally too. In that respect, when it comes to who I am, no other person has been as responsible for the story you're reading than him, nor is there anyone else on earth I've looked up to as much.

My dad worked for the *London Evening News*, which is now the *Evening Standard*. These days he'd be called something like a newspaper distribution operative but what he actually did for a living was drive a van and drop copies of the paper off to all the vendors around the city. He loved it. He was a very sociable man, my dad, and although the money wasn't fantastic it ticked every other box for him. Fresh air, friends, travel – around London – and lots of conversation.

Although it was great that Dad loved his job, I was far more interested in what he did in his spare time, which, as well as listening to The Beatles as often as he could which is something I definitely inherited, was playing guitar in a local skiffle band. He was the first person I knew who had musical ability and having it so close to home was an inspiration. As you know I didn't really take to any one instrument but his passion for music and the guitar rubbed off on me and together with football it became an obsession.

Incidentally, do you know how I knew that I was a Beatles fan? I must have stopped listening to them at home when I was about twelve as I was always out and about, but when I started listening to them again in my early twenties I found that I knew every single word. The Beatles are still a real passion of mine and it's all down to Dad.

As I got older, Dad's influence over me shifted from what he did in his spare time to how he behaved as a human being. He'd always been a very polite and kind man but it was only when

I became an adult that I began to appreciate how that affected, not just his life, but the lives of the people around him. Everybody adored my dad and that made me feel very proud. He was also full of wisdom which was almost always about appreciating what you've got. I realised just by watching him that simple things like kindness and politeness cost nothing and he always believed that if you worked hard and were nice to people everything else will fall into place.

Let me give you an example of how his wisdom helped me.

One of the most stressful things that's ever happened to me is being voted the number one DJ in the world two years on the trot by *DJ* magazine. I was riding the crest of a wave at the time. I was playing to the biggest crowds – stadiums a lot of the time, when I was playing with U2 – receiving the most adulation and making the most amount of money. I was also remixing everyone who was anyone. I'd arguably become, so some people said, the world's first ever superstar DJ and although it felt fantastic most of the time, with that came a price.

Once you get to the pinnacle of your career there's only one way to go and that's down. I remember my dad saying something similar to me when I first won the award. 'Paul,' he said. 'Just be careful, will you. Being voted the best in the world is all well and good, but just make sure you accept the fact that it won't last forever. Be grateful that it's happened at all.' At first I thought he was pissing on my parade a bit and for a short while the whole 'best in the world' thing sucked me in. I don't mind admitting that. 'How am I going to retain my exalted position?' I used to ask myself.

The only way I was going to get over that was by taking a step back, accepting the inevitable and making peace with it. And that's what I did. What I had and still have going for me is that I've never enjoyed staying in the same place for too long, so as much as I was enjoying being on the DJ throne I knew that eventually I'd get bored. Or at least get bored of certain aspects. I like to move around. What this actually did, which turned out to be an advantage, was that it made me think about where I wanted to go next and what I wanted to achieve. It actually galvanised me, in a way, and broadened my horizons. Had Dad not had that conversation with me, which actually happened on many occasions in one shape or another in his lifetime and is just the tip of the iceberg when it comes to all the amazing advice he gave me, then I would have had much further to fall when the inevitable finally happened. Believe me, having somebody close to you who works hard, is happy-go-lucky and is nobody's fool when you're in a job like mine is an absolute godsend.

For his sixtieth birthday we decided to have a party for Dad and so we hired a local hall. He was still friends with the majority of his school mates so with everyone he'd collected in between then it was going to be a big old do. To this day I have never known a couple with a bigger social circle than my mum and dad which is a mark of who they were, or in my mum's case, still is. She's a proper social animal and people just gravitate towards her.

The party was due to start at 7pm and at 6.30pm Dad collapsed from a heart attack and later died. He was just sixty years old. I remember as clear as day receiving a telephone call from my mum to say that Dad had collapsed and then thinking to myself, 'He'll be all right.' The thought of Dad dying full stop, let alone thirty minutes before his sixtieth birthday party was just preposterous and even after I arrived at the hall and was told that he'd died it didn't seem real. I went to where his body was, held his hand and promised him I'd look after Mum, which I have ever since. Not that she needs much looking after. She's pretty tough.

My brother and my sister were both in a terrible state after Dad died so, as the eldest, it was left up to me to go into the hall and tell the assembled guests what had happened. That was a surreal moment. Everyone looked on in horror as I spoke and about half the hall just burst into tears.

What amazed me afterwards was how well my mum coped. I always knew she was stoic – they usually are from that generation – but watching her carry on and rebuild her life while she was obviously still grieving was just incredible. She was an inspiration to a lot of people and I was and always will be proud of her.

Dad's death completely changed my outlook on life. Before him, I'd always fretted about the small stuff and it taught me to just appreciate life as it is, grab each and every opportunity that appeals to you, be grateful for what you've got and look after the ones you love. That was Dad's philosophy.

As stoic and brave as my mum undoubtedly is, over the past four years this has been tested to the absolute limit. In 2018 my younger sister Linda had a heart attack in her sleep and because nobody realised she went into a coma. The brain damage she suffered as a result of this has left her virtually brain-dead so although dear Mum still holds out hope that one day she'll come back to us, realistically that isn't going to happen; to all intents and purposes because of the time it took for her to be treated, she went into a coma. Then, just last year in 2021, my brother Tony also had a heart attack and unfortunately he died. He was the life and soul of every party was Tony and such a big character. I remember Mum calling me up to tell me. Naturally I was devastated because I loved him and he was my brother but all I could really think about was how she must be feeling. Losing a child is the worst thing that can ever happen to a parent but for that to happen twice must be overwhelming. The only blessing, I suppose, is that Dad wasn't around to see it.

I know it's not the same as having Tony and Linda back, but what's happened to them has brought me and Mum even closer together and she seems happy. Or as happy as she can be. Tony and Linda both had kids and they visit Mum all the time. We might not be a complete family any more – we haven't been since Dad died really – but we're extremely close.

You remember I told you about the Ministry of Sound gig I did at the O2 the other day? Well, Mum, who's a very spritely eighty-three, and her partner Sid, who's eighty-eight, came along to that gig and without telling her I was going to do it I introduced her to the crowd and made her stand up and take a bow. You'd think that having to do that in front of 18,000 people might be a bit intimidating for a person of her age but not a bit of it. In fact, had she had a microphone I think she'd have addressed them! She's just the best is my mum.

CHAPTER 25

Bond vs. Oakenfold

One of the biggest disappointments I've ever had in my professional life was when the world premiere of the latest Bond film, *No Time to Die*, was cancelled due to Covid. This wasn't the first time it was cancelled; it was about the third. What was supposed to happen at that premiere, however, which I'll reveal towards the end of the chapter, would have made me officially the happiest man on earth. Even writing about it makes me feel physically sick and having to recall the story always results in a massive swathe of disappointment. You see, I am, and I can say this without fear of contradiction, the world's biggest Bond fan. I have been since I was about five years old and until I shuffle off this mortal coil that title will remain my own.

The only other ambition I had as a child apart from working in the music industry, and becoming a chef for a time, was to become James Bond, or a James Bond-like figure. There are certain dreams and ambitions that you intentionally think about when you're a child and that was always my go-to one. The adventures I used to go on! Also, as I got a bit older, girls seemed less ridiculous and so I even started including Bond girls in my adventures. Nothing happened, but they looked amazing and had lovely smiles.

Although my love of Bond never wavered, as I got a bit older and began working I became less of an obsessive and more of a fan. Dreams I'd once harboured of becoming Bond were replaced by videos and then DVDs of the movies which I watched in no particular order whenever I had time. Actually, the obsessive did creep in from time to time, and still does, come to think of it. I've always considered Bond to be a way of life so whenever I turn up at an especially nice hotel in, say, Hong Kong or somewhere and I'm dressed for the occasion I'll channel a bit of my inner 007 and make like the man himself. I'm well aware of the physical discrepancies, not to mention the verbal ones, but as long as I've got my shades on, am nicely dressed and haven't been stuck on a plane for twelve hours I'll give it my best shot.

Even as my career progressed I never once thought that an opportunity would arise for me to become involved in the James Bond franchise, so when a call came through from my manager one day saying that the producers of Bond had been in touch, my mind went into overdrive. It turned out that they wanted me to remix the Bond theme. Not the latest Bond theme, although I did end up doing that for them, but the Bond theme. The one that Monty Norman wrote back in 1962 and is as synonymous with the character as Ian Fleming himself.

The reason I believe I got offered the job in the first place is because, in addition to having scored *Swordfish*, I'd also scored the big car chase scene in *The Bourne Identity*, the one where they go down the steps. I think my audience might also have had something to do with it as at the time they were looking to appeal to a younger audience. The only other DJ and producer who was really active in films back then was Moby who'd been scoring since the mid-1990s. Unlike me, however, he ended up going full-time and has either scored or contributed to about five hundred movies.

Although I'd written film music before this was on a totally different level. I was being invited to get involved with a series that

I'd almost lived by and if I never worked on another thing ever again I knew that I could retire a happy man. I remember as clear as day putting the receiver down after having been asked to remix the theme. I grinned for about a week. I'm quite a smiley person anyway but this was industrial.

I worked quite closely with David Arnold on the remix, who was the series' main composer for several years, and when it was finally ready for release we had to think of which name to use. Not for the theme, of course. That's as it is and will never change. No, we needed to decide whether it would be released under Paul Oakenfold, Oakenfold or something else. In the end we did what everyone else was doing at the time with regards to a remix which was to have the original artist or band vs. the DJ. So, with that in mind we went with – oh, be still my beating heart – Bond vs. Oakenfold. How cool is that?

About a year after remixing the theme tune I was asked again by the producers if I'd be interested in scoring the official video game for the new Bond film which was called *GoldenEye*. Once again my ticker started fluttering like you wouldn't believe and there have been one or two other opportunities since then. I don't half milk it though. I got given a gold disc after *Die Another Day* came out and every time a new Bond movie comes out I post a picture of it. I'm like James Bond's self-appointed DJ and producer in residence. What's more, I ain't afraid to admit it.

Move forward to 2021 and although things have been quiet on the Bond front for a number of years I'm still a massive fan and have been watching the films on a regular basis. Then, one day in the summer of 2020, the phone rang. It was my manager, Paul Stepanek. 'You'll never guess what,' he said. 'Eon Productions want you to DJ at the premiere of *No Time to Die*.' What this initially did was remind me of my association with the Bond franchise which in turn, as well as making me grin, made me go a little bit weak at the knees. As you'll know by now I'm a bit of a workaholic and have always got several projects on the go at one time. This sometimes results in me forgetting certain things and I've even been known to introduce myself to people I've already worked with. 'Hi Bono, I'm Paul Oakenfold. I'm a big fan of yours.' 'Erm, we went on a rather long tour together in the 1990s?' It's not as bad as that but you get my drift. When it happens I'm like, 'Shit, I am so sorry!'

'What, you mean they want me to DJ the after-party?' I said to Paul. 'Better than that,' he said. 'There isn't going to be an after-party so they want you to DJ the red carpet instead.' 'Really? Oh my God!'

What they had in mind was that as Daniel Craig, Rami Malek and all the other stars and VIPs were making their way from their limos and on to the red carpet while being snapped by photographers, I would be at the top of the stairs outside the entrance to the cinema, which is where the red carpet leads to, doing my thing. This was, without any doubt whatsoever, one of the best ideas I'd ever had the pleasure of being a party to and I almost rang up to congratulate them. It was genius.

They didn't know this but after booking me for the premiere I decided to work on a special arrangement bringing all the different James Bond themes together, culminating, of course, with the original James Bond theme that I'd remixed. When the idea first came to me it felt like I'd won the lottery. I was in bed and just as I was nodding off to sleep it hit me. I don't think I slept a wink that night and spent the next three weeks thinking about it and piecing it together. The last time something hooked me like this was probably the Goa Mix.

Once I'd finished the track, which lasts about fifteen minutes and is a bit of an epic, I sat back in reflective glory and waited for the big day. About three weeks before it was due to take place I received a call to say that the premiere had been cancelled – again – because of bloody Covid. Unfortunately this was the end of the line for me as when the premiere actually did take place in September 2021 I was otherwise engaged. What really hurts is that I can picture the whole thing in my head and every time I do so it gets better and better. I've got to the stage now with my imaginings where Daniel Craig walks along the red carpet and when he reaches my decks he comes around, joins me and we knock back a vodka martini each. It's going to bug me forever, I know it is. Anyway, you know what they say. Bond giveth and Bond taketh away.

CHAPTER 26

What Lies Ahead

The global turmoil of the recent years has been an absolute roller coaster for me, as it has for the majority of people. I don't want to mention it too much as everyone's totally over it, but the effect that Covid had on the club industry has been devastating. The majority of DJs had no other irons in the fire so when the clubs closed down so did their income streams. It's been a massive relief as the clubs reopen, but as I write this, things are still a long way off where they were. We've just got to take every day as it comes I suppose.

If it hadn't been for some advice that my dad gave me many years ago I too would have been up shit creek without a paddle during lockdown because for eighteen months I barely lifted a finger. I'm not after sympathy here, by the way. Far from it. I'm just explaining what went on. When I was small my dad used to say, 'Put a pound away for a rainy day,' and although I had no idea what he meant by a rainy day I took his advice and opened a post office account. Saving money then became the norm for me and it ended up saving my bacon when the shit hit the fan. Despite paying a lot of tax in the USA I got no help whatsoever from the US government despite the fact that I employ a lot of people. Had I not had the savings to dip into (which I'd now moved from the post office account) I really would have been stuffed.

The most important thing going forward is that dance music and the nightclub industry continue to recover, and if the nightclub industry has to make some changes or even reinvent itself in some way then so be it. After all, it wouldn't be the first time that's happened. In the late 1980s it had to be done because club culture was on its knees whereas today it's about keeping people safe. We'll get there though.

Seriously, if you think about how far we've all come since the boys and I arrived back in London from Ibiza in 1987 it makes you believe that together we can do anything. Does that sound a bit corny? Probably. It is true though. If there's one thing I've learned while witnessing the rise of electronic dance music and everything that goes with it, it's that we, as in the EDM community, are much more than the sum of our parts and the community I've just mentioned, which continues to grow daily around the globe, is incredibly strong. If somebody had said to me in the year 2000 that in twenty years' time the biggest music festival in America would be one dedicated to EDM and that the biggest draws on the Las Vegas strip would be DJs I'd have laughed you off the planet. I always knew it was going to get bigger and was determined to be a part of the journey but not even I could have predicted what's actually taken place.

So what's going to be happening with me in the not too distant future? Well, for the last three years or so I've been working on a new artist album, *Shine On*. Given everything I've said in this book about albums I'd be surprised if I did one again, but you never know. I have a kind of love–hate relationship with albums at the moment and whether I do another one or not will probably depend on how I feel about this once it's come out. You get a different kind of nervousness with an artist album. It's obviously very personal so if it does well commercially and is well received by the public then great, but if it doesn't and they all hate it you feel like shit. Everyone has an ego, no matter how humble they might seem, and seeing the reaction to your work unfold like that can get to you. I take it all in my stride these days but with *Bunkka*, for instance, it was a very different story.

The thing that excites me most about the future, apart from the prospect of playing in yet more iconic places (which has become a bit of an obsession of mine) is the prospect of discovering new and emerging talent. That takes up more of my thought time than anything else at the moment and if I were a betting man I'd put a few quid on things continuing to go the same way.

What I really like about it, apart from being around people who have lots of energy and ideas, is that I can get involved with their development on the practical side so as well as advising them I can produce, write and collaborate with them. I can't name any names but I'm adamant that I have recently discovered somebody who, with a little bit of help, could and should become the next big thing. The prospect of this happening excites me equally, if not more, than the prospect of opening my own club did back in the late 1980s. I shit you not. It's the kind of thing that keeps me awake at night.

There's also a documentary covering the first thirty years of Perfecto Records in the pipeline for late 2022. I haven't gone on about Perfecto too much in the book as at the end of the day it's a record label. It is something I'm very proud of though and since launching we've sold well over 10 million records. For a small independent label specialising in EDM that's not bad going.

Something else that I'm excited about at the moment is a new concept involving a seventy-minute movie and fifteen new songs. A few years back I was approached by some people who wanted to make a movie about some kids who travel from Los

Angeles to a festival in Las Vegas which I'm headlining. To cut a long story short they asked me to score the film but what I'm doing instead is providing them with fifteen songs by Perfecto artists. Where it gets interesting is that instead of just using these in the film they'll actually *become* the film. You see, what they're going to do is make a stand-alone video for each one of these songs that, when put together, will form the film itself. As a concept I think it's amazing. The film's titled *The Silent Move: A Dance Experience* and there's an accompanying documentary about the concept and making of the film – *Perfecto Records: A Celebration of Dance Music*.

You may have gathered by now that I'm somebody who thrives on being involved in new concepts and that gives me a bigger buzz, at least professionally. The two main reasons for this are the thrill I've just mentioned and the knowledge that I might just have helped to create something that other people will be able to run with and improve. Do you get my drift? That's why I keep on changing hats, I think, and have such a short attention span. I'm always searching for the next big thing.

One of the greatest accolades I've ever had bestowed on me, which sent this obsession of mine into overdrive, is when, back in 2003, I was recognised by Her Majesty Queen Elizabeth II for being, and I quote, 'a pioneer of the nation'. How about that? I was so excited when I found out that I failed to read the details about the ceremony and called my mum instead. 'You'll never guess what, Mum,' I said. 'I'm only gonna have dinner with the Queen. She reckons I'm a pioneer!' I was like a dog with ten dicks. 'That's nice,' said mum. 'What are you going to talk to her about though? Dance music?' She had a point.

After putting down the phone I slowly read the accompanying information and it turned out that as well as me and Her Majesty having dinner, there'd be approximately three hundred additional 'pioneers' joining us. What quelled my initial disappoint-ment at reading this was the fact that I was being recognised along-side the likes of the great George Martin so I was going to be in good company. Mum was right though, had it just been me and the head of the household, what would we have had to talk about? I could have given her the whole Ibiza story, I suppose, or my adventures with the Happy Mondays. Joking aside, it was nice to be recognised in that way and I even managed to behave myself.

OK, boys and girls, it's time for me to go. You know what they say, places to go and people to see. Before I do go I'd just like to leave you with the advice I always give people who are starting out, such as the kids at the LA Music Academy. I always begin by saying that whatever you do, do your best and be true to yourself. Always be ready to embrace change if you need to – and if you can recognise the optimum time in which to make an important change, all the better. That, as much as important stuff like talent and hard work, is what has given me such a long, enjoyable and of course varied career.

People sometimes assume that I must resent younger DJs but not a bit of it. What they sometimes forget is that I've been where they are now and one day in the future they'll be where I am. The fact that I might even have influenced some of them in some way is a massive thrill for me and hopefully they'll feel the same when they're in my position. The fact that the industry is literally dripping with new talent makes it all worthwhile.

I've said it before many times but I'll say it once again. Whatever our differences, at the end of the day we are all in this together. Long may we reign.

ACKNOWLEDGMENTS

First of all I'd like to thank James Hogg, Tim Bates at Peters Fraser + Dunlop and the guys at Welbeck Publishing for helping me get this thing off the ground and into the shops. Getting me to stop moving for more than five minutes is a feat in itself so how we've managed to put an entire book together I've no idea. Thanks guys. It's been real.

Next I'd like to say a massive thank you and hello to the musician, polymath and expert on yours truly, Richard Norris. Richard's exhaustive authorised biography of me that came out over twenty years ago has been invaluable from start to finish. He knows a lot more about me than I do. Seriously! Cheers mate. I hope you're well.

Where would I be without my brilliant Aussie manager, Paul Stepanek? Paul, and my assistant Ruby, have the unenviable task of putting up with my shit and keeping me on track and this book has kept them even busier than usual. It'll all be worth it in the end my friend. Thanks for everything.

Another two constants in my life are Tariq Ahmed and Mick Jackson who've been by my side for I don't know how long and who I know would do anything for me – and me them. Love you guys.

Last but by no means least I'd like to thank the biggest inspiration of all, my dear mum, Sheila. She takes care of me, makes me laugh (tells me off, lol), and always makes sure I feel loved. Cheers Mum. Love ya. X

PICTURE CREDITS

The publishers would like to thank the following sources for their kind permission to reproduce the pictures in this book.

Section 1: 1, 2 (top), 2 (bottom), 3, 4: courtesy of the author; 5 (top), 5 (bottom): Dolly Ave © Welbeck Non-Fiction Limited; 6: Adrian Batty; 7 (top): Martyn Goodacre/Getty Images; 7 (bottom): Jeremy Simons; 8: Jay Brooks/Pymca/Shutterstock.

Section 2: 1 (top): Mark McNulty; 1 (bottom): Anthony Mooney/ Cream Global Ltd; 2 (top), 2 (bottom): Chelsea Lauren/WireImage/ Getty Images; 3 (top), 3 (bottom), 4 (top), 4 (bottom), 8: courtesy of the author; 5 (top): Steven Lawton/Getty Images; 5 (bottom), 6 (top), 6 (bottom), 7 (top), 7 (bottom): Dolly Ave © Welbeck Non-Fiction Limited.

Every effort has been made to acknowledge correctly and contact the source and/or copyright holder of each picture and Welbeck Publishing Group apologises for any unintentional errors or omissions, which will be corrected in future editions of this book.

INDEX

A&M Records 186

A Split Second 126

Abbey Road Studios 144

Alfredo (DJ) 95, 103–5, 107–9, 111, 113, 115, 121, 125, 182

Amazon rainforest 33–6, 132

Amnesia 98, 102–9, 111, 115, 117, 155, 174, 180

Antarctica 250, 264

anthems 125, 126, 132, 264

Area: One 199, 199–202

Arnold, David 277

artist albums 197, 222–32, 232, 282–3

Balearic Beat 111–15, 120, 174

Bambaataa, Afrika 39, 217

Barton, James 183–92

Beastie Boys 67, 68–71, 74, 75–6, 78–9, 107

Benitez, John 'Jellybean' 42, 73

Big Brother theme 209–10, 222

blagging 48–53, 57

Blitz 87–9

Blow, Kurtis 39, 75, 80

'blue M&Ms' anecdote 184

Bond franchise 33, 53, 230, 275–9

Bond's 42

Bono 93, 156–7, 165–6, 168, 278

Boston Pops Orchestra 217–18

Bowie, David 48, 128, 138, 139, 168

Boys Don't Cry 57, 59–60

Branson, Richard 125, 129, 130–1

Brazil 33–6, 37, 132

breakdancing 40, 56, 73, 75, 77–8, 89

Bruinvels, Peter 70, 71

'Bullet in the Gun' 46, 238–40

Burning Man Festival 197–8, 238, 240–1

Café del Mar 98, 106

Capital Radio 26, 231

catchphrases 124, 128

Champion Records 59–68, 81–3
Chemical Brothers 202, 206
Cher 235
Chicago 80–1, 103
Chillout, Chuck 56, 77
China 28–33, 132, 247–54, 258, 268
City & Guilds 19, 23
City Sounds 27
Clapham Common 207–11
Clayton, Adam 159, 163
Club Amnesia 98
club culture, reinvention of 95–7, 111–17, 132, 181–92
Coachella 202–5
comfort zone 121, 173, 255–7
Conference Division 17
Cool, Kenton 254–6
Corbell, Jeremy 262–3
Courtyard 188–92
Covid-19 245, 267, 268, 275, 279, 281
Cox, Carl 26, 74, 112, 116, 193, 200–1, 206, 261–2
Craig, Daniel 278, 279
Cream residency 45–6, 79, 129, 181–92, 215, 241
cricket 207–11
'crocodile' anecdote 35–6
crowdsurfing 74–5
Crowley, Gary 162
Cure 106, 121, 139, 162

D, Danny 128
dance culture under threat 213–32
Danceteria 42
Davis, Rob 136–7, 141
Deacon Blue 154, 158
Dee, LX 127–8
Def Jam 66, 67–8, 74, 75
Delirium 120
Depp, Johnny 164, 226–8
Desert Move Party 238–9
Diamond, Danny 27–36, 37–58, 73, 75, 76–7, 97–104, 108, 111–13, 115–17, 120, 122–4, 132, 173–6, 253
Digweed, John 193, 197
Diorama 69
Divine 91–5
DJ 270
Donnelly, Chris and Anthony 140
drag queens 91–5, 240–1
Dragonfly Records 173
drug-taking 32, 47, 99–105, 107, 108, 113–15, 114–15, 129–33, 135, 174–6, 180
Duran Duran 87, 94
dyslexia, attitudes towards 7–10, 13–14

ecstasy (E) 47, 99–105, 113, 114–15, 129, 132–3, 135, 174

INDEX

The Edge 156, 158–9

EDM 237–45, 282, 283

Egan, Rusty 86–8

Electra 137

Elementfour 210–11

Elizabeth II 284–5

Elkin & Nelson 113, 136, 137

Embassy Club 75, 86

Es Paradis 106

Essential Mixes 79, 94, 177, 180

euphoria 23, 99, 101–3, 115, 135, 176, 258, 264

Everest, Mt 247, 252–8, 259

The Face 97–8, 129

Factory Records 26, 139, 144–5, 149–50, 193

Fantazia 140

Farley, Terry 127, 261

fashion code 115–17

film/TV scores 1, 2, 209–10, 214–32, 276–7, 284

Flicks 26

Fonsi, Luis 263

football 1, 3, 4–5, 7, 9–11, 13, 15, 17–18, 20, 22, 116–17, 171, 186, 254, 267

Fragma 135

Frenchies 26

Froggy (DJ) 25–6

Fun House 42, 73, 89, 107

Fung, Trevor 27, 38, 73, 86–8, 97–9, 101–4, 107, 111–12, 124, 129, 174

Funk, Farley 'Jackmaster' 74

Furtado, Nelly 200, 225

Future 89, 120, 167

Gabriel, Peter 140, 223

Gatecrasher 183

Gerrard, Gerry 199–200

Gio-Goi 140

'Girls Ain't Nothing But Trouble' 62–4, 135

Glastonbury, 166–8, 167, 202, 205, 234

global turmoil 281–2

Glory's 106

Goa 133, 173–80, 278

Godskitchen 129

Gordon, Eddie 177–8, 179

Górecki, Henryk 229

Grandmaster Flash and the Furious Five 38, 39, 75, 80

Gray, Andy 210

Great Wall of China 30, 31, 132, 247–54, 258

Groove Records 27

Guetta, David 168

Guthrie, Gwen 106

Haçienda 47, 124, 129, 138, 146, 193

Haisman, Gary 124, 128–9
Happy Mondays 26, 63, 138,
 139, 140, 143–51, 153–4, 159,
 164, 285
Harris, Calvin 167–8, 225
Haslam, Dave 47, 140
Heaven 120, 125, 127, 129, 136
HMV 26–7
'Holiday Babylon' article 97–8
Holloway, Nicky 38–9, 97,
 101–2, 104–5, 106, 107,
 108–9, 135
Hong Kong 28–9, 33, 37, 132
Houdini 39, 80, 87
house music, emergence of
 80–1, 103–5
Hudd, Colin 124, 129, 164
Hughes, Darren 183–92
Human League 55–6, 87
Hundred Club 75–6

i-D 129
Ibiza 23, 39, 89, 91–109, 111–17,
 132, 135–6, 261, 282
'immigration control' anecdote
 57–8
Inches, David 120, 121–2, 124–5
International (DJ) 81
INXS 173–4
'Irish mate' anecdote 21–2, 28
Island Records 159, 231

J Lyons and Co. 18–19
Jackson, Micky 164, 170–1,
 215–16, 248, 251, 287
Jane's Addiction 202, 204
Jay-Z 67
Jazzy Jeff & the Fresh Prince 62,
 64–5, 66, 149
'Jibaro' 136, 137
Jingle Ball 232
Jive Records 65
Jones Girls 43, 49
Jones, Grace 94, 128

K-Klass 140
Kathmandu 253–6
Kenji (guitarist) 124
Kevorkian, François 156
98.7 Kiss FM 39, 56, 79, 232
Kiss FM London 79
Kissdafunk 140
KLF 125
Knuckles, Frankie 60, 80–1, 182
Kool Moe Dee 107
Ku Club 93, 94, 98

LA Music Academy 150, 285
Land of Oz 89, 131–2, 135–6, 137
Las Vegas residency 1, 114,
 237–45, 262, 283
law-breaking 11, 57–8
Levan, Larry 25, 44–6, 56, 80–2,
 82, 88, 105, 108, 125, 126–7, 182

Levy, David 183, 186, 189, 190–1
Licensed to Ill 68, 71
Little, Dave 123, 131
Live Aid 168–9
LL Cool J 67, 74, 75, 80, 154, 230
London All-Star Breakers 77–8
London Records 66, 149
London-Sire 223
Lyceum 74, 88

MC Tunes 140
McCartney, Paul 140, 168, 209–10, 236
McGough, Nathan 138, 143, 145, 147, 150, 153
Madonna 34, 42, 201, 222–3, 233–6
Man With No Name 177
Manhattan's 106
Manumission 94
Maracanã Stadium 34, 170
Marley, Bob 49–50, 53, 87, 103
Mastermind Herbie 63, 77
Maverick 222–3, 231–2, 233
Max Q 173–4
Medalie, Mel 59–68, 81–3, 91, 133
Melody Maker (MM) 48
Mercury, Freddie 48, 94
Michael, George 128, 168
Midem 61, 83

Milstead, Harris, *see* Divine
Ministry of Sound 79, 129, 181–2, 213, 273
Minogue, Kylie 135
Mixmag 190, 263
Moby 199–201, 276
Montreux Festival 70

N*E*R*D 217
Net Aid 168, 170
New Order 169, 200
New Romantics 68, 96
New York 36, 37–58, 62, 76, 115, 132, 168, 206, 238
Nicholson, Jack 166, 227
Night Owl 24–5
98.7 Kiss FM 39, 56, 79, 232
NME 48, 53, 106, 148
Noise, Nancy 99, 108, 121, 123, 261
Norris, Richard 126, 178, 287
Northern soul 24–8
N.W.A. 80, 139

Oakenfest 209
Oakenfold, Alice (grandmother) 16–17
Oakenfold, David (brother) 5, 12, 32, 272
Oakenfold, Elsa (daughter) 14
Oakenfold, Linda (sister) 4, 12, 32, 272–3

Oakenfold, Paul Mark:
  birth 3
  Blue Peter badge 1, 78
  chef qualification 16–22, 23,
    30, 32
  childhood 3–14, 32
  DJ'ing career begins 85–9
  education 4, 7–12, 13, 15,
    17–19, 23, 28, 32
  father's death 268–73
  'King of the Pit' 4
  musical tastes develop 6–7, 16,
    22, 24, 26–7, 107
  parental advice 15–16, 270–1
  paternal grandfather's travels
    31–2
  as producer 143–51
  record collection 26, 40
  sets 87, 94, 121, 125–7, 167,
    202, 251, 261
  24th birthday 97
  USP 119
Oakenfold, Roman (son) 14,
  15–16, 267, 268
Oakwood Apartments 146
Olsen, Ollie 173–4
'one-record deal' anecdote
  65–6
'opium den' anecdote 29
Orb 127, 200
Osborne, Steve 26, 137–9, 141,
  143–6, 148–9, 153–4, 221

O2 181, 217–18, 218, 273

Pacha 106
Pandy, Darryl 74–5
Paradise Garage 25, 42–7,
  105–6, 108, 115–17, 120,
  180–2
Park, Graeme 47, 123, 138
Paterson, Alex (LX Dee) 127–8
'Peking duck' anecdote 30
Perfecto Day Parties 243
'Perfecto Mix' 159–60
Perfecto Records 46, 85, 108,
  155, 177, 195, 209, 240, 243–4,
  249, 283–4
Phantasia 131
Pickering, Mike 47, 123, 138, 193
Pills 'n' Thrills and Bellyaches 26,
  63, 143–4, 148–9, 153–4
Planet Perfecto 240, 250–2
Playground 88
Plotnicki, Steve 56–7
private life 265–73
Profile Records 56–7, 60, 66–8
Project Club 73–83, 89, 98, 107,
  111–17, 119, 127
Project Room 116
Psaras, Andy and Dino 176
pseudonyms 221, 222, 240,
  250–2
psy trance 173–80
Public Enemy 67, 80

INDEX

Q 148

Queen 103, 236

Radio London 24, 68, 82

Radio 1 177–80, 211

Radio 2 96

Rampling, Danny 11, 97, 101–2, 104–5, 107, 135, 261

Ranzen (DJ) 253–4

'Ready Steady Go' 224–5

Real World 223

Record Shack 27, 92

remixing 135–42, 153–60, 217–23

Renaissance 183

residencies 1, 45–6, 105, 114, 125, 181–8, 192, 195, 220, 239–45

reunion parties 111–17

Rio de Janeiro 33–4, 37, 132, 170

'Road to Damascus' moments 20–1, 50–2

Robbins, Cory 56–7

Rock Steady Crew 77, 78

Rocky 81–2

Rolling Stone 201

Rough Trade Records 119

Roxy 42, 78

Rumours 86–8

Run-DMC 56, 64, 66, 68, 74, 75, 80

Rush Release 66–7, 91

Ryder, Shaun iv, 145–6, 148, 154, 230

Salt-N-Pepa 65–6

Sasha 193, 197

Save the Robots 42

scouting 57, 60, 66

Section 28 70

'Sermon on the Mount' moment 45

Sex Pistols 87, 186

Shellshock, Shifty 229–30, 232

Shine On 282

shirts theft 11, 57

Shulman, Alon 259–60

The Silent Move 284

Silver, Joel 214–18

SiriusXM 80, 202

Soul II Soul 145, 146

Soul Mafia 26, 27

Sound Shaft 119–22

Soundtrek 252, 254

South London Crew 26

Spectrum 89, 123–32, 135–9, 191

Star Café 109

Stepanek, Paul 277, 287

Stone Roses 139, 140, 161, 162–4

Stonehenge 247, 259–64

Strange, Steve 86–8

Studio 54 42, 48–9, 76, 88, 94

Sun appearances 70, 129
supermodels 163–4, 169, 190
Swedish Egil 202–5
Swordfish 214–20, 276

tabloid press 70, 129
Thompson, Hunter S. 225–8
Thrashing Doves 113
3 Beat Records 46
Thrive Records 197
Tiffany's 24, 25
Tong, Pete 24, 26, 66, 68, 79, 82,
  138, 177
Top 10 hits 65, 136, 222, 232
Top of the Pops (*TOTP*) 64, 74,
  137
Top Rank 24
touring 64–71, 161–71, 193–206,
  232–42, 248–53, 252–64
Trident Studios 136–7
Turner, Nancy, *see* Noise, Nancy

UFOs 263
United States (US) 37–58,
  193–206, 237–45
Ushuaia 250–1
Utopia 238–9
U2 80, 93–4, 106, 155–60,
  161–6, 170, 173, 185, 194, 196,
  200, 208, 214, 222, 224, 231,
  233–6, 270

Vinas, Ricardo 197, 226
Vincent, Robbie 24, 26
Vinyl Mania 46
Virgin 56, 125, 140
'VW logo' anecdote 70

Wag Club 116
Walker, Johnny 97, 101, 107
'Walking on Sunshine' anecdote
  50
Warehouse 80–1
Waters, John 91–2
WBLS 39
'We Call It Acieeed' 128, 129
Wembley 1, 168, 170–1
Wham! 94, 98, 162, 169
Wilson, Tony 26, 139, 144–5
Woodentops 105
Woodhouse 38
Woodstock 198
work ethic 1, 12, 13, 23–4, 32
The Workshop of Forgetfulness
  103

XS 242

Young, Christopher 217–19

Ziggy's 73
Zoo TV 93, 161